BEFORE I WAS I

Judith Allen

BEFORE I WAS I

Psychoanalysis and the Imagination

By
Enid Balint

Edited by
Juliet Mitchell
Michael Parsons

Free Association Books/London/1993

FAB *'an association in which the free development of each is the condition of the free development of all'*

The Guilford Press
New York   London

Published in Great Britain in 1993 by
Free Association Books
26 Freegrove Road
London N7 9RQ

By arrangement with Mark Paterson

Printed in the United States in 1993 by
The Guilford Press
A Division of Guilford Publications, Inc.
72 Spring Street
New York, NY 10012

Printed in the United States of America

This book is printed on acid-free paper.

Last digit is print number: 9 8 7 6 5 4 3 2 1

A British CIP catalogue record for this book is available from the British Library

ISBN 1-85343-187-7

Library of Congress Cataloging-in-Publication Data

Balint, Enid.
    Before I was I : psychoanalysis and the imagination / Enid Balint;
edited by Juliet Mitchell and Michael Parsons.
        p.   cm.
    Consists of papers by Balint written over a period of forty years.
    Includes bibliographical references and index.
    ISBN 0-89862-258-1
    1. Psychoanalysis.   2. Physicians (General practice)—Psychology.
I. Mitchell, Juliet, 1940–   II. Parsons, Michael, 1941–
III. Title.
    [DNLM: 1. Psychoanalysis—collected works.   WM 460 B1855b]
RC509.B35   1993
616.89′17—dc20
DNLM/DLC
for Library of Congress   92-49564
                                                                              CIP

*This book is dedicated to my patients
and my colleagues.*

*If a man will begin with certainties, he shall
end in doubts: but if he will be content to begin
with doubts, he shall end in certainties.*

*They are ill discoverers that think there is no
land, when they can see nothing but sea.*

—Francis Bacon, Advancement
of Learning, *I.v.8; II.vii.5*

Acknowledgments

The person least qualified to identify the connections between papers written over a period of some forty years, and to provide a collection covering such a time span with the coherence that it needs, is perhaps their author. In my case this task, begun in the 1980s by Gregorio Kohon, has been admirably carried out by Juliet Mitchell and Michael Parsons in the 1990s. They have edited the text of the book and supplied thematic linkages between its chapters as well as interviewing me and writing an introduction, clarifying my ideas for the reader in the process. I am deeply grateful to these friends and colleagues. My particular debt to Juliet Mitchell is the most difficult to describe. It includes memories of frequent discussions over the past ten years about the ideas I have been giving much thought to, and her insistence that I should overcome my initial reluctance to write about them. And without my husband's patience and determination this book would certainly never have seen the light of day.

The original suggestion that I should put together a collection of my papers came from Bob Young of Free Association Books.

I owe the discovery of the title of the book to Elizabeth Holder, who drew my attention some years ago to the passage where it occurs, although in a different context, in a sermon preached by John Donne on 24 February 1625.

I am grateful to the successive secretaries who kindly, and often with difficulty, typed the chapters as I wrote them.

For permission to reproduce copyright material I express my thanks to the following: Baywood Publishing Co., The Royal College of General Practitioners, The Institute of Psycho-Analysis, Pitman Publishing, International Universities Press, and W. B. Saunders.

Enid Balint
Ramsbury, Wiltshire

Contents

Introductory notes to Chapters 1–10 by Juliet Mitchell,
to Chapters 11–17 by Michael Parsons.

ERRATUM

Before I Was I: Psychoanalysis and the Imagination by Enid Balint. Guilford Press, 1993.

In the first paragraph of the Introduction, on page 1, "Tavistock Clinic" should read "Tavistock Institute of Human Relations."

ERRATA

Introduction

T he opening chapter of this book is called 'The Analyst's Field of
Observation'. Enid Balint's field of psychoanalytic observation is a wide
one, as the table of contents alone shows. Part I of the book reflects the
core of her work: the psychoanalysis of individual patients. The papers in
Part II show another aspect of her career. For almost thirty years she has
been developing, both with her husband, Michael Balint, and also in her
own right, a group method of helping general medical practitioners look
at what they do in a new way. She also initiated, at the Tavistock Clinic
in 1947–48, the Family Discussion Bureau which became the Institute of
Marital Studies, and the two papers in Part III originate from this part of
her work.

Not many have contributed so fruitfully to such different areas of
psychoanalytic activity, and it is important to emphasise that throughout
this book we see her working *as an analyst*. People may come to her
looking for something different from what a psychoanalyst can offer, but
she says, 'I can only work as a psychoanalyst. If I work in any other way I
am an amateur, like a friend' (p. 121). So it is not a case of the psychoanalyst of Part I turning to other métiers in Parts II and III. Balint's identity
as an analyst is just as essential to her work with medical practitioners and
marital therapists as it is to her treatment of individual patients. It is the
use she makes of herself as an analyst that varies in the different contexts.

Many analysts of her generation were prompted in their discovery of
psychoanalysis by experiences during the Second World War. As she
describes in the interview at the end of this book, it was while organising
Citizens' Advice Bureaux in London and helping families whose homes
had been bombed that she came to appreciate the irrational aspects of
human relationships. This led to contact with the Tavistock Institute of
Human Relations, and there she set up the Family Discussion Bureau,
which later became the Institute of Marital Studies. Psychoanalytic train-

ing followed, and since 1963 she has been a training analyst of the British
Psycho-Analytical Society. The training groups for doctors began in the
early 1960s at the Tavistock Clinic, and in 1980, in recognition of this
work, she was made an Honorary Fellow of the Royal College of General
Practitioners.

Her work is clearly located within the Independent tradition of
British psychoanalysis, while also belonging to no one but herself. The
references throughout this book to the work of Michael Balint and of
Sándor Ferenczi testify to her connection with one particular strand of
that tradition. There is also, however, something very English about her
intellectual and personal style. John Rickman was an important influence;
her work is in constant dialogue, implicitly or explicitly, agreeing or
disagreeing, with that of Donald Winnicott; and she stands in a line of
Independent women analysts such as Ella Sharpe, Sylvia Payne, Marjorie
Brierley, Margaret Little, and Marion Milner. Like every one of these
names, she has a commitment to a shared tradition, allied to an unmistak-
able individuality.

She has played a leading part in the life of the British Psycho-
Analytical Society, particularly in her role as training analyst, and occupied many important positions in it. The quality of her presence, however, in the analytic community has been harder to pin down. When as an
analytic trainee I was looking for a supervisor for my first training case,
my analyst said to me, 'Why not ask Enid Balint? Supervision with her is
a rather particular sort of experience'. And so it was. There are supervi-
sors who show you how to talk to the patient, and those who help you
organise your theoretical understanding. Sometimes she would do these
things but often she did not seem concerned with them, and her supervi-
sions had a curiously elusive quality. There was nothing vague about
them, though. They were somehow elusive and distinct at the same time.
After many months I realised I was absorbing something about the
business of being with an analytic patient, which I could not easily put my
finger on but which certainly made a difference to what happened in a
session.

I think this mixture of elusiveness and distinctness is related to the
subtlety and flexibility with which she uses herself, or lets herself be
made use of, as an analyst. When we come to tease that out in these
papers, Part II makes a good starting point because of what she is clearly
not doing there. She is not teaching psychoanalysis to the doctors in Balint
groups, and although it may look at first sight as if she is supervising them
on particular patients, she is not doing that either. The first case, for
example, in Chapter 13 might seem like supervision, but the crucial
phrase in the account is 'After the discussion in the group he [the doctor]
could see how to help' (p. 168, italics added). Shortly afterwards Balint

says, 'we were not sure whether the results in the long run gave the doctor, and therefore the patient, sufficient satisfaction' (p. 169). The primary focus is not the particular patient under discussion but the doctor's quality of awareness; changing that can make him into a better doctor overall. This calls for a perceptiveness about unconscious processes on the part of the group leader, linked to a particular kind of restraint and capacity to wait. In the third case in the same chapter (p. 170), for example, it is clear that the doctor's hopelessness in the first interview was the result of the patient's projections. The group leader did not interpret this, however, either for the doctor's own benefit or so that he could pass something on to the patient. There was discussion, of course, but as for any explanation or interpretation by the group leader, it seems that, as with a case described in Chapter 15, 'there was no comment' (p. 194). And yet in both cases the next session reported showed that the doctor's awareness of the patient, and of his own reactions and feelings, had expanded and that change was becoming possible. The method 'consists of amassing facts and the feelings about the facts at the same time' (p. 166) and calls for 'a leader trained to observe in a particular way, who can tolerate the absence of a consistent story for a time, and use the muddle rather than try to discard it' (p. 166). In the papers of Part II, then, Balint is describing something which is not psychoanalysis but which is nonetheless founded in her being a psychoanalyst.

The context of the two papers which comprise Part III both resembles and differs from Part II. They are general introductory papers, but rich and subtle in their content. They draw mostly on work done in case discussion seminars at the Institute of Marital Studies. Balint's role there involved a more supervisory function than in the training groups for doctors, but the focus on developing the therapists' self-awareness was the same. As the seminar leader, Balint again had to resist any temptation to teach a debased form of psychoanalysis, while still using herself as a psychoanalyst according to the demands of the particular situation. Some of her conceptualising in Part III is overtly psychoanalytic. For example, Chapter 17 is explicitly based on theories of instinct, transference, the repetition compulsion, and unconscious over-determination. There are two main reasons, I think, why psychoanalysis seems nearer the surface in this context. The social worker therapists were more psychodynamically sophisticated than the doctors; and the clinical situation in question, that of marital disharmony, intrinsically involves psychological conflict. These factors mean, however, that the seminar leader has to be even more alive to the differences from psychoanalysis. In the final case quoted in Chapter 16, for instance, we read that 'The point here is that the neurotic form of satisfaction did not have to change, but both needed to

be made aware of some unconscious feelings before they could enjoy it'
(p. 206). In individual psychoanalysis we might blink at the idea of
helping a patient to enjoy neurotic satisfaction rather than change it, but
that may be the very way that psychoanalytic understanding can allow a
marital therapist to help a marriage. Notice also, in Chapter 16, how
ordinary and apparently unpsychoanalytic are the five crucial questions
for the diagnosis and treatment of a marriage. Again we see Balint
illuminating, as a psychoanalyst, situations which are not going to be
treated psychoanalytically, and using her identity as an analyst to help
other sorts of therapists to develop their own identities.

The thread which joins Parts II and III to the more overtly psycho-
analytical work described in Part I is sometimes very evident. When
Balint writes of the need 'to be able to observe phenomena which are
strange and not to obscure complexities and paradoxes in human relationships because they do not make sense; or perhaps at any one time do not
seem to make sense' (p. 128), this recalls the group leader 'who can
tolerate the absence of a consistent story for a time, and use the muddle
rather than try to discard it' (p. 166). Perhaps the clearest connection
comes at the end of Chapter 4. Speaking of the kind of participation
which the mirror metaphor implies, Balint says:

> This finding is highly important for our analytic technique. Beyond its
> importance for psychoanalysts this sort of thinking begins to influence the
> whole of modern medicine. . . . If any progress beyond these confines [of
> 'illness-oriented medicine'], any development aiming at 'patient-oriented
> medicine' is contemplated, it must be based on a new class of observations
> by participating observers. (p. 62)

This explicit link between Part I and the rest of the book points to
something crucial in Balint's view of the analyst's role. It is the *nature of
the analyst's participation* that matters. After warning us against oversimplified views of what it means for the analyst to be close or distant,
she concludes that the value of the mirror model is in enabling the analyst
to be 'neither distant nor close, but just there' (p. 59).

The discussion of what this means is one of the central themes of the
book. In Chapter 8 we find another description: 'It is essential at these
times for the analyst to be quiet and not intrusive, but also absolutely
there. It is hard to describe this, but what matters is for the analyst simply
to go on breathing. He must not put anything into the patient's mind; the
patient is occupied in finding his own words or actions' (p. 102). This
apparent inactivity still requires from the analyst the methodological care
and the accuracy of attention illustrated in the clinical vignettes of

Chapter 1. Non-intrusiveness is one of Balint's basic essentials in analytic work, but significantly she refers to it 'after I have stressed the need for a basic and thorough training in psychoanalytic theory and practice' (p. 121). She closes the papers of Part I with an insistence on the same balance. 'Imagination is a precondition of the creative life. It can be safely used only if the structure and training are there; but the structure and training are useless if the analyst's imagination, or the patient's, is imprisoned (p. 129).

We begin, perhaps, to grasp something of the elusiveness. Balint is exploring a technique in which what the analyst does not do may matter more than what he does, and it is more important for him to remember what he does not say than what he says (p. 126). This is no empty passivity. It is founded on the strictness of a discipline which is kept, however, for the most part invisible. This comes across most clearly in the last four chapters of Part I. Chronologically they stand together and show the recent development of Balint's thinking. She sees analysis 'more like the process of learning a language than as a joint journey of explanation or research' (p. 129), and in these papers she seems to invite the reader to share a language with her in which to think about psychoanalysis. 'As writers it is equally important for us who try to describe our analytic observations, to use words that are right for ourselves but which are right for the audience too. They must not be integrated into a concept before both writer and reader are ready, so that the concept does not seal off further creative work' (pp. 102–103).

In this group of papers Balint is particularly concerned with questions of existence. Does this man exist in his own mind? Did his parents exist for him? How can he come to exist, and possibly to have had some parents? For this woman does the analyst exist? Is there anyone alive in the consulting room or not? Balint avoids a conventional use of theory to translate such questions into something more apparently comprehensible, and insists that the analyst should not say or do anything which might seduce the patient, or herself, into a more manageable kind of dilemma.

This does not mean she is not using theory. We note, for example, a sentence like 'In the transference projective mechanisms were very active and had to be followed minutely' (p. 106), or a passage where she spells our points of theoretical agreement and disagreement with Winnicott (p. 101). There is an illuminating paragraph in Chapter 1 (p. 12) on the changing relation of analysts to their theories at different stages of their analytic development. In Chapters 7–10, however, the main function of theory is a silent one, to avoid endowing patient, analyst, or the analysis itself with an existence that would be premature and false.

The central concept in Balint's notion of existence is 'imaginative perception'. This is 'what happens when the patient imagines what he perceives and thus creates his own partly imagined, partly perceived, world' (p. 103). It gives reality to the outside world, to the people to whom we relate, and to our own selves. It is the essence of creativity and indeed of being truly alive. Without it, the mere registration by the senses of things and people around us and a self-awareness which is purely automatic give no real sense of being. A fundamental aim of Balint's analytic work is to facilitate the emergence of imaginative perception. She relates it to Winnicott's account of creativity and also to her husband, Michael Balint's, notion of the Area of Creativity (pp. 102–103). He only sketched out the concept (M. Balint, 1968, chap. 5), and one of the important achievements of these papers is in Enid Balint's own development of the idea.

She believes that 'the first imaginative perception can only arise out of a state of eager aliveness in two people, the infant with the potential for life and the mother alive inside herself and tuning in to the emerging infant' (p. 102). A developmental approach explicitly or implicitly underlies much of her writing. It is overt, for example, in Chapters 5 and 6, and the analysis of Sarah described in Chapter 3 is conceptualised almost entirely in terms of her developmental history and her relationship as an infant to her mother. Balint had not at that stage formulated the idea of imaginative perception, but in this account we already find a picture of the 'void' experienced by the infant, or the patient, if the mother, or analyst, does not see her in that way (pp. 43, 46).

It is fascinating to discover such pre-echoes, and reading the book through a second time with eyes and ears open for them gives a powerful sense of the development of a psychoanalytic mind. At the beginning of her career, for example, in the paper she wrote to qualify for full Membership of the British Psycho-Analytical Society, Balint says of her patient, 'I find it difficult to say in what way she showed the world that she was a stranger in it' (p. 23). Already this turn of phrase shows the vivid, individual perceptiveness which throughout her work she applies to both her patients and herself. Of the same case she tells us: 'The only factual material I was given is that when she was one year old her mother had to spend some weeks in hospital and that when she came back my patient did not recognise her' (p. 24). More than thirty years later, Balint was to write 'Memory and Consciousness', 'Creative Life', and 'Unconscious Communication'; and here is this first case of all, turning on the question of recognition between a mother and her infant daughter!

This is an introduction, not a comprehensive survey of these papers. I have highlighted particular aspects of them and made certain connections so as to draw out some underlying themes. Many other pathways through them remain for the reader to trace, with, I am certain, a continually growing regard for Enid Balint's originality and creativity as a psychoanalyst.

Michael Parsons
London

chapter 1

'The Analyst's Field of Observation' offers a clear account of analytical work for a lay audience, and a simple and lucid introduction for the general reader. Enid Balint sets out the aim of analytical observation, discusses its nature, and distinguishes it from the also necessary use of inference: 'It is important to realize that the patient has not been observed trying to please the analyst. What has been observed is a polite remark. That she is trying to please the analyst is an inference' (p. 12).

'The Analyst's Field of Observation' can be interestingly compared and contrasted with 'One Analyst's Technique' (Chapter 10). In this introductory paper, Balint is setting out common ground, although it is characteristically distinctive of her own particular stance. She stresses the general truth of the hard work and intensity of the analytic process. This work is in a special type of 'open' concentration. But then she emphasises that what is missed may well be more important than what is seen, certainly more important than what is too clearly understood. Even in this relatively simple exposition we can find the underlying importance for Balint that 'too much light darkens the mind'.

Nearly twenty years after this lecture, the role of observation has become a topical question. Many trainees in psychoanalysis and analytic psychotherapy observe developing babies. Child therapy in particular involves observation of behaviour. Balint's reminder is a timely one, that like all scientists the psychoanalyst must both observe and make inferences, and distinguish between the two. Beyond that, however, she emphasises that, for the psychoanalyst, this work must be done always and only in the light of the understanding of unconscious processes. Freud (1905b, p. 133) wrote in the 1920 preface to *Three Essays on the Theory of Sexuality*: 'None, however, but physicians who practise psychoanalysis can

---

'The Analyst's Field of Observation' was delivered as a public lecture at the Middlesex Hospital, London, on 20 February 1974; it has not been published previously.

have any access whatever to this sphere of knowledge. . . . If mankind had been able to learn from a direct observation of children, these three essays could have remained unwritten'. Seen in this light, the title of Balint's lecture takes on fresh meaning. The analyst's field of observation is not the interpretation of behaviour but the understanding of the manifestations of the unconscious mind.

The Analyst's
Field of Observation

In trying to decide how to open this discussion on the analyst's observations, I have been debating with myself what aspect of my subject I most want to emphasize. Where do I want to direct your attention, your arguments, your curiosity? Of course I shall go off on tangents, but I must try to engage you all in a *relevant* discussion with me. What, then, is relevant?

First I must set out what is perhaps the most important of our working hypotheses: the conceptual framework, or general theory within which we operate. We assume that there is an unconscious part of the mind and that unconscious mental processes exist. This part of our mind and these processes influence our thoughts and actions all our lives but, by definition, we cannot be aware of them. Once a part of our unconscious mind becomes conscious it need no longer influence us in the same way, although the process of change is slow and a theoretical understanding of some unconscious thought is seldom enough to bring about a change in our behaviour or even in our conscious thoughts themselves. Freud's interest in this idea was a practical, not a philosophical, one. Without making this assumption he was unable to explain, or even describe, a large variety of phenomena he came across. Making it, on the other hand, he found the way open to immensely fertile regions of fresh knowledge.

Analysts work within this basic assumption and gain evidence which confirms or refutes the theories they have learned about the structure and the working of this part of the mind. They may then formulate their own theories, which in turn have to be retested, reformulated, or abandoned; and so on ad infinitum. In *The Interpretation of Dreams* Freud (1900) was beginning to work out what the unconscious is like and how it functions, and this process of discovery still continues today.

I want now to try to convey something of the nature, the quality, and the intensity of an analytic session. My remarks will mainly concern individual sessions, the down-to-earth, day-by-day work of a patient with an analyst, rather than the process of a whole analytic treatment, although it will be impossible to exclude that altogether.

After that I want to open up, but not necessarily discuss fully, three interrelated problems which, although shared between patient and analyst, are essentially the preoccupation of the analyst. These are: (a) What does the analyst observe and why does he choose to observe some things and not others? (b) How do his theories help and how do they hinder him in his observations? (c) The difficulty, shared with other sciences, of distinguishing between observations and inferences.

I will start by offering two examples to show the kind of processes that go on in the analyst's mind. The first illustrates the questions that occur to the analyst. It is Monday morning. A man in his twenties who started analysis six months ago comes in looking dishevelled. He lies on the couch and says it has been a bad week-end. He cannot get himself comfortable on the couch and wriggles about. *Question in analyst's mind: why does he find the couch difficult to settle down on this morning? Is it connected in his mind with the bad week-end or was the week-end felt to be bad because of the patient's feelings about the analysis? Or is this irrelevant?* Soon the patient puts his hand under his head between it and the cushion (a rare thing for him to do) and starts to talk, telling the analyst about a girlfriend whom he took to visit his mother at the week-end. *Question in analyst's mind: what is the patient going to tell her about women, perhaps including herself? Something about how uncomfortable he is with them?* There are no inferences yet, only questions. The analyst says nothing and waits; but these first observations, made in a matter of seconds, of the wriggling around, the way he puts his hand between cushion and head, and of what he said, will probably not be unimportant. The analyst must not infer too much from them, however, or become incapable of following the rest of the session because of them. They will stay in her mind latent, arousing curiosity and a kind of readiness to hear more, but must not obscure anything else.

The second example is about the analyst's inferences. A patient who has been in analysis for three years, and has recently been away with her husband and thus missed some sessions, says before lying down how pleased she is to be back and how much she has missed the analyst. The analyst notices that her voice is rather forced and that she lies as far away from her as she can. She says how well the analyst looks. *Inference: the analyst is being well treated but thinks that the patient may tell her later that she prefers being with her husband, or that she is fed up with trying to please the analyst but will continue to do so (an old theme).* The analyst is not sure that this lies behind what the patient is saying and doing, and will have to be careful to see whether in fact it does, and if not, what may account for the rather forced cheerfulness and the unusual way of lying.

It is important to realise that the patient has not been observed trying to please the analyst. What has been observed is a polite remark. That she is trying to please the analyst is an inference.

As the student's own personal analysis is probably the main part of the analytic training, the analyst begins by being a patient, not an analyst. It is as a patient that he first of all learns about and observes the quality of the analytic session. In addition he is expected to read a great number of books, by Freud and many others as well, and to attend lectures and seminars. The student is thus introduced to analytic sessions and theories about the unconscious mind in two ways: through having an analysis and through lectures and reading. The theories often overlap with one another, are frequently contradictory, and are difficult to absorb and co-ordinate. If the student thinks he has absorbed one particular part of the theory, he will usually find later on that it was a gross over-simplification and at the next reading or the next thinking he will grasp something which he did not understand before.

When an analyst starts out in his own consulting room he will find it difficult to distinguish between the observations he makes and the theories that he thinks should explain them. This continues to be so, but at the beginning it is particularly hard to make use of a conceptual framework. If theories are used at all they are often used rigidly. A young analyst can therefore be hindered in his observations if he tries to bring forward his theory and fit his observations into it. This makes him unable to test and retest either the observations or the theory. The best thing an analyst can do to begin with is just to make observations and not be too worried if he cannot fit them into any particular theory. He often does extremely well with his patients at this stage if he can do just that. His abilities to observe and to communicate are of paramount importance and they need to grow. At a much later stage he begins to question the theory and to collect observations of a certain kind without, perhaps, consciously deciding to do so; but if he is interested in a certain aspect of theory he will probably find he is collecting observations around that. Only much later in his career, however, can he discuss with others a theory and the observations on which it has been built, and reformulate it; or even discard it for another theory put forward by himself, which later he may in turn also discard. I need not tell you how difficult this process is, but it is essential that an analyst should test and retest both his observations and the inferences from them which may lead him to construct theories. He must also ask himself why he is observing some processes but totally missing others, and whether he is therefore misunderstanding his patients.

Here is an example where I observed a process which turned out to be the wrong one for the patient and my work with her. During the first year of work with a woman of twenty-five I thought we were making very good progress. I was able to analyse some aspects of the relationships with both her father and mother and to see the conflicts she had with her mother over the mother's relationship with her husband and other men. I thought I was able to trace the ways these conflicts were interfering with the patient's relationship with her own husband and with the analytic process too. I was observing what the patient said from the point of view of the processes in the so-called Oedipal phase of the patient's development. I was quite satisfied with this work. But when I realised just how satisfied I was with the treatment, I began to question whether the process I was following was the important one. Was it really helping the patient and helping the work to proceed? At that point I found a new process, which was that the patient's main aim was to please me and keep me satisfied so that she could continue her life with men as before, in a promiscuous and self-denigrating way. Before I had realised this I was allowing my theories about the Oedipal process to obscure the more important observation about the patient's wish to satisfy her mother and the analyst and keep them at bay without changing her way of life. I communicated my new discovery, or inference, to the patient, who became dissatisfied and angry in the sessions, being frightened that I would find her out and make her even more anxious and secretive than she had been before. After this we were able to get down to work and see how much she had to cheat, lie, and denigrate herself, while at the same time not being able to sleep or ever accomplish anything satisfactorily. My theories had not been wrong in themselves, but irrelevant. The patient's anxieties at that time were of a more primitive and less organised sort.

I did not, of course, derive any theory from this. I could not say that all patients come to treatment unconsciously to satisfy their analysts or to fool them; but I could become more watchful of myself when satisfied.

It is difficult to describe the seriousness of each session for both patient and analyst. If an analyst tries to describe what he does, it sounds either trivial or pompous. It always appears that much ado is made out of nothing, or that the analyst is lacking in feeling and is using the patient as if he were an inferior being. Aristotle spoke of a curiosity which is a kind of wonder, and Bertrand Russell (1946, p. 58) said: 'In studying a philosopher the right attitude is neither reverence nor contempt but first a kind of hypothetical sympathy, until it is possible to know what it feels like to believe in his theories, and only then a revival of the critical attitude'.

These viewpoints are relevant for the analyst in his way of relating to his patients.

One of the difficult things about analysis is its asymmetry. The analyst is in a different position from the patient. He knows about both positions because he started by being a patient himself; but however serious the analysis is for him, it is serious in a different way for the patient. The patient can seem to be in a less favourable position, having apparently so much more at stake than the analyst. In his own way, however, the analyst also has a great deal at stake, and nothing is ever trivial to him. The slightest communications and gestures are important to the analyst, however trivial the patient might consider them. The patient may think he is wasting time by talking about something stupid; but the analyst will never think of it as stupid. Although the patient's wish to communicate is encouraged, he often thinks it is more important to get the analyst to talk. This is seldom true. At each session some part of the patient wants desperately to convey something, but it can take a whole session or longer for the analyst and patient to find out what it is. The analyst must also notice in what ways the patient defends himself against communicating. It is for this reason that the analyst's observations are so crucial.

If an analyst begins a session feeling light-hearted and inattentive, or depressed and inert, he will soon find himself listening intently and remembering snatches of dreams and associations from previous sessions, even if he would prefer not to, because what the patient communicates on any one day is not just out of the blue at random, but part of a line of communication which starts at the beginning of the analysis and goes on until the end. (This also is a working hypothesis.) Few of us can help remembering snatches from the past, and the analytic process is not usually interfered with so long as the analyst is not distracted but listens and watches intently to what is happening in the present, and can see how it varies and in what way it is unique to the present. His ears and eyes are not the only organs he uses. His own feelings, or lack of them, in response to the patient have also to be taken into account.

Everything that is observed is part of a process which has probably happened before and which is being repeated in the relationship with the analyst. This is only one of the possibilities; there are many other theories and hypotheses to explain why a communication is made on one day and not another. It could be, for example, that the patient wants to cheer up, comfort, hurt, or infuriate the analyst, and the repetition aspect is relatively unimportant. An analyst can often see what is happening without being able to understand the reason in repetition, or transference, terms. When this happens *he must not guess*.

Many observations do not appear relevant when they are made. The analyst inevitably selects what he thinks is important at the time, according to what seems to be part of an ongoing process or else a defence against it. Meanwhile he stores up thousands of small observations which he may use at a later date, perhaps without even remembering when he made them. Something the patient says weeks, months, or years later may call them to mind and the patient, too, will probably remember them when reminded. The analyst makes interpretations or comments only if he thinks they will help the patient further in the work, by facilitating the process that he thinks is important. This would be dangerous if the analyst were working in isolation from the patient and could not hear the patient's responses as communications about the importance of some different process. Patients, in fact, have quite a lot to do with what is observed by their analyst. They will probably not let him get away with too much fitting observations and inferences into a preconceived theory. They will go on and on trying to show the analyst what it is that they really want to say. It is probably true that all analysts often miss what the patient is wanting to say; and, of course, the patient himself will not consciously know what that is. This is one reason why it is so hard both to make analytic observations and to convince others of their validity. The patient is not conscious of what he wants the analyst to observe, and yet the two together have to find out.

I notice certain things: a patient wants to satisfy me, or a patient's hands and words do not seem to be in harmony, or the words and actions do seem to be in harmony. We do not consciously register everything we see and hear. We may only later recall some important fact. For example, it took me quite a long time to realise that one patient always hid herself from me and even when coming into the room or going out of it did not let me see her face, keeping her hair over it or hiding it in some other way. This was a particularly attractive young woman who thought herself to be absolutely hideous and whose mother also thought she was hideous. So although every time she came she looked absolutely gorgeous and very well dressed, she did not want me to see her. For a long time I had the impression that she was afraid I would look at her, but the opposite was also true. She wanted me to look at her, otherwise she would not have dressed so well. What I had to realise was that she was in a state of conflict about this, a conflict that she could find no healthy way of dealing with and which was contributing to her illness.

All this assumes the existence of transference phenomena and is thus based on a theory which some of you might think is so flexible that it is impossible to disprove. For example, I had been away on an unexpectedly long holiday. One patient began his session by talking about his work as an engineer, and how complicated things had become with some of his colleagues. He then switched to a snippet about his father who was his usual disagreeably fed-up self; but the patient added, 'Who can blame him? My mother is ill and unavailable as well'. He then said, 'I suppose you will say I am talking about you', meaning I would try to brainwash him as usual, and then returned to a snatch of associations about his girlfriend who tried to comfort him when I was away, but who, as I knew, was unfaithful to him from time to time. He supposed this was his fault as he was also unfaithful to her. I commented that the transference communication seemed to be about infidelity and unavailability on both his and my part, just as he and his mother had withdrawn from one another. The patient appeared to ignore this comment but went on to talk about an old girlfriend who, as I already knew, had been unfaithful to him while they were together in the same house, before his eyes. He said he could never forgive her.

I noticed this because it was part of a process I was following, with which I was already familiar. But why do I choose particular processes? For instance, I will notice with some patients more than with others how they come into the room and lie on the couch, although this may be important with every patient. If, however, I decide for an experimental period to notice it for all patients, my mind will be switched on to this and I will miss many other things. So I cannot even start to tell you what I observe without introducing the fact that I inevitably select and, further-more, I think I should. Freud's dictum that the analyst's attention should be free-floating still seems to me to be true, and perhaps his most important contribution on technique. If the analyst is on the look-out for something he may find it but he is bound to miss something else, and it is my experience that what he misses is likely to be more important than what he sees. I have to qualify this at once, though. Once the analyst realises that he has missed something, such as that a patient is trying to please him and nothing else matters, he must still watch out to see whether or not what he missed is relevant. However, the reason I missed what I did with the patient who satisfied me may have been because my mind was too interested in theories so that I was hampered in my ability to observe. Of course it can easily happen the other way round too. The activity of a patient can disguise or make unbearable the content of her verbal communication; and, as I have shown, one can often wrongly follow unimportant processes.

So how can the analyst know what is important? I think we can only answer by assuming that the analyst, like the patient, has an unconscious which selects, thinks in a particular way, and builds up a picture of the analysis. The analyst's unconscious chooses a process to follow and then checks this activity. The analyst has to be aware of what is happening to him and use his conscious knowledge and skill to check his own unconscious processes with the patient. First he has to identify with the patient and then he must constantly 'revive the critical attitude' both to himself and the patient.

In summary, then, the analyst observes what the patient does, says, and feels, and he observes his own feelings about his patient. He may not observe at all what does not seem part of the particular process he is studying and thus he may fail to notice other, different processes. His theories will help him to make some observations but they may prevent him from making others where no theory is available. I have, however, suggested that this happens mainly in the early years of work, when theories obtrude and the analyst cannot yet entertain them while still attending to areas not covered by them. Because the analyst inevitably selects his observations it is difficult to distinguish between inference and observation. The patient can help here, but only insofar as his mind is allowed free rein and understanding, with defences that are not too strong and if the analyst is free enough as well.

Finally, I think that theories from other disciplines can also sometimes hinder rather than help the analyst. It is hard enough to cope with our own theories and keep an open mind about them. If theories from other disciplines as well intrude on our minds while we are working with our patients, there is a danger that our analytic theories may either get turned into dogma or be abandoned, without, in either case, being properly scrutinised. There is also the danger that we may stop observing the analytic process itself. None of this means, of course, that an analyst should cut himself off from current thought; he must keep in touch with the world and the cultural milieu in which he lives. His central task, however, is to observe with a free and curious mind and not to be distracted by theories and the easy solutions they may offer.

PART I

The Analyst in the Consulting Room

Balint qualified as an Associate Member of the British Psycho-Analytical Society in 1952 and two years later, which was the minimum required time, received her full Membership with the presentation of this paper, 'Three Phases of a Transference Neurosis'. The occasion of its presentation has a historic significance as it was the last time that a Membership paper was read, discussed, and defended before the entire society. The nature of the situation necessarily meant that Balint showed due acquaintance with the theories of senior colleagues and that her overall interpretations were presented, as was then customary, at the Oedipal level. She refers to both Melanie Klein and Anna Freud, and clearly accepts aspects of Klein's work on pre-Oedipal or early Oedipal states and mechanisms. Thus she refers to the Kleinian 'depressive position' in which the baby has overcome the paranoid anxieties and defensive splittings to integrate good and bad aspects of the object but feels guilty because of the attacks it feels it has perpetrated and now wants to repair.

However, behind a typical modesty Balint is already placing different emphases and suggesting ideas which were only to be expressed by others much later. For instance, she established the hallmark of her own influential later technique at this early date: 'I took this as a defence . . . but this did not make sense to her and I really only bewildered her by my interpretation. I responded by remaining quiet, giving her the opportunity to talk or be still as she wished' (pp. 26–27). There is a quiet emphasis, even in subdued opposition to Anna Freud, who was present when the paper was given, that for any psychic change to take place it must be experienced, even enacted, within the analytic transference. This is the significance of the motif of 'acting out' which runs through the paper. Acting out (p. 27) is the compulsive enactment in the present of unconscious desires whose source in the past the patient cannot recognise. It is

---

'Three Phases of a Transference Neurosis' was read as a Membership paper to the British Psycho-Analytical Society in 1954. It has not been published previously.

often frowned upon as the analyst is conventionally supposed to enable the patient to remember and speak rather than act.

The patient of this chapter was a 'training case'. While training for Associate Membership of the British Psycho-Analytical Society, which constitutes qualification as a psychoanalyst, students, who are also called 'candidates', take two patients in supervised, five-times-weekly analysis. These patients are treated under the auspices of the London Clinic of Psycho-Analysis. Patients pay a fee related to their means for their analysis with a student, who receives no payment. The student sees the first patient for a minimum of two years and the second for at least one year, usually on the clinic premises. After these periods the patient may be seen privately in the student's own consulting room. (Nowadays this may be so from the beginning of the analysis.) This is the move referred to on page 27. One or the other of these patients may later be described as here in a paper presented for the analyst's qualification as a full member.

The significance of the spellings 'fantasy' and 'phantasy' which occur in this chapter is explained on pages 94–95.

Three Phases of
a Transference Neurosis

I wish to describe the analysis of a woman who started her treatment with me when she was thirty-eight. She had previously had two-and-a-half years' analysis with another student analyst.

I propose to discuss three phases in the analysis which, although different in many ways, have certain common features. I shall leave it until later to consider what these similarities are; all I want to say here is that they were the most intense phases of the treatment so far, and I should like to examine the value, if any, of this intensity and to consider its theoretical and clinical significance.

Miss A is a slightly built, nondescript-looking person with an attractive smile. She has a goitre. She used to wear a frightened, rather bewildered expression on her face. She did not look normal; but I find it difficult to say in what way she showed the world that she was a stranger in it. When she came to analysis she was, in fact, a stranger, feeling lost but determined to find her way. People were, on the whole, intruders to her and she kept them out of her life. In some ways she seemed extremely wise, in the sense used by Ferenczi (1923) when describing the fantasy about the wise baby. She was sensitive to what was going on in other people's minds, and her likes and dislikes about me and my surroundings showed a good deal of taste and discrimination. On the other hand, in superficial ways and in describing everyday occurrences she was often intensely petty, silly, and irritating. One felt there were two entirely different people in her, and I was puzzled at first as to how it came about that she could be at the same time so wise and so stupid.

Miss A came to analysis for a second chance in life. It would have to provide her with what her parents had not given her. This was thought of at different times as the opportunity to take in all the knowledge in the world, since she felt she had been taught nothing and knew nothing; and the chance to get hold of all the precious wisdom which was already inside her and without which nothing made sense. Later it also appeared that she came for analysis unconsciously wishing to be simultaneously both a man and a woman. This aspect of her illness, and her homosexuality, though linked with the rest of the material, cannot be dealt with in the present paper.

My knowledge of the early events in Miss A's life is the result of analytic work. The only factual material I was given is that when she was one year old her mother had to spend some weeks in hospital and that when she came back my patient did not recognise her.

She is the second of three surviving sisters; one sister is three years older, the other two years younger. A fourth sister was born when Miss A was five and died one year later. The family lived in various small towns in the north of England. The father appears to have been an intelligent, bright but rather unreliable man who loved his daughters in his own way, but without ever being in touch with their needs. He owned in turn two small shops, and when my patient was grown up he built himself a cinema. This cinema was never a financial success but it was his pride and joy. All three daughters were made to help him run it and my patient felt that they were all sacrificed to it. It was sold a year before he died, which was when Miss A was twenty-five. He died quite suddenly, probably from a thrombosis. The mother, who is still alive, emerges as a confused, anxious, uneducated, very simple woman who has never been able to look after herself or her family without considerable support. Miss A says that her mother makes very little contact with other people and only chatters in a confused way when anybody is there. When the father died it was my patient who had to take charge of her mother and deal with a difficult financial situation.

The children had all been taken away from secondary school when they were fourteen. Miss A greatly resented this. She had wanted to stay on although she was an unsuccessful scholar. She tells me that she could not actually remember anything. Facts made no sense to her. She was, however, very good at arithmetic, particularly mental arithmetic. Her chief interest, though, was in games and sports. She describes herself as a perfect hockey player. There was no question about it as far as she was concerned; everything she did when playing hockey was absolutely right. She, too, was absolutely right. In her last term she hoped that a miracle would happen and that she would be allowed to stay on at school. No miracle occurred and when she found that her schooldays were indeed over she was numb with misery and felt that she had lost everything. She had had some boyfriends but she stopped seeing them and withdrew miserably into herself. Immediately afterwards her menstrual periods started and this threw her into even greater despair and confusion. She had to stay at home and help her mother and thus she began what she felt was a life of drudgery. At some later date she asked her father to give her a training as a gym mistress but this he refused to do. Before their father died, however, my patient and her older sister did manage to get trained as shorthand typists, and since his death they have managed to keep themselves through this kind of work and even to help their mother to some extent.

Towards the end of the war Miss A joined the armed forces and spent some time abroad where she managed fairly well, although there is some suggestion that she nearly had a breakdown. She had one important friendship with a boy some years younger who wanted to marry her. This came to nothing, partly because of her jealousy of her boyfriend's friendship with another man. After that she had various boyfriends who meant nothing to her. She refused to have any sexual relationship with them, and although one or two of them attempted to seduce her they soon gave up trying, and left her frustrated and miserable.

After demobilisation she had a severe nervous breakdown and became confused and desperate for about a month. During this time she received out-patient treatment consisting mainly of occupational therapy. Finally, after some attempts to re-establish herself, she was taken on for a year of vocational training in a residential college. It was there that she decided that she needed further psychiatric help. Her elder sister had already been in analysis for some years and she decided to apply for analysis. She wrote to the London Clinic of Psychoanalysis saying that she could not bear the thought of going through life much longer in her present state; she also complained of bouts of exhaustion, feelings of inferiority, self-consciousness, and loss of memory and concentration. She was diagnosed as having a moderately severe hysterical reaction and after a six-month wait was taken on by her first analyst, a man.

During the first six-and-a-half years of analysis, two and a half with the previous analyst and four with me, very little happened to Miss A in the external world. She made few friends and has indeed had very little social life. When she started her treatment with me she was in a poorly paid job earning only about £3 ($5.00) a week for part-time work. After about a year the firm offered her a much better position and she started to work full time. She has now taken a job where she is earning a little more than £8 ($13.50) a week.

At the beginning of her analysis the only person she saw often was her older sister, about whom she talked with dislike and disdain, but whom she found it difficult to leave alone. She also had a few women friends whom she met occasionally and respected, but apart from this she seemed frightened of the world and lost in it. She felt that everybody in it would waste her time and would be an obstacle to her progress. The older sister and she live in separate furnished rooms; neither seems capable of making a home. Until recently they lived in the same street but now my patient has moved to another neighbourhood. Their mother used to live nearby, but a year or so ago she moved out of London to live near the youngest sister, who is married and has a house but no children.

I shall now describe three phases of work and set them into the general course of her analysis so far.

When she started Miss A was frightened and quiet. She behaved like a startled animal waiting to be attacked and prepared to attack. She always seemed to be crouching, although actually she lay still on the couch with her hands in her pockets. She said very little and spoke with difficulty in a stilted voice, her sentences coming out jerkily. She spoke chiefly about her dislike of me and her love of her previous male analyst. Inasmuch as I existed at all, I represented to her a soft, empty, and flabby woman; that is, her mother. She herself had something good, hard, and valuable inside her, or in her hand, and I would certainly want to take it from her. I interpreted that she thought only one of us could have anything valuable. In any two-person relationship one was on top and the other subjugated. Ideas of mother and father together were intolerable, and there were no three-person relationships. I naturally interpreted all this in terms of Oedipus conflict and and the castration complex. I do not know whether it was due to this kind of interpretation, but after about four months with me she became less frightened and it was then that the first intense phase started.

During all this time, outside the analytic situation she felt that I was a rather silly woman of poor intelligence, incomparably worse than her first analyst. In the sessions themselves things were quite different. It was a precarious situation and if I even moved in my chair I spoiled the session for her. By moving I reminded her that I was not, as she had thought in fantasy, and as in the beginning she had imagined her mother to be, completely fused with her. She did not dare to become aware of her separate identity, and when she had to, it seemed as if a different personality took over. She spoke in a different voice and lost all her zest and eagerness. These observations are in agreement with the idea of primary love as described by M. Balint (1952). I felt that she must have had to become aware of her separate identity too soon, with the period of primary love ending prematurely for her and being followed by a period that meant disaster.

I continued to interpret that she was defending herself against the perception of reality, to which she responded by telling me that I was going too fast. I took this as a defence against recognising the external world where there were two separate people, a father and a mother, with separate interests from hers; but this did not make sense to her and I really only bewildered her by my interpretation. I responded by remaining quiet, giving her the opportunity to talk or be still as she wished. Through my not interfering with her acting out, her compulsive need to control both me and the course of her analysis became clearer and I understood her demand not to be interfered with prematurely. She then talked in a soft, childish voice and gradually began to notice things about herself and later about me. First, for instance, in her fantasy there was a thread joining us. Then suddenly she noticed she had a mouth and later that she was hungry. She thus showed me that she was experiencing separateness from me. At times I represented her faeces to her and she was sorry for me as I was only half alive. She then began to look around the room, which she had not been able to do up to now. After a time she started to look in a less confused way at the real things in the external world and it was then that she started going to picture galleries and attending classes on the history of art. There were moments of vital pleasure when she discovered she could look at a particular picture without confusion. I took this to mean that during the acting out phase she succeeded in a rudimentary way with her attempts at sublimation, which is tantamount to some integration of her ego.

All through this phase of her analysis she has been attending evening classes, studying chiefly the history of art and in that connection looking at pictures. In doing this I think she has been trying to find out, as she does in her analysis, how to understand and live in the world, and how to make new identifications. Marion Milner (1952, p. 85) writes of 'the possibility that some form of artistic ecstasy may be an essential phase in adaptation to reality, since it may mark the creative moment in which new and vital identifications are established'. I feel Miss A's search has been for this chance, both in the analysis and in the external world, and in this way the evening classes could be thought of as acting out. All the time she has been trying to find something that made sense to her.

Emergence from this intensive acting out phase probably started spontaneously but it came to an almost traumatic climax when I announced to her that I would soon be leaving the clinic and she would have to come to my home for her sessions. She became terrified that I would leave her as she thought I was pregnant. Her phantasies about anal birth, her identification with the baby inside me, and her fears of being stuck half in and half out were analysed and brought with them memories and fantasies of her younger sister's birth and of sitting on her mother's lap and noticing that she was pregnant. I assume that this refers to her experiences at the age of about two. All this was interpreted and worked through in an unregressed, less intense atmosphere.

Soon after emerging from the first phase of intensity and acting out, Miss A was able to enjoy some social life and she became more active and efficient in her work and was offered a better job. Incidentally she made friends with a man but soon got frightened and gave it up. This comparative ease lasted for about six months. During much of this time Miss A seemed unreal and her conduct was often manic and defensive. This was interrupted by a physical illness. By now Miss A had been in analysis with me for about a year and a half and she was nearly forty.

This brings me to the second intense phase. It was centred round the physical illness, a lump in her breast which was first diagnosed as mastitis and later as cancer. While I was on holiday she was advised by her doctors to have a biopsy and if the result was positive to have the breast amputated. She refused all this and after some time she refused medical help altogether. Instead she put herself under the care of nature cure practitioners.

This seems to be a case of negation as described by Freud (1925a). The patient said, so to speak, 'There is a possibility of death by cancer, but not for me'. In a posthumous paper Freud developed the idea of negation further and discussed the effect of denying some external event which the ego feels as painful. He says (Freud, 1940a, p. 204):

> Whenever we are in a position to study them [denials] they have turned out to be half measures, incomplete attempts at detachment from reality. The rejection is always supplemented by an acceptance; two contrary and independent attitudes always arise, and this produces the effect of a split in the ego. The issue once more depends on which of the two can command the greater intensity.

Melanie Klein, in discussing early anxiety situations, contends that if anxiety is too great, projective mechanisms can be put out of action: 'The person thus affected denies, and to a certain extent eliminates, not only the *source* of his anxiety but its *affect* as well' (Klein, 1932, p. 205). Anna Freud, however, considers that the mature ego resorts extensively to denial only if its relation to reality has been greatly disturbed (A. Freud, 1936, p. 90).

Miss A interrupted her analysis on the advice of the nature cure practitioners. She went away for a month to a nursing home where she was dieted very severely. She came back into analysis looking extremely ill and painfully thin. For more than a year she refused to see a doctor and lived largely on a diet consisting of fruit, salad, a small quantity of brown bread, and some milk. Her associations showed no fear of death, but only of being maimed which meant, on one level, the fear of castration. Once this was superficially abated by the reassuring opinion of the nature cure practitioners, her whole life became centred around eating and looking after herself.

Her previous medical doctors had thought that Miss A would die of cancer within a year and of course I was extremely anxious to get her to see a doctor as soon as possible. At first I felt that this was my duty above all else. Two alternatives were open to me: to refuse to continue treatment unless she agreed to accept medical care, which would have been responding to her acting out in kind; or to carry on in a strictly analytical way, limiting my responses to interpretations and to tolerating her acting out; and this I decided to do.

Her fears in connection with the threatened amputation were clearly partly castration fears on the phallic genital level. This was interpreted but these interpretations gave her no insight and made no change in her mood or behaviour. Nearly two years later we were able to get back to her castration anxiety and I could then make use of much of this material. At the time, however, her whole being was absorbed in the regression to an exciting, impulsive feeding situation, to the complete exclusion of any other interest. While in the previous period she had regressed to a specific form of object relationship, now the regression was to the instinctual aim of gratification. Then her relation to the primary object, that is to me, had been fairly simple, but during this second phase there were complicated denials, splits, and idealisations, and the playing off of one object against the other.

During this phase she behaved in a very childish way in the sessions. She had to have the electric fire pulled up close to the couch whatever the weather was like, and she covered herself up with a rug. Often she brought warm, fresh brown bread into the room, and she spoke almost entirely of the food she had eaten or would eat, and of the forbidden foods that she craved and did in fact eat in large quantities. This forbidden food was chiefly soft chocolate cake and Mars bars. She feared I was getting very thin and would fade away, which made me realise that the chocolate and Mars bars represented the inside of my body and my faeces. If she was particularly greedy on any one day, she dieted strictly on the next, often starving herself entirely. It appeared that she could re-experience in the analytic situation the early oral phase of her life only on condition that an external controlling object, the nature cure practitioner, was there all the time to prevent her either getting too dependent or eating too much. He was also needed to prevent me from retaliating by cutting out the lump or amputating the breast, which represented at different times both the penis and the baby which she had stolen from my insides. The emphasis here was on activity and excitement whereas before it had been on inactivity and tranquillity.

I could not have understood this material without the help of Melanie Klein's work concerning the infant's sadistic impulses and fantasies directed against the mother's breast and the fantasies of entering the mother's body and robbing it of its contents. Equally helpful were her ideas about denial and splitting as two of the main defences against these anxieties.

One characteristic example of the split belonging to this phase is as follows. Miss A brought only one part of herself to me, the part that attacked, and ate forbidden food; while she took the other, the child who never ate impulsively, to the nature cure practitioner. By this split she avoided any guilt caused by her greedy oral impulses.

This phase ended when Miss A reacted violently to an interpretation given her, not for the first time, pointing out this kind of split. Possibly the reason for the violent reaction at that moment lay in my increasingly tense counter-transference. For all I knew she might have been dying of cancer and I felt she was playing silly games with me instead of taking her illness seriously. This feeling might have coloured my attitude. In any case she said that I was not part of her any more but was standing outside, jeering at her. She withdrew from me and complained bitterly that when at last after all these years she had managed to get to where she wanted I had spoilt it all.

Her fury, hatred, and resentment following this bitter ending of what seemed to her in retrospect a blissful period lasted for about four months. I wondered whether the hatred was also determined by my having brought her out of her regression too soon, or too suddenly. Michael Balint says that hatred is always a denial of and defence against primary love; while Winnicott says that anger follows a period of full regression to dependence and has little to do with initial failure. Probably the hatred here arose when my patient started to bring together the split in her ego and in her objects. This enabled her to experience by projection the fury and persecutory anxiety against which she had defended herself during her illness.

A non-regressed stage followed lasting for about a year. I have no time to describe in detail the work that we were able to do during this period. Among other things we worked through Miss A's fear of killing people, particularly with her mouth, her very marked persecutory anxieties, and her wish not to get on in the world. She repeatedly said she did not want to work and that it was my job to give her the money to go back to school and make a fresh start. We also dealt with her omnipotent fantasies and her fury when she found she could not control me. I started to be a real person to her and in her fantasy she began to be concerned about my husband and me being together, having rows, and getting over them. One day she asked for a pencil and paper in the session because she could not say what was in her mind and she wrote 'I love you'. Nevertheless her persecutory anxieties persisted and she was still unable to have any relationships other than the precarious one with me.

One result of this work was that, to my great relief, Miss A visited the doctor, who told her that the lump had almost disappeared and that no operation was necessary.

Soon after this she decided to look for a better job. I felt this was done to please me; that is to say, external reality was accepted as a necessity but it still had no meaning for her. She did, however, start to learn languages at this time with great enthusiasm: first French and later Latin. Learning languages became as important for her as looking at pictures.

My patient gradually became aware that all she wanted was to be what she called 'the little girl who was three'. This was not new material; the novelty was that she could talk about it more freely. If analysis was not going to help her achieve this, she supposed she would have to go on but it was no good. When I interpreted her wish to be dependent on me forever she replied that she was sitting on top of the world and was not in it, and that it was moving along too fast for her.

We both realised that we had the problem of how to enable the grown-up woman to live a real life, with external reality being worthwhile. This task led to the third, most intense phase, which lasted only ten days. It seemed literally to overwhelm her, although never to the extent of making her incapable of looking after herself. When she emerged from it she was different in her relation to the world. During this phase she produced four dreams, all of them dealing with the primal scene and the difference between the sexes. One could say that she was overwhelmed by the dreams; but it might be more correct to say that she dared to have them only after she had reached a point in her analysis when she could risk being dependent on me. The regression started when she developed a cyst on her eyelid. She was asked at the office to type some accounts. She could not see the figures and was terrified of looking. She then discovered that she could hardly see at all. Her fear of doctors reappeared and in the session that evening she was frightened and shivery. She thought I would make her go to a doctor and would be angry because she could not do the typing properly. Though I did not understand the full meaning of her fear I interpreted that the page of figures represented some terrifying spectacle she would rather not see, a spectacle connected with the fear of being maimed or blinded. I added that the figures looked disorganised and messy, like the female genital, and she feared that I would punish her because she could not understand the mess; that is, she could not type the page of figures representing an injured, castrated genital.

Next day she brought two dreams. In the first one *she was in a locked room with a naked man. He was coming towards her with a small instrument like a potato peeler in his hand. She did not know what to do but remembered that he had a hollow near his groin which would hurt if she put her hand into it. This she did, but he then found her hollow and it was so terrifying that she woke up*. This was followed by the second dream, which was even more terrifying. *A man was pushing up against a door*. In her associations she kept trying to remember an old, forgotten dream in which there was a door which she could not open and a long corridor. I recalled it for her, and she said, 'That was not a dream; it was a memory'. She became terrified and suddenly remembered that she was rushing from her parents' room down a corridor towards her own room and saw the knob of her door but could not reach it or escape. Her father was coming after her. I interpreted that she was running away from the sight of parental intercourse, and from a man with a weapon in his hand which represented an erect penis. She then said that while remembering the corridor she thought of the word 'hymen'; but she saw a navelcord. She went on to tell me about a blind woman whom she had helped across the road. She had seen this woman later on and felt she ought to help her again when, to her great relief, the blind woman was helped by someone else. I interpreted that she had never until now been free of the compulsion to help her mother, who had been blinded, castrated, by her father. I also said that her inability to look at the figures was caused by her fear of seeing her mother's genital. A part of herself had become identified with the castrated mother and was continually frightened. This had prevented the little girl from growing up. Another part of her was identified with her father, the man with the weapon in his hand who castrated her mother. I then linked up the idea of the parental intercourse and her fear of pregnancy and birth.

These dreams were reported on a Friday. On the following Monday she told me that she had wanted to come and see me over the week-end but was too frightened to telephone. I said I thought the reason she wanted to come was to protect me from my husband; she agreed and added that what she had wanted to say was 'Don't let him do it to you. Don't let him do it to you'. Then she reported the third dream of this period. In this dream *her father was a gorilla and was climbing up on something*. She woke up so frightened that she turned on the light and then thought she saw, almost as a hallucination, a woman coming towards her who she was afraid would throttle her. In fantasy she then went into the street and met a man carrying a gramophone in his arms. She banged him on the head, killed him, and took the gramophone from him. I interpreted that she had in fantasy taken her father's penis from him, perhaps in order to restore it to her mother, and was now frightened of looking at the genital of either parent.

During the next week Miss A was overwhelmed by fantasy and for the first time since the beginning of the second phase she could not go to work. She said that the little girl had taken control and that she wanted to be allowed to come to me all the time. She had never been dependent on

me in this way before and she did not like it. She said she had been
stubborn and stupid in wanting to revert to the little girl, who now spent
all her time crying in a kind of whimper and kept on saying 'What shall I
do? Where shall I go? What is to become of me?'

She then began to talk about her fear of having to do the accounts at
the office. The next day she reported the fourth and final dream of this
phase. *She found herself in bed with somebody behind her whom she referred to as
'it'. 'It' was curled up in a ball and when she moved and touched it, it stretched out.
She then found she had come up to it and that their lips met and that "it" was a man.
She went to sleep and when she woke up her mother came into the room and told her
to type a map. As she already felt in disgrace, she felt she must do it and she did not
know how.* She then woke up. I said that the thing was a penis which
stretched out and became erect when she kissed it. She had been in bed
with her father. The map that her mother asked her to type was a map of
a castrated genital which she could not bear to look at, having seen and
kissed and perhaps swallowed the male genital.

For my interpretation I took into account earlier material connected
with her oral fears and especially with her urge to eat anything she loved.
I also used some previous material about her goitre, according to which
she had swallowed something which she wanted to exhibit and to hide at
the same time. She accepted the interpretation, and confirmed it by
adding that the thing she kissed had been cylindrical and prominent, more
like a penis than a mouth.

Bringing together the four dreams, I pointed out that she always
wanted to become the little girl of three, but this time she was doing it in
relation to me. I was felt to be a safe and stable primary mother but at the
same time represented the Oedipal mother who was in danger of being
attacked by my husband and was also capable of attacking her. She
dreamt about her father first as a danger to her mother, then later as
castrated by her. I reminded her of the feeling she had often mentioned,
that she was really the superior-member of the family, and I added that
she had never been able to deal with the guilt about this superiority.

After this piece of analysis her anxiety diminished and she was able
to return to work. Simultaneously she felt well again and was delighted
to find that this could happen to her. She realised with sudden surprise
that she had not made friends at her evening classes; now she wanted to.
She said to me, 'I used not to be there, so I couldn't know any people'; and
later, 'I used to know nothing, so I couldn't learn anything'.

Her relation to me became different and gradually she began to
show signs of depression. She mentioned this to her sister, who replied,
'You have always been depressed'. Miss A asked me if this was true and I
asked her what she thought. She said, 'You can get into a depression and
then you can get out again; but you have to be brave to get in'. I felt that

my patient had, in reaching the depressive position, now become more integrated; that although the anxiety she had experienced in the analysis during the past years was certainly not all dealt with, she had taken a step forward and had, for the first time, begun to make real relationships in the world.

She still resents her dependence on me and this is one of the main topics in the analysis at present. There are days when she shows regressive tendencies and these are accompanied by an increase in the intensity of the transference neurosis, but they are transitory and can be dealt with by interpretations. She talks now about the end of her analysis and thinks that she will go to Canada so she can speak French and make some money at the same time. She promises to come and see me or write to me once a year but not more often, as she insists she must be free. I tell her that she fears I will get too dependent on her and will never set her free.

I shall now briefly summarise the three phases of analysis and compare them and discuss their theoretical significance.

In the first phase Miss A was confused and easily frightened. She was incapable of accepting external reality in the analytic situation or of recognising my separate existence. Any clash in our interests was a shock and produced anxiety, anger, and hatred. She never brought together her two worlds: the external one outside analysis and the internal one that she was acting out in the transference. She attempted to experience an identity of interest between herself and her most important object, and establish a relation in which there were no frustrations. Unfortunately she could only achieve a labile and perilous union and a fear of discovery of separateness. Insofar as I tolerated her attempts and did not try to overwhelm them prematurely by my interpretations, I allowed the episode to deepen and to be acted out in the sessions. This produced regressive features.

This first phase may have ended with the repetition of a trauma. The demand to accept a change of environment recalled the memory of her mother's pregnancy and forced her to recognise her own separate existence. During the intense phase she began to be interested in my body and simultaneously to look around my room. This amounted to a sublimation and enabled her, as I have previously mentioned, to look at pictures which eventually became a source of great pleasure. The dramatic end did not disturb this gain but led to the emergence of phantasies about anal birth.

In the second phase there was acting out both in and out of the transference. During what was considered a very serious illness Miss A denied the possibility of death, over-cathected instead the fear of being maimed, and became compulsively interested in eating. Food was all-important but dangerous. External help was needed to prevent her eating too much, or poisonous, food and to stop persecutors from robbing or maiming her body. I tried but failed to stop the regressive acting out by interpretations. In fantasy she often felt she was playing on my lap, eating forbidden foods, and so on. This phase ended abruptly and there was no immediate therapeutic gain, except insofar as she was able to bring hatred, rage, and persecutory anxiety into the transference where they were fully experienced. In the previous period any hatred had caused anxiety and been inhibited.

The third and last phase was characterised by the prevailing fantasy of the little three-year-old girl and an accompanying hysterical conversion symptom of inability to see. The dreams produced during this period, dreams which Miss A could now tolerate, were all of the kind typical for a three-year-old. Freud describes how between the ages of three and five, when the sexual life of children reaches its first peak, they begin to show signs of an activity which he says can be ascribed to the 'instinct for knowledge or research' (Freud, 1905b, p. 194). This so-called instinct makes use of the energy of scopophilia. My patient's search for sexual knowledge at the age of three led to traumatic discoveries, and in the period of analysis when they were uncovered the scopophilic instinct was predominant. The resulting ambivalence about seeing might have been hysterically converted to an inability to do so. The anxieties of the period were intense but could be dealt with by interpretations. There was, however, a short but dramatic regression and memories were uncovered in dreams and fantasies. Her fears of her own oral aggressiveness and of being castrated could be interpreted and understood in the transference. This phase brought with it an immediate change towards maturity in Miss A's relation to internal and external reality.

Each phase was characterised by dramatic and intense visual excitement and some acting out. Rosenfeld (1964, p. 204) thinks that 'it is the patient who is strongly fixated in the paranoid-schizoid position and has turned away from his primary object with intense hostility who tends to act out excessively'. Miss A was fixated at the pre-depressive position when the acting out took place, and no excessive acting out did occur once the depressive position was reached.

Greenacre (1950) says that a special emphasis on visual sensitisation produces a bent for dramatisation which is a derivative of exhibitionism and scopophilia. She thinks that the tendency to act out usually results from disturbances in the second year of life and is accompanied by a distortion in the relation of action to speech. She links this distortion with difficulties in the patient's life at the time of transition from pre-verbal to verbal forms of communication. Miss A is definitely a visual type and her two main fields of sublimation have been first, enjoying pictures and second, learning languages. During the analysis Miss A's ability to verbalise her thoughts and to accept interpretations has developed. She had been almost entirely silent with her first analyst for about a year and seldom spoke freely. She spoke with difficulty when starting with me and has only recently been able to talk and listen in a more adult way.

I would like to put forward the hypothesis that she was exposed to traumata in the transitional period from pre-verbalised to verbalised thought. This had the effect of stunting her maturation, both in terms of ego development and in her object relations. In view of her previous history it is fair to assume that between the ages of two and three her ego was insufficiently integrated and too weak to master the anxiety caused by the traumata of her mother's pregnancy and the sight, or fantasied sight, of the primal scene. After this age she was unable to make real emotional progress. Her early introjections were frozen and it was not possible for her to absorb any further objects into her ego. It was only after three years of analysis with me that she could introject me as a whole person without being swamped by persecutory anxiety, and so to reach and maintain the depressive position.

I have not yet tried to evaluate the usefulness of the three intense phases. Anna Freud (1936, p. 23) points out that acting out in the transference brings only small therapeutic gain. Here, certainly, very little gain could be observed during the period of acting out. After each phase, however, I had the impression that work was possible that could not have been attempted before, and I should like to ask whether the acting out periods could be considered as providing an opportunity for ego consolidation and maturation that would have been difficult without them.

Winnicott (1954) discusses the therapeutic effects of certain kinds of regressive experience, particularly regression to full oral dependence. He thinks this experience is sometimes necessary in the analysis of psychotic patients. Although there was no regression of that kind in the work described here, there were phases when an understanding of his ideas was very helpful. I think the chief difference is that my patient's ego was weak but accessible, and contact of a real kind could be made from the start.

From the point of view of regression, perhaps the function of the two first phases was to enable the patient's ego to develop sufficiently for the analysis of the Oedipal anxieties to be undertaken. She had to go back in order to come forward, the *reculer pour mieux sauter* which Michael Balint often referred to when quoting Ferenczi. The relationship to her primary object had to be stabilised so that it could be maintained when the Oedipal anxieties and the rivalry with her mother were experienced and worked through. In other words there had to be a relationship simultaneously to the primary and to the Oedipal mother.

chapter 3

'On Being Empty of Oneself' is a pioneering paper in the study of the very earliest object relations in a severely ill patient. Through the transference it appears that a quality of inner emptiness can be linked with the misrecognition of the state of being of the post-natal baby. This is a mismatch of infantile experience and maternal perception which has become known by the title of one of Michael Balint's books as the 'basic fault' (M. Balint, 1968). 'Fault', in this instance, is used as a geological metaphor and not a term of blame. Misrecognition rather than maternal absence sets up a void within, which is repeated as an experience in the patient's later life. This has consequences for analytic technique: instead of interpretations which can only be grasped by thought processes, can the analyst provide a patient-elicited feedback to the baby in the internal world of the patient, who apparently has never had this crucial response? The two *activities* of patient and analyst may be able to achieve the 'recognition' from which the person can grow. Balint asks, as she is to do again with yet more certainty in later papers such as 'Memory and Consciousness' (Chapter 7) and 'Creative Life' (Chapter 8), whether misrecognition and its consequences form a condition prior to, and quite different in its feel and the implications of its mood from, the earliest paranoid-schizoid position described by Melanie Klein, with its massive projections and splittings. Balint suggests that the sense of emptiness would pre-date the onset of envy as the patient is empty of internal objects either good or bad. There is nothing either to envy or to be envied.

In this paper Balint distinguishes between 'self' and 'ego' in a way which she was not to do subsequently, but even here we should not

---

'On Being Empty of Oneself' was read to a Scientific Meeting of the British Psycho-Analytical Society on 20 February 1963. It was subsequently published in the *International Journal of Psycho-Analysis* 44 (1963), 470–480, and in *The World of Emotions* (ed. Charles W. Socarides, International Universities Press, 1977), a collection of seminal clinical essays. Copyright 1963 by the Institute of Psycho-Analysis. Reprinted by permission.

mistake the 'self' for the 'self' of self psychology. It has more the meaning of 'subject', as one might be (or not be) the subject of one's own history. Although it is not her concern here, Balint wonders if her patient Sarah's specific experience of being misrecognized might not be of more general importance for the psychology of women, insofar as it emerges from the pre-Oedipal or even neo-natal (and pre-natal?) mother–daughter relationship. She will develop this thought in Chapter 6.

It is interesting that Balint's ideas on infant-elicited feedback response were being developed alongside Bion's notion of the mother's alpha-function responding to the beta-elements of the baby (Bion, 1962, pp. 34–37), and Winnicott's thoughts on the mother's 'holding' function for the baby, who cannot exist in isolation (Winnicott, 1960). One feels that although all three writers may have been working with comparable material, the male analysts, Bion and Winnicott, put more stress on the role of the mother and the analyst, while Balint's interaction with her patients leads her to a theory that stresses the activity, and necessary passivity, of *both* participants: baby as well as mother, patient as well as analyst. Where Winnicott (1960, p. 39) famously asserted that there is no such thing as an infant without a mother, Balint reminds us that there is also no such thing as a mother without a baby.

On Being Empty
of Oneself

There is an English phrase 'He is full of himself' which means that the person in question is happy and proud, having accepted himself and his achievements. In other words he is identified with himself, either permanently or, at any rate, for the moment. The opposite phrase—'He is empty of himself'—does not exist in the English language, but related ones such as 'He doesn't look himself today' or 'I don't feel myself today' are quite often heard. They always mean that there is something wrong with the person, and the last conveys in addition that a feeling of uneasiness is present. It is not clear whether the ego or the self is wrong, but what is clear is that one feels the other to be dystonic.

This paper brings some clinical material to bear on a very complex area of psychoanalytical theory, the relation between the ego, the body, and the self. Here highly uncertain boundaries separate the various concepts proposed. To mention a few: Freud (1923a) introduced the concept of the 'body-ego'; later Federn (1926, 1932) speaks of 'ego experience' and 'ego feeling'; Schilder (1923) of the 'body schema' and later (1936) of the 'body image', which was later taken up by Scott (1958). Hartmann (1950, 1955) and others speak of the self and of self-representations, and the relationship between them and the ego. Since I do not intend to start my paper with a number of intricate definitions, I shall use only the concepts of self and the development of the self, and will not either clearly delineate or even touch upon the parallel and possibly even sometimes identical processes that lead to the acquisition of a properly functioning ego and superego.

In our clinical work we quite often see people—either moderately or severely ill—for whom the description 'he is empty of himself' might be helpful. The feeling of emptiness may be rather mild or very severe. To mention a few of their characteristic difficulties: these people do not

like to be left alone, and they find it difficult to do anything for themselves by themselves; in spite of this, they often dread human contact and
resent being helped by others. They may appear mildly inhibited; they are
perhaps shy in company, easily embarrassed, awkward with their hands.
In some cases they can hide and even overcome to some extent their
inadequacy and feeling of emptiness, and can be active and successful,
though never satisfied with their activity. Under favourable circumstances they are also able to keep up a more or less normal social life,
where they can be very popular.

At the other end of the scale, these people have to withdraw
completely from everyday life, but this withdrawal, instead of helping,
aggravates their state and may lead to a sort of confusion. If he is
hospitalised at this point, the patient's confusion may be halted or even
diminished, because he is cared for without any obligation to those caring
for him. Thus the patient is not alone, but not actively with anyone.

How can one understand the co-existence of these two apparently
unrelated conditions: 'being empty of himself' and the need to have
somebody there, although this does not make him feel better or more 'full
of himself'? I wish to stress here that the presence of a real person may or
may not improve the situation in mild cases. In severe cases, however, it
never does.

I suggest that this disturbance in the relationship both to the self and
to the environment originates in a fairly early phase of human development; perhaps in the area of the basic fault (M. Balint, 1958) or before or
during the onset of the paranoid-schizoid position (Klein, 1946). Several
authors have contributed to our understanding of this period, amongst
them Ferenczi in the late twenties, Melanie Klein and Michael Balint in
the early thirties, Winnicott, Anna Freud, Hoffer, and Greenacre in the
late thirties and in the early forties, and more recently, Gitelson, Little,
James, Khan, and Laing.

What I can add to their ideas are some clinical observations on the
possible psychogenesis of this feeling of emptiness. As will emerge in my
discussion, this psychological condition is closely related both in its nature
and in its chronology to the importance for the child of communication
with his mother and her ability to provide for him a feeling of time for
growth and development.

These observations might also contribute something to our knowledge of the special psychology of women. In my clinical experience the
feeling of being empty or of 'being empty of herself' is more frequently
found in women than in men, as already noted by Erikson (1950). Further,
this disturbance may be linked with another, which in my experience is
also encountered more frequently by women than by men; namely that
they are full of rubbish, which is valueless and lifeless, like sawdust in

their teddy bears. Such women often say that they feel stuffed and uncomfortable, even after a small meal. From here various threads may lead to a theory of the symptomatology of anorexia.

Much help in understanding this condition can be found in the Kleinian literature, with its dynamic approach to the inability to take in and keep alive good objects inside the self, and its ideas on the early onset of envy. These ideas, though valuable, seem insufficient, since the patient described in this paper was troubled more by the lack of self than of objects good or bad inside herself. True, she could not take in good objects. This could be connected with her oral attacks on her objects and later on her envy of them. In my opinion, however, the envy seemed only to arise after feelings of being empty of herself had been overcome (that is, after the patient had acquired a feeling of self) and appeared to be connected with a more advanced stage in development than the one which I shall be describing.

The question arises here: have these patients ever felt that they were 'full of themselves', that they were really living in their bodies and were the same people, whom other people would recognise if they saw them from day to day; that is, did something occur to them in their development that created the feeling that their essence had been taken away from them, although they had once had it?

My paper is based mainly on certain aspects of the developing transference of a patient, whom I shall call Sarah, who was twenty-four when she was referred to me for analysis. I shall attempt to show the ways in which I understood these aspects of the transference, and how I used them for therapeutic purposes. This selection cannot, of course, be taken to mean that other aspects of the transference were absent, or were not observed or used; only that I needed these in particular for my reconstructions and theoretical conclusions. I am stating this in order to avoid giving the impression that this analysis was one-sided, or that it consisted mainly in the aspects which I shall be describing.

Sarah's parents were well-to-do professional people from abroad. Her father was described both by my patient and her mother, whom I saw when she came to England during the analysis, as a man with a violent temper who was never able to control himself. He was disappointed when his third child, my patient, was born a daughter, although his two elder children were sons. The mother seemed a depressed woman with precarious self-esteem, who relied on her children to take her side in her stormy marriage.

Sarah was breast-fed and, according to her mother, there was always a plentiful supply of milk, and Sarah was a perfect baby. Very early she started to play with her brothers, who were only a few years older than herself, climbing trees and competing successfully with them in every way. She did well at school and at games, and was good at horse riding. Her mother showed me a photograph of Sarah aged seventeen, so that I could see what a beautiful and glamorous girl she had been until the breakdown, which occurred soon after she arrived in London and which brought her to analysis. Sarah's mother could not understand how her daughter could have changed so much, and stated emphatically there had been no trouble at all until perhaps a year before the breakdown. The breakdown was put down to the fact that at that time Sarah's father had been particularly violent, and this might have worried his daughter. Sarah's mother's pride was deeply hurt by her daughter's illness. She was sure that if Sarah was spoken to sensibly she would be quite all right again in a few weeks' time.

During analysis, it became clear that Sarah had in fact always been in difficulties. She described how at a very early age she lay awake terrified in bed, frightened to call out, listening with panic to her heartbeats in case they stopped. From transference reconstruction it also appeared that from still earlier times she would lie rigidly in anticipation of some object descending upon her from above, and crashing on to her head. This object was sometimes described as a rolling-pin, sometimes a rock, and sometimes a cloud. I also have good evidence for believing, although for much of the analysis I was very doubtful whether this was phantasy* or a reality, that when she was about six or seven years old, the younger of Sarah's two brothers had intercourse with her, and continued to do so until she was about twelve. Her mother's failure to recognise the trouble her daughter was in at that time, as well as at an earlier age, was worse for my patient than the experiences themselves. Sarah saw herself at best as scorned, but usually as not recognised, not seen. In fact, as I will show later, one of the main themes in her treatment was the difficulty one person must experience in recognising another (see also Laing, 1960). She could never understand how I should know who she was when I went to the waiting room to fetch her for her session.

Sarah came to England when she was twenty-four years old, in order to undertake some post-graduate training, but almost at once she became confused and acutely anxious and had to abandon her training. She managed to move to the house of some elderly relatives near London, and got herself referred to a psychiatrist. Once she broke down she was unwilling to work or to do anything except bring herself to analysis each day. She wore the same clothes all the time, winter and summer, and for most of the analysis did not take off a thick cardigan. She managed, however, to appear normal enough to travel on the train and underground. The relations with whom she lived tolerated her queer behav-

*For the significance of the spellings 'phantasy' and 'fantasy' see pages 94–95.

iour, with some support from me and from the doctor who referred her for analysis.

After the first few months of treatment and during the first phase, which lasted for about one and a half years, Sarah covered herself up with a rug and turned away from me. There were long strained silences and sometimes some violent outbursts of feeling, but usually a rather flat atmosphere was maintained; feeling was mainly shown when Sarah had to cover the distance from the door to the couch, which she did with some difficulty. During this first phase, Sarah experimented with my ability to tolerate her confusion and withdrawal. Her transference reaction was to expect that anything that happened between us, either her associations or my interpretations, would have no meaning. She said, as some other patients do, that she was sure that I must repeat the same interpretations automatically at the same time in the analysis of every patient, and that perhaps I kept records of different sessions and played them over again in turn to each patient. But instead of being contemptuous and angry as some patients are about this, she accepted as inevitable the fact that our relationship was meaningless. This material was interspersed with fairly coherent normal Oedipal material, which demonstrated very strong penis envy, and also with accounts of many homosexual and heterosexual exploits. Her associations, though, were for the most part about, for instance, the wild animals which encroached on the city where she used to live, and how children were often swept into gutters and never seen again, and how frequently snakes were found and killed in the city. There was always a danger that termites might burrow under the foundations of houses and trees, and cause them to collapse. She was frightened of undermining me and of being undermined by me. I was seen as a whole separate person or animal, and she expected me to see her in the same way. She frequently said she would kill herself. At this stage she never looked at me, except for brief moments, but she constantly tried to find out if I would know when she was really frightened and when she only pretended to be so and, on the other hand, whether I would force her back to work and, in so doing, into her mother's world, which she experienced as a complete void. She dreaded the void more than anything else; much more than her own nightmare world. She was constantly strained and had difficulty in living—moving about—getting up—going to bed: everything caused strain and anxiety.

During this first phase of analysis Sarah's mother came to England and tried to remove her daughter from treatment and turn her back into the normal girl she really was. I had hoped she would look after her daughter for a time, but this was clearly out of the question. Sarah, though, was determined to stay in analysis and managed to take matters in hand. She passively resisted all attempts to make her go to parties and

buy new clothes, but agreed to be seen by a very undynamically orien-
tated psychiatrist. She was clever with the consultant, appeared to outwit
him, and led him to tell her mother that he could not take her daughter
away from analysis for six months at least and that she should not be
forced to work for that period.

Soon after her mother left England Sarah's only intimate friend
committed suicide. Sarah gave up attempting to look after herself, became confused, terrified, and withdrawn, and I had to refer her to a
mental hospital. She stayed there for three months and I was able to visit
her occasionally. On entering hospital she was described as 'depressed,
inert with marked volitional disturbances. No evidence of psychotic
experiences'. Her personality was said to be schizoid and mildly obsessional, with suppressed aggression and superior intelligence.

Shortly before this period of hospitalisation, after about one and a
half years of analysis, the second phase of treatment started, when one
day Sarah noticed a piece of paper and a pencil on a table near my chair.
She asked if she could take them and, when I agreed, she put the paper on
a table near the couch where I kept an ash tray for her, and she began to
draw. Her drawing was made up of little lines and dots and, although
disconnected, gradually they filled up the whole sheet of paper. She then
took another sheet and did the same thing again. This activity was not
undertaken easily, as if giving pleasure or satisfaction, but with intensity
and great effort.

After this, she spent part of each session drawing in this way. I
interpreted this activity as an attempt to communicate with me and show
me herself and her sensations and how scrappy and bitty they were,
because she could find no words to describe them. It was not important if
I did not then or later understand and interpret her drawings; but I had
always to recognise them as communications, respect them, and respond
to them. On some days when I was perhaps less responsive, she would
notice this and would withdraw but say nothing. I did not notice this for
some time, but later she told me about it and said that it was all right
because she now knew that I would probably be more alive the next day,
even if I seemed rather remote on that day. The rest of each session was
spent in normal analysis; Sarah started to recollect her dreams and to
associate to them.

I kept her drawings in a portfolio in my room. Later, when she
brought me paintings, I also kept her paintings, and it gradually became
understood between us that she was giving me bits of herself, of her body,
and that I was collecting them and keeping them in one place in my room.
As time went on, the paintings, which of course she did at home, became
more integrated, but not until towards the end of the analysis, in the third
phase, did they represent whole objects; in this, the second phase, they

were quite often clearly distinguishable part objects, breasts, penises, ovaries, and other parts of the body. Sarah had studied biology and used some of her knowledge, but nothing was ever complete, and nothing ever joined up with anything else until the final phase.

It was only during the third and the fourth phases of analysis (i.e., from the fourth year to the sixth) that Sarah was able to *speak* about her body. Before that she spoke of events and activities in her head, but these events belonged to the nightmare world in which, for instance, wolves constantly and ceaselessly chased round inside her head, or in which her head consisted of hundreds and hundreds of little bits like mosaic, each with a most elaborate picture on it.

This period, the third phase of work, was characterised by violent changes of mood, which were repeated session after session. Many of the sessions seemed to fall into three periods; the first a violent one, during which Sarah hit the couch or the cushions, clenched her fists, flung cushions on the floor, tore up her drawings, and crouched away from me sobbing. After about ten minutes—when I had interpreted this behaviour—the second period of the session started, and Sarah almost seemed to collapse on to the couch. She then started to suck her fingers or some part of her hands, or she left her mouth open making sucking movements. She became quiet and then only after a time she started to speak, and the third phase of the session started. Her associations were of this character: she said she wished that she were a bat so that she could come into my room and sit on the ceiling, or that she could be a monkey jumping from branch to branch. She described how at the beginning of analysis she used to sit up on the ceiling, or on a cupboard in the corner. I had not realised, she said, that on the couch was only a shell with an eye in it. Or she would talk about beautiful streams, which were clear and good on top but poisonous lower down. She expressed vehement fear of death, of killing, and in particular of being poisoned. In this period, as in the previous one, she repeatedly threatened to kill herself. More meaningful work could then be done on her fear of her oral impulses and on the danger of projecting them into me and into her environment. At one point during these associations Sarah often turned round so that she could see me. She began to speak about her need for me always to be the same and about her astonishment that I could recognise her day after day. She was still terrified of living in a void and of not being recognised.

By this time, I was beginning to understand something of the meaning to her of this void. During the third phase of treatment, towards the end of the session, Sarah sometimes turned away from me in a withdrawn way, looking frightened, angry, and pale. I came to realise that this behaviour related to my impatience of her continued illness, or occurred when I appeared to think that she was exaggerating or pretending to be iller than she really was, or the reverse, when I took her condition more seriously than it actually warranted. By the material which followed these episodes I learned that she felt deserted by me, and felt that if she did not withdraw and go back to her own nightmare world at these times, she would once more have to live in a void. *The void in fact was caused by my presence when I did not understand her,* because that meant that I saw only the external shape of her body, so to speak, but not what really mattered—herself. We were strangers: I became alien to her. I will discuss this topic more thoroughly later. It gradually transpired that she felt in a void or empty of herself, or both, in the presence of people who were, so to speak, in another world but did not recognise this fact, or failed to recognise that she was in another world.

In the period of her withdrawal what was libidinal satisfaction for me had ceased to be libidinal satisfaction for Sarah. Similar behaviour occurred if I was ever carried away by my 'understanding' of some material which at that time was quite irrelevant to Sarah's real communication.

At about this time in the treatment, during the fifth year, Sarah recalled a dream which she had first told me about a year before. In the dream a dog came out of the sea and bit her and then disappeared. This reminded her of a previous dream in which a bird swooped down, gashed her on the head, and disappeared. In this earlier dream she said that what had hurt her most was that the bird never turned back; it was quite unconcerned, indifferent. She then went back to the dog dream and said that when the dog bit her he took away her uterus, but now she had got it back again and could feel it inside her.

At about the same time she began to feel her hands as alive and belonging to her; until then they were often experienced as if lifeless and made out of steel. The common denominator of these two and many other similar experiences is that she could not have anything inside her because there was nothing to feel it with. I was reminded of Hoffer's (1950) ideas concerning the primary sensation of self being conveyed by the first hand-to-mouth sensation.

The theoretical question arises here—was this loss of feeling a secondary defensive mechanism against an earlier paranoid persecutory position and her own destructive urges? My impression is that it was not so, but on the contrary, it perhaps prevented the development of one. Admittedly, the patient's statement that her hands were of steel is a possible indication that the syndrome described in this paper was a secondary defensive development arising out of an earlier disturbance suffered at the time of the prevalence of the paranoid-schizoid position, and not a precursor or a mechanism to avoid its onset.

However, I would like to point out here that before this rediscovery of her own uterus in her body, Sarah showed only a manageable amount of hostility or resentment in the transference, nor was she often unbearably afraid of me or of her hostility towards me. One might almost say that as soon as she rediscovered herself and, so to speak, filled herself up, she became terrified of her own hostility to me and, of course, parallel with it, of mine to her. Her projective processes began to operate and this part of her analysis was accompanied by the emergence of intense paranoid projective phantasies. Before this discovery, in contrast, her relationship to me and her expectation of me was of an empty and lifeless person. Her anger was despairing and aimless.

A week after the reanalysis of the dog dream, she reported another dream, in which she was asleep and awoke to find that the light on the ceiling in her bedroom was on fire. She rushed to her parents' room to call for help. Her parents did not come, but her brother came instead and, as he was tall, he could reach the fire and put it out. When he left her he warned her never to touch the bulb again or to turn on the light. I knew enough at that time to enable me to interpret her fear that she had now turned on the light again and had got the bulb, globe, uterus, back inside herself and was in danger of catching fire. In response she told me other dreams in which it appeared that if she was empty she and presumably her objects were safe; if she was full with feelings, urges, desires, she felt she might catch fire, and although a man might come and put out the fire, he would later ignore and leave her, taking away what she had inside her, and she would be empty of feeling once more. She became very disturbed here, and this material was repeated again and again in different forms and could be worked through in spite of great strain. Her fear that if she had any feeling it would be 'put out' and she would then be deserted could be tolerated so long as she knew that I saw her distress but did not try to change her, to 'extinguish' her feelings. Although at this time—in the fifth year—Sarah knew that she could only have about a year's more analysis, any movement from me, which could be interpreted as my wish to make her well or get her back to work and so-called normal life, heralded a period when she was withdrawn, lifeless, and hostile.

The decision to fix a date for terminating analysis had been made three and a half years after the beginning of treatment, when it was decided to terminate at the end of six years, namely in two and a half years from that time. The reasons for this unusual decision were many. Perhaps the most important was my feeling, at that stage of my development as an analyst, that I could not stand an interminable analysis with this patient, and Sarah was aware of this. But, on the more practical side, there were reasons also. Sarah's father was unwilling to pay and, in fact, as it turned out, refused to pay for the last year's treatment; and secondly, the relations with whom Sarah was living were beginning to feel the strain of looking after her; although they stated their willingness to continue, it became doubtful whether they would be able to do so, as one of them became physically ill; in fact at the end of the analysis they sold their home and moved to the country.

Returning now to the case history, this working through period was brought to an end when Sarah recalled one day going into her parents' bedroom in great trouble. She thought she must have been about six, and it must have been the first time that her brother had had intercourse with her. Her parents had noticed nothing and she had said nothing. They had treated her just as usual; this had made her feel utterly alone and empty. To begin with, she had accepted this loneliness, but in time it had become a terrible struggle even to get up each morning and almost impossible to go into a shop and ask for anything, because she did not expect to be seen, recognised, or understood.

The principal phantasies about the loss of feelings and about being empty were expressed by Sarah in genital terms, that is, by the loss of her uterus. The connection between these phantasies and aphanisis (Jones, 1929) is obvious. In spite of this, I have the impression that the expression in genital symbols is a secondary phenomenon. A possible theoretical explanation for the use of genital symbols may be that the basic distur-bance happened at such an early stage and was so traumatic that a long time had to elapse before the patient could allow it to emerge into consciousness; by that time the language of genital symbolism had been established. Sarah's associations and behaviour in the transference give support to this theoretical construction. Her behaviour for most of the analysis was highly primitive, and can only be described as pre-genital: for instance, her intense urge to suck, which itself could only be reached after a long period of analysis. Only after these critical periods had been worked through did the patient begin to have feelings inside her body, which, remarkably, were soon expressed in genital terms. Prior to this, she had clearly shown me her desire for the breast and her wish to get it inside herself, and her attacks on it which prevented her doing so, but I had not understood her wish to get her feelings of herself back inside her body. When she began to speak about her uterus, however, it did, clearly, at that time, symbolise her whole self, but she began to talk about it only when she felt that I would understand this. At this time, she brought a very small pear-shaped pebble to show me, which she had found on the beach before she came to England. It came, in fact, from the beach where the dog came at her in her dream. She was able to show me the pebble when she knew I would recognise it as a symbol of her uterus and of herself.

Before summing up, I wish to report very briefly on the end phase of the analysis and on a follow-up of more than two years. During the last, the sixth year of her treatment, as I have said, Sarah experienced violent aggressive-paranoid feelings, but was able to contain them in the analytic situation. Normal analytic work continued, centring particularly on Sarah's relationship to her father and brothers. She tried to get a job but failed, probably partly because she interviewed badly. She finally decided to take a secretarial course, so that she could at least earn money in case, as she hoped, she could return to England. Her mother visited London again at that time; I saw her and she expressed pleasure at her daughter's improvement. During the sessions at this time, and though only for brief periods, Sarah was very angry, disturbed, and withdrawn. We did a considerable amount of work on her anger at being forced to go home, at being deserted by me, on her intense fear that she might lose herself again, that is to say, have 'herself' taken away by someone; and also on its meaning in terms of projection, and chiefly her fear that her impulses were too disturbing to be projected into the external world.

When she left we agreed that she would write to me from time to time, which she did. To begin with she lived at home and was unable to settle in a job. In a letter written about a year after the termination of her analysis, she reported a dream which was an obvious continuation of the 'dog dream' and which I was therefore able to interpret in terms of her fear of loss of self and body contents.

In answer, she wrote that my interpretation was right. She had now reached the decision to move to another town and live with a woman friend; the following week she started a job, using her university qualification for the first time, which she has kept ever since (about one and a half years). Two months later I received from her mother, who had visited her, a letter in which she said: 'Her first few months here imposed a strain on her, but I was delighted at the self-control she was able to command'. And another passage added: 'To me she seems perfectly relaxed and is entering more and more into everyday affairs of life. I do feel now that the long years have not been in vain'.

I have also had letters from the friend with whom Sarah lives—a university professor—in which she expresses appreciation for the work of analysis. She has asked me whether analysis always achieves such good results.

To sum up the course of the analysis:

Phase I. Lasting about one and a half years. A feeling of being empty of herself. The world is a void. Horror at having to do anything in it. No genital symbolism. Perpetual fear of the emergence of a catastrophe, or of creating a catastrophe. Much mental activity, which acted as an outlet for her destructive wishes.

Phase II. Lasting about one and a half years. Drawings, first of dots and dashes, recognised as communications about body movements and sensations, gradually developing into part objects and genital symbols. No attempt was made to understand the drawings in any other way. Analyst was allowed to keep her drawings. A false relationship was avoided as far as possible. The patient was able to store some of her feelings in the external world.

Phase III. Lasting nearly two years. Violent mood swings. Parallel with this, sucking movements predominated. She began to have feelings in her body and with them genital symbolism emerged, to describe the loss of feeling. As she filled up, the world filled up.

Phase IV. Lasting nearly one year. Paranoid persecutory anxieties became prominent; genital symbolism and body feelings continued, though not without anxiety. Some adjustment to reality.

A follow-up lasting more than two years. Adjustment to reality developing. Professional and social life developing.

Let us now reconstruct Sarah's development on the basis of the material obtained in her analysis, supplemented by the data obtained from her mother. I shall, of course, have to draw on somewhat more material than I was able to report in the paper.

1. Although there was plenty of milk and she was a good feeder, and on the surface developed satisfactorily, there was apparently a vitally important area where there was no reliable understanding between mother and daughter.

2. Although the mother tried her best, she responded more to her own preconceived ideas as to what a baby ought to feel than to what her baby actually felt. Possibly Sarah's innate ability to bear frustration and to adapt herself was limited. Possibly this experience formed the basis of the ever-recurring theme in Sarah's analysis—of not being recognised. Probably Sarah's mother could not bear unhappiness or violence or fear in her child, did not respond to it, and tried to manipulate her so that everything wrong was either put right at once or denied.

3. What was missing, therefore, was the acceptance that there might be bad things, or even good ones, which must be recognised; that it is not sufficient merely to put things right; moreover, that the child was neither identical with her mother, nor with what the mother wanted her to be. It was on this basis that the painful situation developed, where neither would identify with the other. The mother coped with this painful situation by denial, and the daughter by becoming 'empty of

herself', which probably also served as a method of dealing with her anger.

4. Although I have not presented the clinical material in support, I would like to add a further aetiological factor: the mother's inability or unwillingness to provide unhurried time for the development and integration of the feeling of self.

I now wish to attempt to express these reconstructions in the terms proposed in this paper. Sarah's mother was impervious to any communication which was different from the picture she had of her daughter and, in consequence, Sarah could not understand her mother's communications and felt that her mother never saw her as she was; neither found an echo in the other; and consequently only a spurious interaction between the growing child and the environment could develop. The mother and child could not, in Winnicott's phrase, 'live an experience together' (Winnicott, 1945). I envisage this experience as the child finding an echo of herself coming from her mother; or as the mother accepting her child's as yet unorganised feelings and emotions and, by her reactions to them, enabling the child to organise them into a self.

I propose to call this process a 'feed-back' which starts in the child and acts as a stimulus on the mother, who must accept it and recognize that something has happened. Her recognition results in a kind of integration, and this is then reflected, fed back to the child, in much the same way as on the biological stage the baby's sucking acts as a stimulus for milk production. This feed-back process presupposes an interaction between two active partners which, I think, differentiates it from projection and introjection in which one of them is only a passive object.

Sarah's mother's unwillingness or inability to understand her daughter was evident even at the time when she came to see me in London. I was unable to make a workable contact with her myself, and it was clear that she was unwilling to try to understand anything about her daughter, or even to consider anything worthwhile listening to, that did not link up with her own ideas. She was in another world, incapable of enlarging her own experiences or taking in anything that was unfamiliar. I realize that it is impossible to draw a conclusion from this alone and to state categorically that this proved that Sarah's mother had been impervious to communications from her infant. My impression, however, was that for her mothering was an enveloping manipulating activity, where the infant herself had no potential, but was a kind of empty object into which she could or even must put her own self, so as to gain satisfaction and reassurance; she could not see her child as an independent person in her own right. No doubt this can also be seen in her unhappy relationship with her husband and her inability to make a relationship with him.

We can now see why having somebody around her was not necessarily helpful to Sarah and why in fact, in many cases, it even aggravated her illness, although she could not bear to be entirely alone because if she were alone there was no confirmation at all of her continuing existence. What was needed was a human being who realised that she was in another world and did not force her back into his world. I would like to add that the relatives with whom Sarah lived played this part to perfection. They recognised her singularity, but did not try to force her to live in their world, nor was their world quite 'conventional'. Neither they nor Sarah forced their own world on the other.

I wish to illustrate these ideas further by some brief clinical material from Sarah's analysis. For instance, the way I responded to her drawings allowed her to feel that I accepted her and did not try to force my standards of goodness and interpretability on to her and her pictorial expressions. In this way my reaction was acceptable to her and was even sometimes perhaps a proper feed-back.

My last illustration is a general observation about children. It is interesting to note how important it is for healthy children to be able to show a hurt part of their body to parents. When they hurt themselves, even if it is only in a very minor way, they usually run to their mother to show her what has happened, and she must accept it. They can then run off and play again. A proper feed-back is when the mother receives the hurt, recognises it, does not make too much fuss over it, but just accepts its reality. It seems as if it was in this situation that Sarah's mother failed her.

By the way, lack of proper feed-back may also lead through a deficiency or superfluity of adequate stimulation to ego distortions. Parts of the ego may over-develop in trying to cope with the situation, while other parts may under-develop or become retarded. I cannot elaborate this theme here, which is, of course, only one of the causes of ego distortion, which have recently received much attention in the analytic literature (Gitelson, 1958; James, 1960; Khan, 1962).

To return to my main train of thought. Because of the lack of proper feed-back, the child, as well as the environment, got poorer; this ultimately resulted in the void outside and the emptiness inside, with life only being lived in a fantastic and nightmare world dominated by id impulses, but out of touch with body sensations and feelings; or, to paraphrase Ferenczi (1933): in a world of 'thinking without feeling and feeling without thinking'. The infant tried to communicate, but got no response; nothing came back, everything faded; nothing was fed back, or what came back was not an echo or a response to what the infant felt or was trying to communicate. This lifeless relationship with the environment continued until a breakdown occurred, when Sarah was seventeen.

What was left in my patient was only aggression out of despair. One could interpret the meaning of the wolves chasing round inside her head as representing the patient chasing her mother, or the mother chasing her child. This activity, however, only expressed endless futile anger and despair. After a time, with no real feed-back, the object that was chased, or the object that was needed, became unimportant; no particular object was worth chasing or worth being angry with.

In addition, since time was not punctuated by periods of good and bad feed-back, the patient gave up hope that time would do anything for her, that there would be time to do anything in, or that time would bring about a change or growth.

For Sarah, the nucleus of herself was not based on feelings arising out of body-self-sensations, reinforced and enriched by responses from her mother to them, so her early introjections were felt to be alien, threatening to swamp her self. Healthy projective and introjective processes were stunted. The infant remained isolated from reality. In this connection see also Erickson (1950) and Searles (1961). Hoffer (1952) also points out that in a child's development many situations of stress amounting to a loss of the feeling of self may arise. The patient cited by Anna Freud (1954, p. 613), an adolescent girl who had been a victim of the Nazi régime and who was smuggled out of a Polish ghetto as an infant, told her analyst that she could not be analysed unless her analyst spent the whole day with her as she was a different person in different places. Miss Freud says that she asked the therapist 'to offer herself in the flesh as the image of a steady, ever-present object, suitable for internalisation, so that the patient's personality could be regrouped and unified around this image. Then, and only then the girl felt, would there be a stable and truly individual centre to her personality'. She demonstrates the predicament of a girl who as an infant did not have the opportunity to develop a coherent self because of the lack of one single person with whom she could relate.

Since the early work of Freud, the paramount importance of a good mother–child relationship has been stressed. The difficulty, however, is sometimes to define or specify exactly what 'good' really is. In this paper I have stressed that aspect of a good relationship where the mother is stimulated by her baby so that her reactions will be felt by her child as an echo or a proper feed-back.

SUMMARY

Reconstruction of Pre-analytic Developments

1. Sarah's mother did not notice, or ignored, or could not respond to, her daughter. She could therefore not provide the proper feed-back or

echo which was needed. This faulty relationship continued during Sarah's childhood and throughout her whole life.

2. Because of this lack of feed-back Sarah felt that she was unrecognised, that she was empty of herself, that she had to live in a void.

3. If she was empty of herself, no one could recognise her; she was ignored, alone, and relatively safe.

4. To have something, Sarah created a nightmare world which she felt was located in her head. This also served as an outlet for her aggressive impulses.

5. In order to try to satisfy her parents, Sarah did well until she was about seventeen, although constantly suffering from strain and feelings of impending catastrophe, which went unnoticed.

6. Finally the feeling of unreality became unbearable, and when she arrived in London (where she knew analysis was available) she broke down.

Developments During Analysis

1. During analysis she became aware of her feelings of being empty of herself, expressed often as seeing herself outside her body. She felt that on the couch she was a shell with an eye in it. Inside she was full of dead people and objects.

2. She then began to experiment with putting bits of herself into me (and my room) and getting my response to them. She gave me drawings, representing sensations, movements, and parts of her body which were collected in my room; she also felt her associations were collected inside me, as I demonstrated when I remembered them.

3. Sarah began to have body feelings—that is, she felt herself to be inside her body—and parallel with that the external void began to fill up.

4. This led to fear of losing herself again and to a phase of paranoid anxiety.

Theoretical Conclusions

1. It is well known that the ego and the self develop in certain respects spontaneously or autonomously by what is called maturation. In other respects, however, their development depends on a proper interaction between the growing individual and its environment.

2. In this paper I have tried to describe one mechanism of the interaction which I have called an echo or feed-back. The infant, by his behaviour, stimulates the environment, and foremost his mother, to various reactions. Echo and feed-back can be described as what the mother contributes to the stimulus and reactions out of her self.

3. The infant then gets to know what he is like in terms of someone else's—the mother's—experience, as the mother lends her ego to integrate and reflect back the child's communications. The infant therefore gets to know himself, and his mother at the same time, by how she reacts to him. If the mother's reactions do not make sense to the child because, for instance, she is too preoccupied with her own ideas or feelings, then it is not a proper feed-back. On the other hand, good mothering, or proper feed-back, is what makes sense to the child.

4. There is no possibility of the development of a healthy self when there is no proper feed-back at acceptable intervals. My idea is that these need not be at fixed moments or periods. A few may be enough—and each can be valuable and start a development. (Possibly even a rejection or a reproof may be experienced as a feed-back if it makes sense to the child.)

5. These ideas lead to interesting problems regarding technique, such as the difference between interpretations and feed-back, and the different treatment necessary for withdrawal or secondary narcissism.

To end my paper, I would like to say that in general, if the interaction between the growing individual and the environment leads to severe disappointment, two reactions can be observed:

a. The increase of aggressiveness and hatred in the individual.
b. Deficiency symptoms in his or her development. Sarah's analysis enabled me to isolate (more or less completely) this deficiency reaction, and led me to the theoretical conclusions which I have just summarised.

chapter 4

Balint summarises her reflections on Freud's two crucial metaphors for the stance of the analyst thus: 'Without participation, that is, introjection, identification, and reflection, there can be no analytic work' (p. 62). Anticipating current developments, she concludes that this concept of participant observation is the scientific way of the future.

Typically, Balint has used her deep familiarity with Freud's work to show both her respect for it and how, within that respect, she has at the same time made it her own. This brief paper written for non-analytical practitioners has the 'surprises' that characterise Balint's work. She derails the reader's expectations, quietly challenging the assumptions that could arise from her own predicates. Thus having demonstrated how necessary is a degree of identification with the patient, she says that the patient will feel more alone, lonelier, if the analyst is friendly, as the ill part of the patient, the part that needs treatment, may feel neglected and ignored by such friendliness. She thinks it is the analyst, not the patient, who wants the soft opinion of friendly communication rather than the very hard work of listening for the significance of free associations. The analyst may also be tempted to opt out of the difficult task of enabling another person ultimately to feel recognised. Interpretations at certain points may show the analyst's intellectual understanding but not an understanding of the needs of the patient, who may at that moment need not to be disturbed by 'understanding'.

The biphasic stance referred to in this paper reappears in another context, that of training groups for general medical practitioners, in Chapters 12 and 13.

The Mirror and
the Receiver

Ever since Freud (1912, p. 118) advised that 'the doctor should be opaque to his patients and, like a mirror, should show them nothing but what is shown to him', analysts have followed, discussed, re-evaluated and sometimes even disagreed with this recommendation, although Freud made it clear that unless an analyst obeyed this rule he 'should know that his method is not that of true psychoanalysis' (Freud, 1912, p. 118). The functioning of the analyst as a mirror has been understood in a variety of ways, partly perhaps according to how much the analyst's own character, training, and ability allowed him to follow Freud's advice, how much he was able *not* to introduce any of himself, his own views, character, and ideas to his patients during the analysis, and partly because his experience with certain types of patients or at certain periods of the treatment convinced him that this technique did not lead to the desired results. In the 1920s, some analysts began to inquire whether conscientious adherence of the mirror model was appropriate to, or even possible with, all kinds of patients. Ferenczi (1933) pointed out that by following this model too rigidly the analyst might repeat some of the traumas, the consequences of which had brought the patient to analysis.

This leads to my subject, which is to inquire what sort of patient or which period of the treatment may call for a different kind of technique or for permission for a different kind of relationship between patient and analyst to develop.

Freud's original recommendation was not based on ego psychology, as it was made more than ten years before the publication of *The Ego and the Id* (Freud, 1923a). In spite of this, it carries with it the assumption that the healthier the patient is, the more danger there is of ego distortion through analysis; that the fairly healthy neurotic patient, in comparison with the borderline or near-psychotic, might not be able to resist being influenced by the analyst's personality, whereas, surprisingly, the less healthy patient is in less danger. It is thereby implied that a patient of the latter sort, because of his less integrated ego, is less likely to be influenced by the analyst's personality, or perhaps that he might even benefit from it. A problem may be hidden behind this apparent non sequitur.

My understanding of the mirror technique is that it is a biphasic attitude in which the analyst first identifies with the patient and then, by his interpretation, shows what the patient's thoughts and ideas 'look like' to him. Ferenczi (1919) also described such a biphasic attitude. As I see it, the stress is on the assumption that the analyst's ideas and thoughts do not distort or colour the picture he reflects back to his patient. This assumes a high degree of identification by the analyst and a minimum of projection. It assumes also that the analyst can, after introjecting the patient's communications, build up a whole object out of them in a reliable way and identify himself with the introject without endangering its similarity to the original. It does not assume that the analyst is inhuman; only a human being can identify with another human being. However, if the analyst is incapable of this kind of identification or for some reason thinks it inadvisable, the mirror model breaks down; if we take Freud's 1912 dictum seriously, the method is no longer that of true psychoanalysis.

As far as I know, the question of the timing of reflections, i.e., of interpretations, was not discussed by Freud in this context. His idea of using the metaphor, and stressing the opacity of the analyst, was to make it clear that the analyst's personality and opinions should not be shown to the patient, nor should he give advice, sympathy, or consolation. His job was just to reflect back to the patient what he was able to understand. True, the mirror reflects immediately and all the time, but I do not think Freud meant that; since the analyst waits for his interpretation until a favorable moment, he deviates from the mirror model. Of course, the analyst's decision to wait rather than to make an immediate interpretation inevitably influences the effect of his verbal interpretation, as do the tone of his voice, the rhythm of his speech, and so on.

As Freud was well aware, the analyst inevitably responds as a person, but this does not mean that he thrusts his personality on to the patient or that he thinks it of help if he does so. It is our general experience that in the ordinary way, unless the analyst gives advice or more or less forces the patient to see what kind of person the analyst is, the patient will not perceive him as he is. The patient's ability to perceive reality varies during different periods in the analysis. Different patients see us differently, and we will be seen in at least as many different ways as we have patients. We will be seen as a cold, rigid person by one patient, and a more warm, motherly one by another; our ages will be seen to vary greatly, as will the colour of our room and our clothes. For long periods in many analyses, we may not be perceived as people at all. Nowadays we sometimes tend either to overemphasize or oversimplify the effect that the analyst's actual personality has on the treatment. Provided the mirror model is followed, I think this is unjustified. More than the patient, it is the analyst who has difficulties in adhering to the mirror model. When we are tired and not on our guard, we may find ourselves paying less attention to the association of ideas, which is hard work, and instead discover that we are listening to a description of events in the patient's life which we might like to respond to in a friendly way. If we do this, we show the kind of people we are: we deviate from the mirror model; but more often than the patient, I think it is we who wish to deviate from the model.

May I now introduce a new idea: the distance of the analyst from the patient? Is an analyst felt by a patient to be near him when he is friendly and sympathetic, and distant when he is keeping to the mirror model? My idea is that a patient may feel more alone, more isolated, more distant from the analyst, when the analyst is friendly or sympathetic and thus deviating from the mirror model, because that part of the patient which needs treatment, the part that is more ill, may then feel left out of the sympathetic, friendly relationship. Although the other, the healthier part, of the patient may feel some satisfaction or even gratification from the sympathetic friendly analyst, the ill part of him, which is seeking help, may feel out of contact and not reached, even ignored (for instance, the aggressive, resentful part).

In my opinion, the mirror model enables the analyst to be neither distant nor close, but just there; when necessary, perhaps, as the primary substances, such as the air we breathe, described by M. Balint (1959, p. 66). It follows, possibly, that patients do not often try to change us into friendly and sympathetic analysts. This could be particularly true of severely ill patients, who, as we know, sometimes have difficulty in differentiating themselves from their environment and therefore cannot relate to it because this increases their confusion. They need the analyst's opacity and a mirror model in order to help them achieve some separateness. The apparent success sometimes achieved by friendliness may be because it enables the patient to get away from the task of clearing up his confusion. This might make him feel better for a time, but it cannot have any permanent therapeutic results. If real work is to be done, it is particularly important for these patients to have an analyst they do not experience as being close to them; whose identification with them does not go beyond the minimum needed for the recognition of this patient as a person; who relates to them, one can say, at a respectful distance, and who displays a receptive waiting, not an outgoing, identifying attitude.

At these periods, any verbal interpretation may be felt as 'obtruding' (Eissler, 1953) on the patient, as at such times the patient may be so preoccupied with keeping in touch with what he feels he has inside him, and solidifying it, that he defends himself against having it understood, added to, or disturbed, disrupted, or ordered. Any disturbing ideas coming in from outside are felt to be disruptive, even harmful. If interpretations are made, they run the risk of being experienced as distortions, partly because of the patient's paranoid anxieties; or, in fact, they may even be distortions, because at these times it is very difficult to interpret accurately. Any real distortions in the mirror, any projections of the analyst's own feelings and ideas on to the patient, will be almost unbearable at these times, as they will be felt as signs of intolerable hostility or intolerable seduction.

It often happens that the analyst discovers it is inadvisable to reflect back to the patient the unorganised thoughts in an organised way; instead, he may have to reflect the specific difficulty, for instance, that the patient cannot tolerate interference.

Another way of describing the same clinical observations is that the patient's ego is inaccessible: it cannot be reached. I think this might be true if the analyst only offers the voice of reason, i.e., his own perception of reality. Patients at this time can only tolerate very small doses of 'reason'. They need first to organise and then to communicate their reality to the analyst before they can accept even small doses of the analyst's reality. Any external reality cannot be forced on such patients.

With this we return to my remarks that Freud did not discuss the question of timing of reflections, i.e., of interpretations. In fact, in the same paper he used another metaphor: the analyst as a telephone receiver adjusted to the transmitting microphone. These two ideas taken together go beyond the metaphor based on the reflecting optical mirror. Any system using mutually adjusted microphone and receiver presupposes a built-in selective amplifier.* This must be either construed or instructed so that it disregards disturbing signals although very loud and impressive and can pick out faint but important signals. When studying the possibilities of brief psychotherapy, we called this function 'selective attention' or 'attentive neglect'. This sounds formidable, but it is nothing new. Often in a dream interpretation, one neglects very impressive details while finding the clue to the understanding of the dream wish in a faint detail in this general background. Looking from that angle, this selective attention and selective neglect is only a more specific reformulation of Freud's free-floating attention.

---

*I am indebted to Dr. W. Blomfield of Melbourne, Australia, for this suggestion.

If we agree, then, that many borderline or near-psychotic patients, although at times they need an analyst who behaves as a carefully timed mirror and has some of the characteristics of a finely adjusted receiver with a built-in selective amplifier, never need an analyst who abandons the mirror model, what kind of patient, if any, needs the latter? What kind of patient needs to know what his analyst thinks and feels, and which kind of patient is in need of sympathy from his analyst?

In Chapter 3 I described a patient who, for a short period of her analysis, needed me to respond to her communications in a way which showed not only the content of her communications but the effect they had on me. This period followed a long phase in her analysis when she could take nothing from me, and where my task was to accept incoherent and disjointed communications, remember them, and wait until the patient and I could talk about what she had been unwilling and unable to verbalise before. One could say that here I was not a mirror but a repository or filing system which only later was fed into the mirror. Following this period, the patient needed me to reflect back to her, i.e., to interpret, in the normal way, except that at this time she could not work unless she was also in touch with my feelings. I do not mean by this that I had to tell her what I felt about her, but that she turned around on the couch and looked at me and was at this time aware of my mood and tone of voice. (I must add that remarkably often she was accurate in her assessment of them.) She showed that she needed an analyst whom she saw as a concrete person she had not destroyed in the earlier phase, so that she could discover the effect of her behaviour and communication on that part of the world (the analyst) from which she had previously withdrawn. She would reach out to me. I, of course, must not reach out to her. She could then proceed, and during the following phase she could accept the reflection and criticise me and be angry and destructive without too much anxiety. All this was impossible in the earlier phases.

This amounts to agreeing with Eissler (1953) and many other analysts that there are processes in analysis when variations in the opaque model may be necessary. My example shows that they may be needed when the patient is on the return journey to health after a period of threatened ego disintegration. After overcoming the threat, the patient may need to have some response from the analyst, which may become his first introject of the new period, an introject the ego can accept without fear of further distortion or disruption. I have not found that an analyst needs to express sympathy except when things go wrong in the conduct of the analysis itself.

In conclusion, we have come to realise that the implications of Freud's metaphor about the mirror are more far-reaching than one would think at first glance. It was on the basis of this metaphor that all we now call the analytical situation, the analyst/patient relationship, and so on, have developed. A further consequence of this metaphor is the professional duty it imposes on every analyst to scrutinise every detail of the patient's communications, verbal and non-verbal, and to give equal and serious attention to every minute detail, undisturbed by the analyst's own private priorities and weighting system.

These consequences of the mirror metaphor are to my mind more important than the more often quoted rule also derived from that metaphor, that the only tool an analyst needs to accomplish his task is that of verbal interpretation.

Our train of thought leads us to a surprising result if we reformulate our findings using somewhat different words. The mirror model presupposes not a detached, but a participating observer, where participation, however, is strictly limited. Without participation, that is, introjection, identification, and reflection, there can be no analytic work. This finding is highly important for our analytic technique. Beyond its importance for psychoanalysts this sort of thinking begins to influence the whole of modern medicine.

Our researches have shown that in spite of its enormous successes, present-day medical thinking based on the data supplied by 'scientific', this is, objective, non-participating observations, has to accept certain limitations, the sum total of which we call 'illness-oriented medicine'. If any progress beyond these confines, any development aiming at 'patient-oriented medicine' is contemplated, it must be based on a new class of observations by participating observers. Such observers must use in addition to the scientific objective, detached observations, introjection, identification, and reflection.

chapter 5

Enid Balint's husband and colleague, Michael Balint, died in December 1970. After his death she found an envelope marked 'Fair Shares' containing notes made by them both and a few pages of typescript on a theme they had discussed intensively and extensively; she organised and added to these notes to produce this brief paper.

She presented 'Fair Shares and Mutual Concern' in July 1971 at the 27th Congress of the International Psycho-Analytical Association in Vienna, to which she travelled on the same plane as Anna Freud, who was returning to her home city for the first time since her exile. The starting point of 'Fair Shares and Mutual Concern' could be said to be Michael Balint's notion of the state of harmony he called 'primary object-love', a hypothesis which he preferred to that of primary narcissism (M. Balint, 1937). It develops, however, into a discussion of an important theme of Enid Balint's: the growth and central importance of mutual concern between mother and baby, and also patient and analyst, and the part played in this process by the presence in the inner world of significant other people.

The educational reflections in this essay have come to be a focal point of debate today. Demand-feeding as discussed here is the infantile background to so-called 'child-centred' education. In counterpoint to it, the Freudian theory of the superego corresponds to the education that asks the child to internalize the rules and regulations of an adult authority. Balint sees that these should not be mutually exclusive alternatives. There are always two people involved, parent and baby, teacher and child, analyst and patient; and mutual concern necessitates transcending any theory which gives priority to one at the expense of the other.

'Fair Shares and Mutual Concern' was presented in July 1971 at the 27th Congress of the International Psycho-Analytical Association and published in the *International Journal of Psycho-Analysis* 53 (1972), 61–65. Copyright 1972 by Enid Balint.

Fair Shares
and Mutual Concern

This paper is based on notes written some years ago, mostly by Michael Balint, some by myself. They were kept in a large envelope labelled 'Fair Shares', together with a few pages of typescript dictated by Michael. The notes were made following long discussions between the two of us, over the years. The discussions were of two kinds, but the problems they approached were the same. The earlier was concerned with what happened in the early life and education of one particular individual that enabled him to stand up to tension, to overcome the inevitable setbacks, frustration, and seemingly unfair treatment which he met in life. Was there a link between these qualities and the ability to be passionate and concerned for others, or are these qualities biologically determined, met with in different kinds of people and not connected?

The second arose out of our discussions about the upbringing of our grandchildren.

There are many psychoanalytical concepts relating to our questions. We talk about personality, character, individuality, identity, ego, and self—and there are many theories to explain individual differences, particularly the individual's capacity to develop a strong enough ego to tolerate tension. Very broadly speaking, we based our discussions on two theories: the first, one of Freud's earliest theories, namely the theory of the superego, in which laws are given and prohibitions are set. This theory, which has its origins in the theory of the primal father, is based on ideas about identification and idealisation, of the child's relation to his external father, who is much loved, hated, and envied. The child's conflicts are eventually solved, and laws are accepted which reflect the father. This acceptance can lead to underground rebelliousness, reaction formations, and so on. The individual is never quite free, and his relation to external reality is to some extent imposed. The laws given to him are not individualised laws; that is, they are not related to his particular ability to stand frustration or pain at any given time, but are, as are all systems of education, an attempt by the older generation to form the character of the newer generation according to their own ideas or ideals. However, in this theory the father has laws, which he believes in, can say 'thou shalt' and 'thou shalt not', and can train the child to behave in a certain way. He takes responsibility for seeing that the child does what his laws require.

Our contrasting theory was based not so much on the child's relation to the father and his laws, but more on his relation to his mother, and what we, over the years, came to call the theory or law of demand-feeding. In this we included not only the earliest phase of education—that between a mother and her baby whereby the baby is not fed according to the mother's or physician's timetable or schedule but according to the baby's so-called demands—but also a whole theory of education which has seemingly arisen out of these ideas. In exaggerated form it could be said that according to this theory the child creates the laws and the mother obeys them; that here, too, there is no individualisation, but it is the mother who has to obey and the child is educated to disregard everyone else—only his own needs matter. In addition, the law dictates that there is no possibility of waiting. In fact, according to this theory any increase of tension is felt as an injustice and therefore an attack on the individual by the world and therefore intolerable. We could say that here, too, the parents give laws—but in this case the laws dictate that the child must not be frustrated because it is frustration which gives rise to hatred and ambivalence and malformation of character. However, as with the theory of the superego, no parent can ever adhere strictly to this law and few parents would think that a child should never be frustrated, nor could they keep to the law, nor know for how long they should try to avoid frustrating him. The question is more when, at what stage, and how, should demand-feeding he given; also, who takes responsibility for knowing?

There are many people who consider that any outside interference in the self-regulating system in the child is harmful to the child, and that he should be left to develop with as little interference as possible. Interference leads to repression, distortion, reaction formation, inversion of the ego, etc. There is certainly some truth in this theory, for experiments have proved that if children are allowed free choice—if, for instance, they are allowed to eat as much as they want—they soon adjust to their needs and do in fact eat the right proportions of various foodstuffs. Or, secondly, if left alone they probably sleep the right amount of time; and toilet training sets in spontaneously. In fact, one could say that biological functions do possess built-in regulators.

Assuming, then, a fairly normal life, can parents leave children to educate themselves, find ways of acquiring skills and information, manners and morals, by identification, imitation, and so forth? Is this true for all social adaptation? Is there then any problem of discipline or of concern for others, or does a natural discipline and concern develop, and does the parent only have to protect his children from certain dangerous objects—fire, water, motor cars, etc?

Do these ideas lead us inevitably to follow the laws and theories of demand-feeding? Our idea is that this may be so for many, even the majority of, human functions which possibly possess built-in regulators—but not, perhaps, for social functions which develop as a result of adaptation to the human environment.

I do not think we shall get any further with our problems with the help of either of the theories I have briefly described. Neither of them, as described by me, involves object-relationship. Both involve laws and demands given by one person (either the parent or the child) to another person. Our problem can only be approached if we introduce ideas and a theory of object-relationships, and regard parents and child as equally involved human beings, not thinking that only one of the partnership is human, with drives and needs, or that fully reciprocal needs always exist between a mother and her child. We then have to ask the question about how much tension and frustration parents (as well as children) can support, and under what conditions. What satisfies them, what frustrates them? Does it give any particular mother more pleasure to 'demand-feed', to be used, and to be the sole object of the child's drives, than to curb them? How much should the child be her sole object, and for how long? Does she show concern when she satisfies, or when she curbs? These questions arise only if one assumes that the balance of satisfaction is usually not reciprocal as between mother and child at all times, in spite of the biological basis for their interdependence. From our observation as analysts we know that the amount of frustration and tension and satisfaction that is tolerable for us with different patients varies enormously according to our own personality and character, and I think it is not going too far to assume that the same thing happens with parents and children. What is felt as fair and acceptable in one analysis for the analyst as well as the patient is not in another, by either partner or both. The theory of the superego, which teaches that if each is treated equally, and obeys the laws given by the father, he gets a fair share, is felt to be true; and of course in any case in the pre-Oedipal phase the laws have not yet been introjected, so any frustration is felt by a child to be unfair. Depending on how the child experiences frustration, he may feel he is not understood or loved (and develop paranoid anxieties) or he may feel it is all his fault because he is so bad (and develop guilt feelings and depressive anxieties).

Under the law of demand-feeding the mother also feels it to be 'unfair'. Equal shares are not of course the same as fair shares: needs vary. And even if equal shares were fair, and 'what is good for the one is good for the other', the way they are given varies, as well as the way they are received. If we do assume that there are differences in satisfaction between a mother and her child at different times, this will inevitably lead to differences in the relationship between the giver and the receiver on the next occasion and we find ourselves studying an object-relationship and not a theory, either of good or faulty laws or demands or fair or equal shares.

We cannot understand the reason why one person can tolerate tension, be passionate and active, either by studying superego education or demand-feeding education. We have to study object-relationships to find out what leads to the ability to stand tension and acquire concern for the object.

One way we can approach the problem is by turning to Michael Balint's (1952) early theory of object-relationships—that of primary love. We then have to study the development that takes place in the relationship between the mother and her child which enables it to change from a primary object-relationship, in which mother and child are need-satisfying objects, and objects requiring satisfaction from each other, to a relationship in which they are objects of mutual concern. I wish to stress that both mother and baby can be, and often are, either or both need-satisfying objects and objects needing satisfaction. Although the mother probably never qualifies fully as an object of mutual concern, and always wishes to be, and is, experienced as a primary object to some extent by her children, it is through the relationship to her, as well as to the law-giving father, that the child becomes able to give up his quest for a primary object only (i.e., for an object whose needs are no concern of his) and to acquire concern for his object. In his International Conference paper read in Paris Michael Balint (1938, p. 208) said, 'The endurance of strain does not only take place at the command of the superego, but . . . it can also run counter to any such command and constitute an autonomous function of the ego'. We see this, then, as one demonstration of ego rather than of superego development. This involves both mother and child in the development of skills in being able to distinguish between themselves and their object and is also thus one aspect of the development of reality-testing. At one and the same time the child and the mother begin to separate from each other and become aware of their different interests while experiencing other relationships where differences of interest are already established, such as between a mother and a father. The relationship between the primary object, the mother, and the law-giver, the father (although usually of course both parents combine both functions), is of more importance in this developmental process than the kind of laws and demands given and received by both parents and child. The quality of the object-relation, both in reality and as perceived by all three, between the mother and the father, and between the mother and the child and the father and the child, is more important than what the laws are. What the individual will expect from his environment will depend on how the laws were introduced, or felt to be introduced, and not so much on how his needs were met; perhaps also more on how the mother herself was feeling than what she was doing, and how the child consciously and unconsciously was able to perceive and introject and later identify with her. It is important to stress here the difference between the way the object-relations are experienced by the observing adults and by the child himself. These experiences and perceptions will depend on the projections by both partners on to the others, which in turn distorts what is already introjected. This of course influences both the intrapsychic life of the individual and the way he relates to people and thus to future introjections.

The quality, then, of the object-relationship between the mother and the father, as seen and felt by the child in the degree of their capacity to convey mutual concern and fair play, is a more important introject than the function of either parent taken individually, either as introjects or as external objects. Our theories concerning the child's introjection of the parents perhaps belong here, but this process is usually examined in the setting of the solution to the Oedipal conflict, whereas our emphasis is on the importance in the pre-Oedipal as well as in the later phases of development, of the beginning of the awareness and the introjection of private and intimate, almost unobservable, collusive, mutually acceptable activities between the parents themselves and between the parents and the child. (For the sake of simplicity I am leaving out for the time being the existence of siblings.) Once the endurance of this strain has become tolerable to the ego, there is then the possibility of the development of the idea of fair shares. This, however, is more exacting, more dependent on the individual's (as a rule the mother's) capacity to tolerate and enjoy close proximity without restricting too much the partner's freedom. She has to tolerate proximity without satisfaction and without the control which goes with being desired as a need-satisfying object.

We now return to our idea: that given a fairly normal family life we can leave children to educate themselves. We may go one step further and assume that in these circumstances a child will not be overwhelmed by impulses that are too strong or that, if he is, the parents will be able to participate in, but not interfere too much with, the crises, and be proper partners, not too much or too little involved. It may be that three factors only are essential in education: (a) tolerance of the spontaneous development, of 'natural' control and discipline; (*b*) normal emotional life in the parental home so that the child has a chance to be loved, and can identify with a loving environment where he is not abandoned, left alone too long, or interefered with too much, nor compelled to witness too much parental disharmony, unhappiness, or excessively stimulating or passionate scenes; (*c*) not too much primitive satisfaction is sought from him by the parents themselves. However, will this amount of education prepare the child for strenuous effort towards tolerating serious unhappiness in himself as well as in others, and in coming gradually to understand real passion? Will he be able to make efforts when it will be a long time before he can see or experience the satisfaction that they give? Will he learn to tolerate tension and to accept severe frustration of his wishes, and that others are more talented or more successful than himself? If the parents demonstrate by example that such tensions are bearable, and if they participate in the child's crises as proper partners in them and thus do not shame the child—need they prepare the child in any other way? In participating in this way one can say that the parent prepares the child for a world where he will expect to receive and give fair shares, where he will be capable of giving and expecting from others mutual concern. He will certainly expect concern from his environment, but will it prepare him for tolerating and even enjoying the satisfaction of another at his own expense?

Winnicott (1963) approaches this problem by describing the child's relation to two different aspects of the mother: the object mother and the environmental mother. He suggests that the child can develop the capacity for concern when his sense of guilt in relation to his id drives towards the object mother becomes modified and when he can become responsible for them and the functions that belong to them. The environmental mother's presence is needed for the development of this sense of guilt and reparation and for the consequent development of the capacity for concern. This is an important observation and assumes that the child can develop the capacity for concern in such a relationship alone, that is, in a two-person relationship. Our question is, whether this is true or whether a certain kind of multi-person relationship is also needed. We are now considering a process which starts in the two-person mother–child relationship but needs, if it is to develop fully, a particular kind of multi-person relationship, the structure of which has not been described but which deserves serious study.

Can we therefore now approach our problem, not from the setting of a family of two or three, but from another—that of group therapy? This of course will lead us back to the family, but to a family where there are more than three people and where the phase of a two-person relationship has been replaced by a phase where the individual can relate to more than one or two people at a time. In a therapeutic group, although the amount of time and consideration given to any member of the group varies enormously from time to time and its variations are usually well tolerated without much trouble by the rest of the group, the group is very sensitive that, on the whole, time and consideration should be given to each member in fair shares. This never means in equal shares, but always that what each member receives should be in relation to his needs at that time on the one hand, and the needs of the other members at the same time on the other. If the therapist does not see to it that this happens, a serious upheaval may follow. A comparison of the results of psychoanalysis proper with those of group therapy conducted by psychoanalysts was described by us in 1961. Here we said that, 'after a successful psychoanalytic treatment a patient is definitely less neurotic (or psychotic) but perhaps not necessarily mature; on the other hand, after a successful treatment by group methods the patient is not necessarily less neurotic but inevitably more mature' (M. Balint and E. Balint, 1961, p. 5). The reasons we gave for this were that whereas during psychoanalysis the patient receives full and undivided attention in a very close two-person relationship, in the group therapy setting every patient must accustom himself to the idea of fair shares. We stressed the fact that the setting in which the treatment is carried out appears to have an important bearing on the therapeutic processes and the therapeutic results.

In the setting of group therapy the patients are helped by becoming aware that other people also have to tolerate tensions. We might question here whether, in a child's relation to the parents, this can be experienced without a traumatic outcome. Certainly in psychoanalytic therapy our patients are not always helped by becoming aware of the analyst's emotions; neither, of course, are they helped by seeing him as incapable of emotion. Can, perhaps, the toleration or even enjoyment of witnessing the satisfaction of another at our own expense only be established in a multi-person relationship, where laws are developed by a group of equals and are not given by one 'superior' individual, either the 'superior' child or the 'superior' parent? Certainly both in a therapeutic group and in a family setting the existence—the presence, even—of a parent is essential. But the climate of concern in the group appears to arise more as a result of relations between the group members than of that between the group leader and group members, and does not appear to arise, as Freud (1921) suggested, only as a reaction formation against jealousy, which amounts to a demand for *equal* treatment for all. In the setting of a family, too, it is often the parents rather than the children who become anxious unless all have equal rather than fair shares.

I do not wish to suggest that in a group setting primitive emotions and impulses are not experienced by members of the group towards the group leader, or that his love is not sought by all, as in a family setting; or that there are not many mechanisms which arise in this setting which attempt to deal with primitive conflicts belonging to two-person psychopathology through the relationship to the group leader. But group members will also, sometimes in a very quiet, almost imperceptible way, show concern for each other and will help the group leader to give more or less what each member needs (and will include the needs of the group leader in their endeavours).

I do not know if this is possible unless there has been a good enough early two-person relationship, although we do know from work with patients during psychoanalytical treatment that these structures arise from very early life. A child's wish is not only to get, and in my opinion this is much helped if the mother's wish to give is not over-strong. Perhaps a group leader is also helped by group members because his need to 'cure' is shared by others.

Summary

In the study of human ease and contentment on the one hand, and dis-ease and discontent on the other, in recent years more and more attention has been given—in addition to the favourable balance between gratification and frustration of instinctual drives and the healthy development of ego functions—to the importance of satisfactory object-relationships between the individual and his fellow human beings.

Our thesis is that the two factors in the structure of human relationships which we have been examining have their origins in primitive conditions, which means also that they contain a fair amount of unconscious elements and phantasies. In this paper I have not examined the development of these phantasies. This would have to be based on clinical material which I have no time now to present. Usually, only the secondary aspects of these two factors are studied, those which are developed as a reaction formation to primitive and aggressive tendencies. Over and above these, fair shares and mutual concern in children, adolescents, and adults can be better understood, also, as direct derivatives of primitive emotional attitudes which, although observable from the earliest stages of human existence, often seem to disappear, and when they emerge later are seen as reaction formations which, if they lack spontaneity, do indeed demonstrate their defensive structure.

chapter 6

'The Analysis of Women by a Woman Analyst: What Does a Woman Want?' is an important, highly original understanding of the early formation of a woman's desires and her internalised object relations. The springboard for this work was an observation which is a hallmark of Balint's technique. The two analyses described here were proceeding very satisfactorily; in fact, all was too satisfactory: something must be wrong, something crucial was being missed. These patients were satisfying the analyst in a regular but remote way; this led to the understanding that they had not been able to identify with bodily introjections of their mothers, whom instead they satisfied from a distance, so that although there was a primary heterosexual urge there was no integrated inner sense of being women. The patients were keeping their mothers quiet, or keeping their own antagonisms to their mothers at bay. As a result they had to have similarly quiet, empty marriages.

A number of ideas developed here both pick up earlier reflections and foreshadow their later development. In different ways the concepts developed in this paper are all concerned with the complexity of the relationship between body and mind and between pre-verbal and verbal psychic processes. In Chapter 10 this relationship appears as one of Balint's central, continuing concerns. The observation in this paper (p. 79) that where one would hope to find an internalised mother in the patient, there is instead a frozen 'foreign body', also relates to the discussion in Chapters 9 and 10 of how an introjection can be identified with and thought about only if it is imaginatively perceived.

This paper was originally published under the title 'Technical Problems Found in the Analysis of Women by a Woman Analyst: A Contribution to the Question "What Does a Woman Want?"' in the *International Journal of Psycho-Analysis 54* (1973), 195–201, and also in *The British School of Psychoanalysis: The Independent Tradition* (ed. Gregorio Kohon, Free Association, 1986, pp. 331–343). Copyright 1973 by Enid Balint.

Another later theme, closely connected to the one just mentioned, also emerges in the present paper. The analytic relationship can create something from material that is already existent but has not so far been imaginatively perceived by the two people who are always necessary for such perception. Balint once more can be seen to be pushing our understanding back behind the hitherto mandatory early Oedipal view of the baby's need to satisfy a depressed mother.

The Analysis of Women by a Woman Analyst: What Does a Woman Want?

Strachey (1961, p. 244), in a footnote to his introductory remarks to Freud's 1925 paper on female sexuality, quotes Ernest Jones as saying that Freud said: 'The great question has never been answered—what does a woman want?' Freud's most important additional contributions to the subject of female sexuality concerned the little girl's pre-Oedipal attachment to the mother which, he said, was stronger and of longer duration and richer in content, and left behind many more opportunities for fixation and character formation, than he had previously realised (Freud, 1925b, 1931). He stressed also that the girl's sexual aims in regard to the mother are active as well as passive and contain a wish to give her a baby as well as to bear her one and that she fulfils them in indirect ways. Freud also admitted that we know less about the sexual life of little girls than of boys, and that the sexual life of the adult woman is a 'dark continent for psychology' (Freud, 1926, p. 212). In spite of much recent research into this subject, this is still largely the case. In this paper I shall concentrate only on the many obscure aspects of a woman's attachment to her mother which are a part of this 'dark continent'. These need to be clarified if we are to understand more about her sexual life and approach the question 'what does a woman want?'

The problem of what brings the powerful attachment to the mother to an end has often been discussed. It involves more than a simple change of object (i.e., from mother to father) and often ends in hate of the mother, which may last throughout life although it is usually carefully over-compensated for in adult life. In Lampl-de Groot's (1928) important contribution to the subject, she gives clinical material to illustrate the immense difficulty a little girl has in giving up her possession of her

74

mother and changing from possessing her to having her solely as a loved object to be identified with. The little girl feels that the possession of her mother can only be maintained if she, the girl, is not castrated, but has a penis. It follows therefore that if the little girl cannot give up the possession of the mother, she denies castration and either forms no relationships with men at all and keeps her mother as her most important possession, or, while secretly denying castration, forms relationships with men with whom she is frigid but still remains inwardly attached to her mother. In my experience, however, as I hope to show, such women are not necessarily frigid. They never identify with their mothers or with any mature woman, but, in spite of this, can establish satisfactory relations with men in many ways. However, the men are never really at the centre of their lives; their real preoccupation remains with women and how to care for and satisfy them; but on the condition that their own bodies are for men: they do not give or get any direct physical bodily satisfaction with women; they wish to care for them but at a distance. Lampl-de Groot speaks of one of her own patients who wished to become an analyst, not so that she could identify with her, the analyst—but so that she could get rid of the analyst's analyst (a man) and thus take his place by herself becoming the analyst's analyst, and thus care for her in a non-sexual or sexually inhibited role.

Helene Deutsch (1946) describes the woman's struggle to get away from her mother while at the same time showing an intensified and anxious urge to remain under her protection. She also sees the attachment to the mother as continuing in adult life, and says that:

> In all the phases of woman's development and experience, the great part played in her psychologic life by her attachment to her mother can be clearly observed. Many events in that life are manifestations of attempts to detach herself, attempts made in thrusts, and the woman's psychologic equilibrium and eventual fate often depend on the success or failure of these attempts. (Deutsch, 1946, p. 16)

Deutsch thinks that if the little girl cannot detach herself from her mother successfully she will continue in adult life to need a considerable amount of tenderness and motherly protection and find life unbearable without it. In the analyses of the women on which I base this paper, this wish is shown as having been reversed; namely, these women avoid motherly protection and wish instead to give it to other women and perhaps enjoy it vicariously.

This problem first came to my notice during the analysis of two women patients who, although dissimilar in most ways, seemed to present similar features in the transference and also in their relations to men. In both analyses the work apparently went well; they did not make me feel frustrated or inadequate. In fact, I often felt I was doing well with both of them, particularly during the hour itself. During the work some of their conflicts in relation to men were made conscious and some resolution of them took place. However, one area of work was repetitious and unfruit-ful; namely that in relation to their mothers. Although they spoke about their mothers, little unconscious material came to light, either in fantasy or in memories, and little change occurred in their feelings about or their attitude to their mothers, or to me. Furthermore, although each patient presented very different (almost opposite) transference patterns, in neither analysis did these problems vary from day to day.

My feelings of unjustified satisfaction during the sessions put me on my guard and I gradually came to see this as a major technical problem. It appeared that both patients wished to satisfy and please me but since their wish was acted out it was difficult to analyse: in one it was erotised, in the other not. Both patients felt in different ways that coming to analysis regularly and producing dreams and free associations satisfied me—who was seen as the mother, seldom as the father—and thus their major problem was solved day by day. In addition, as this desire was satisfied in the transference their relationships with men became less tense and artificial, although on the whole their unconscious relation to objects remained the same. I was doubtful whether they would ever be enabled to introject their mothers—or if they had done so, to identify with the introjects in a way which would enable them to give up their peculiar distant, though intimate, satisfaction from trying to please and care for them, and come to value men in a wholly satisfactory way.

Both these patients were married women with children; both had lovers; both were referred to me because of 'marital problems'; both liked their husbands and thought that they were nice, good, even interest-ing men, but both were cool and critical of them while being capable of being warm, intimate, and loving with their lovers, with whom they had good relationships—not only sexual. Neither saw her lover as superior to, or even nicer than her husband. There was plenty of evidence to support the hypothesis that they were in the sexual phase dominated by the Oedipal complex which should present no particular problem to the analyst. For instance, they denied that their mothers were satisfied by their fathers or had ever had satisfactory sexual relationships with them. In this way they denied their envy of their mothers, or hostility to them. They both also denied feelings of guilt because of their relationships with their fathers, although they admitted to fantasies about being given babies by them, and of being preferred by their fathers. Both valued their vaginas, but there was evidence of a denial of castration and an avoidance of penis envy. Both patients were girlish in their appearance and manner, although one was in her forties and one was in her thirties, and it seemed as if neither could really show herself to be a fully adult woman who could be satisfied genitally by her own husband, that is, by her children's father. They could, however, as they had in fantasy with their own fathers, have their husbands' babies and be mothers of their children. They denied guilt but could have no pleasure from their husbands. One of them concentrated on pleasing (erotically to begin with, and later in a more caring way which was only sometimes a reaction formation against hostile feelings); the other one on utterly failing to please—their mothers and me. Their mothers were more important to them than their husbands although they could give pleasure to and receive pleasure from men if they were not their husbands. They appeared to have less severe super-egos than I at first suspected and were thus able to enjoy some relation-ships in spite of their hostility to their mothers. Both these women had older brothers with whom they had been intimate when they were young, and perhaps they had thus to some degree solved their Oedipal problems by transferring some of their sexual strivings from their fathers to their brothers, thus diminishing the hostility and guilt they felt towards their mothers at the Oedipal level.

During the first few years of the analyses I worked with these ideas to which both patients agreed in an unconvincing way, with little protest (although one as I will show became confused) but the work did not change their attitudes to their mothers or to me. Their analyses remained repetitive. One patient's attachment to me was based on an aim-inhibited sexual drive and a hope of overcoming my hostility, and the other on a hopeless attempt to be near to me which sometimes involved a search for a penis with which to do so.

I will now give some material about the two patients separately before coming back to theoretical considerations.

Early in her analysis Mrs. X acted out her wish to satisfy and please me—the mother analyst—in a teasing erotic way, secretly imagining that I was satisfied each time she entered my room. She thus identified with a penis; I was related to as an external object and simultaneously as one who could be identified with (Freud, 1923a). She dreaded touching me but entering my room symbolically represented entering my body and giving me pleasure and so set her free to have pleasure with her lover. She was anxious when she left my room, which she did with the greatest care and tact. She never touched me and lay on the couch as if she were not really supported by it. She told me that she hated men when they withdrew after intercourse, and was sad and never happy after inter-course because she would then have to wait until the next time before she was needed by a man again. He would be indifferent to her for the time being and would go to sleep. She wanted to be wanted all the time, to be the need-satisfying object for her lover, which was easy (because she had a vagina); and for women, which was more difficult as her vagina was no good to women. In spite of this the task was not felt to be hopeless or impossible. Early in her analysis she had many lovers, as she thought that I would be aroused and stimulated and amused by stories of them as her mother had appeared to be by her childish sexual games. She never for a moment risked my envy as it was always made abundantly clear to me that men did not really matter to her, which was in a way true. However, she herself enjoyed her relations with men in a rather offhand way. When later in her analysis Mrs. X realised that her sexual aims in relation to women were unrealisable, I was given up as an external sexual object and she began to get in touch with an early, more primitive, repressed introjected object who was felt to be truly feminine and for whom she could feel concern. This object represented her nanny who had looked after her from the age of two and a half years until she grew up and withdrew from her. The patient had been truly dependent on this nanny, who had been strict and thus felt to be caring and dependable. The patient had identified with the caring nanny and was herself able to look after— that is, to care for—her when she in turn was ill. A relationship of mutual concern, as described in Chapter 5, had developed between them. The nanny had responded to the patient's care unlike her mother, who had not. It may be significant that until this nanny's arrival the patient had been looked after by a series of nannies and that her mother had breast-fed her with frequent interruptions for test weighing. She was given the breast, taken off it, put back, and later given a bottle to supplement.

Freud (1923a) discussed the problems which arise when the ego's object identifications are incompatible with one another and said that this may result in a disruption in the ego. Mrs. X was saved this disruption, perhaps because she did not introject her mother but kept her as an external sexual object. The nanny was therefore the only real feminine introject and her individual with this introject was kept apart and secret. Soon after the identification with and relation to the nanny was remembered, the mother (as well as myself) was given up as a sexual object and the patient then tried to care for, and love, her mother in a non-exciting, non-sexual way. The mother then withdrew from her. The patient responded by resorting again to attempts to please her mother erotically. She tried to hide her emerging femininity; became very thin and started to dress like a boy. When this too failed, she behaved like a stupid hysterical girl, making scenes in public, once more hiding her maturity and her pleasure in being able to relate to her husband and children. Following this episode Mrs. X went through a period of grief and hopelessness in the analysis until she accepted her mother's rejection and started liberating herself from her. She then slowly began to change: she dressed like a woman and let me see how much she loved and valued her husband. During this time she seldom related to me as she had before but started to show her care and love for me, which I saw now not as a reaction formation but based on her emerging ability to come to terms with reality. The transference manifestations changed from time to time but on the whole she related to me as she had been related to by her nanny. She also stopped treating her husband as she felt her mother had treated her and her father, as inferior beings and objects needing continual sexual stimulation.

The second patient, Mrs. Y, was aged 43 when she came to analysis. Her mother had died a few years before the beginning of the analysis. The mother had probably been a lifelong depressive. This was revealed by her diaries which, although in the patient's possession, were only read by her after many years of analysis when some resolution of her problems had taken place. The diaries described her mother's struggles to make a close relationship with my patient, her only daughter, and to be able to hold her close when feeding her. This the mother failed to do and in order to bear the strain of feeding her baby at all she had smoked cigarettes and read continuously during the feeds.

Mrs. Y had few memories of her early relationship with her mother but the analysis soon uncovered memories of early relationships with her brothers and father. When she was very young her older brother, John (which was the name of her lover), cared for her, although later he became the main object in the Oedipal phase. Her relationship to her mother was unreachable. She was represented in dreams as a frozen, icy box or coffin or an unreachable bare room. This part of her inner world was not related to her other love objects—nor was it integrated into her ego—and seemed a foreign body frozen and untouchable inside her.

Mrs. Y had been told that analysis was a painful treatment and she thus knew that if she was upset and hurt I was a good analyst and was doing my job properly. I would therefore be happy, so she was content. Although I was seen as an ugly hunchback she did not mind; in fact, her hostility and envy of me was thus diminished. I was felt to be near to her when she was upset and she felt adequate so long as this situation continued. According to the patient her brothers and her mother and father were all intelligent and she was the stupid member of the family. However, during the analysis she felt that if she understood me and I was willing to work with her she could not be so stupid after all; otherwise I would be bored with her. To her stupid meant castrated.

However, she could not bear it if I showed her the Oedipal conflicts expressed in her dreams, nor when her dreams and associations led us to her earlier experiences with her mother. Still more difficult was it for her when I linked the conflicts of these early years with the conflicts she was having in her present life with her husband and with her lover. When these interpretations were made she got confused, felt attacked, and could not understand me. In spite of this she continued to give me dreams and associations in which her present life was connected with her past and with the frozen, isolated part of her inner world which represented her mother. I tried to help her feel her sorrow and her need to warm her mother, but this also made her feel that I was attacking her and was angry with her; and that I too would therefore become distant. She could not accept or really understand the meaning of my words; they became part of the isolated, frozen past. One day, however, she dreamt about her search for a penis and went to buy one at the chemist's shop. With this she could warm up her mother: she was then able to remember some of her mother's clothes, the contents of her cupboards and the books on her shelves; these representations of her mother gradually became familiar objects, and not part of the frozen mother inside her. When these became loved and grieved over she began to take her memories of her mother out of cold storage.

Mrs. Y always dreamt profusely and usually wept when telling me her dreams; however, one day she came into the room looking happier than usual and told me that she had a truly marvellous dream—quite different from the usual ones.

It was about a piece of marvellous velvet, the most beautiful material, texture, colour, she had ever seen; but it was not hers. It was Hope's (the name of a friend of hers). Here the patient wept. She, the patient, could not have the velvet, or touch or stroke it, unless she were Hope—and she was not. 'But still', she said, 'it was a marvelous dream. I never imagined such beautiful stuff'. She then spoke about her mother and soon realised that the velvet represented her mother's body. She went on to speak about her father's attitude to her mother when she (the mother) was 'blue' (her phrase—I did not yet know the colour of the velvet which was first said to be golden—but later became a lovely blue colour like her mother's eyes). Father could do nothing for mother and so when she was depressed he used to go to his shed and mend his boat. The patient then wept again, and spoke about hopelessness. No one could cure or soothe or stroke her mother—only Hope could stroke her. Later in the same session Mrs. Y spoke about her lover who often stroked her but did not touch his own wife; nor could she let her husband touch her.

The meaning of this dream was, of course, over-determined: it proved a turning point in the analysis which for some time became centred on the theme of hopelessness. This was connected with not being able to help or care for or satisfy mother, or to get near to her. I, the analyst, was no longer seen as the angry hunchback, and gradually the frozen isolated part of the patient, the unloved frozen mother, receded. Mrs. Y later began to form relationships with women and she cared for an old, angry woman whom she tended before she died. Later still she was able to let her husband leave her. This involved being able to release him and let *him* give up the hopeless relationship with her and his hope of pleasing her. She is still in analysis and is discovering what it is like to be a woman and to be able to relate to the world—which involves giving up her relationship with unhelpable people—and to be able to receive help from the analyst.

Theoretically the question is: was Mrs. Y's inability to accept and give satisfaction to her husband based on the early failure with the depressed mother who fed her? Did she in this way act out and preserve her relationship with her mother, so that her husband had to relate to her as she had related to her mother and was not allowed to warm her or leave her? Or were her strivings based on a later structure, the result of her Oedipal wish to have her father and give up her attachment of her mother? Her relationship with her husband enabled her to postpone the acceptance of her failure to revive her mother, and her relationship with her analyst enabled her to deny her failure to be nourished by her. She had first to feel the hopelessness and then give up centring her life around it before she could give up her hostility and fear and perhaps reach the depressive position, thus making reparation possible.

THEORETICAL CONSIDERATIONS

I have presented material to illustrate some of the difficulties encountered by a woman analyst when analysing women patients whose mothers were either depressed or withdrawn. These patients' main preoccupation is with the satisfaction of their mothers without giving up their pleasure in their genitals with which they satisfy men. They enjoy and value their vaginas but not their total femininity. This dual aim (the satisfaction both of their mothers and of men) necessitates: (a) a denial of castration; (b) the undervaluing of husbands, who represent fathers; (c) a particular form of relationship with the women who, they feel, do not have the sexual pleasure they have. They have a horror of touching these women but want to render them harmless and to warm or stimulate them.

My thesis is that a state of primitive concern is one factor in the structure of human relationship and can be reached during the analysis of some patients once their defences against their hostility, their reaction formations to their aggressive tendencies, and a period of hopelessness are overcome. Their early primitive emotional feelings can then be used in mature object relationships.*

It is open to question whether these patients should be thought of as latent homosexuals. In my opinion they should not because, although they are preoccupied with women, this is more because of their love and fear and pity for their mothers and their wish to keep them alive, than because of their libidinal drives, which are directed towards men.

In the analysis these patients have first to accept that they cannot satisfy their mothers sexually: they then internalize them (if they have not already done so) and feel love and concern for their introjects. Lastly, they have to go through a period of hopelessness and grief because their love and concern are useless to their mothers. They do not then turn to another woman to satisfy sexually, but find other women to care for and love. I do not see this as connected mainly with guilt feelings. They can also then form loving and not only sexual erotic relationships with their husbands. It should once again be noted that these women do not turn to women for sexual or body satisfaction. They relate to women as love objects—and objects for mutual concern—but not mainly as drive-satisfying objects.

These patients illustrate the technical difficulties inherent in the analysis by a woman analyst of those women patients whose preoccupation it is to satisfy a depressed mother while having sexual lives of their own. I have tried to show how difficult it is to follow the threads of their instinctual life and how these run parallel with the ego's struggle to maintain its object relationship. The analyst has to understand the conflicts appropriate to the Oedipal and pre-Oedipal phases and see how they relate to the primitive object relationships in which the origins of mutual concern can be traced. In the patients I describe the instinctual drives do not deviate but their failure to satisfy their mothers is acted out in their relationships with their husbands and lovers, who are kept as necessary but only partially satisfying objects, and with their analysts whom they feel they can satisfy for ever. I have emphasised these patients' needs to care for their mothers and not what I assume to be the earlier need to be cared for by them.

Before summarising my paper I want to make an attempt at some generalisations, in order to give a partial answer to the question in

*John Klauber made a valuable contribution to this paper when I read it to the British Psycho-Analytical Society and gave me permission to refer to his ideas. He restated the underlying problem as being connected with the way the judgements of the ego impose themselves on the drives and with the important role played by the ego in coming to terms with the realities of the mother's character. This in turn he saw as depending on the basic health in the child which can survive the bad parts of its early experiences and eventually utilise the good parts for mature object relationships.

my title—'What does a woman want?' I am (I think rightly) afraid of generalisations because I believe they tend to blur the clinical material on which they are based and inevitably omit many important issues, but perhaps it is appropriate at this stage to try to make some.

I suggest that women want, in their relationships both with men and with women, to use that primitive structure in human relations, namely the capacity for mutual concern (discussed in the previous chapter). Owing to its primitive nature it can only be satisfactorily expressed by the body itself, or by feelings in the body based on inner representations of the body and by body memories. The vagina is that part of a woman's body which is felt to be the most important area with which to express mutual concern with men (this does not exclude the use of the rest of her body). However, in her relation to women she is at a loss to know how to express it unless she has herself introjected and identified with a woman's body which satisfied her and which she felt she satisfied when she was an infant. I assume that if she was satisfied by her mother's body she rightly felt that her own body satisfied her mother. I do not think it is adequate to think in terms of identification with parts of a woman's body or of the environment created by the mother. Furthermore, I suggest that unless a woman can experience mutual concern with women her relationship with men is likely to be impoverished and men may be undervalued and not experienced as objects for mutual concern.

Summary

1. Some technical problems connected with a woman's attachment to her mother in adult life can be hard to detect by a woman analyst in the analysis of women patients, but if not detected can hold up treatment and the analysis can become repetitive.
2. This tendency shows itself in many ways. For instance, the most important part of the session can be the way the patient comes into and leaves the analyst's room, and the verbal communication is meaningless unless the real meaning of entering the room is understood.
3. The patient's feeling that the analyst looks to the patient for satisfaction and is excited by her has to be understood not only in terms of a wish to satisfy the mother and the analyst, but also as the method the patient adopts in order to keep her own femininity, and prevent the mother from being too envious of her as the possessor of an exciting, excited vagina, which she feels her mother does not have and which is useless in relation to her mother.

4. This can be understood as a form of latent homosexuality but arguments have been put forward to suggest that the heterosexual strivings are primary and are not a defence against homosexuality. The wish to care for the mother arises partly because she (the mother) was depressed or withdrawn when they were young, and partly because of the hostilities of the Oedipal phase. These women are able to do so after some analysis because there was some early object who cared for them and once the reaction formations against hostility have been overcome.

Such patients do not repress their heterosexual drives and the pleasures their vaginas can give to men. In spite of this they can be seen to centre their lives around their mothers and to choose their husbands in order to repeat a pattern that they had with their mothers, in which they, like their mothers, cannot be satisfied. At the same time they secretly satisfy other men, not their husbands. It is possible that this also repeats the pattern which they had as children when they satisfied their brothers. In consequence the lives of these women are split into two apparently disconnected parts in which women are valued but unsatisfied and unsatisfiable, and men are undervalued but some are satisfied and satisfiable.

chapter 7

How can one understand the loss of language and of memory brought to analysis by a patient who manages outside the analysis to lead a successful professional life? The idea of imaginative perception was latent in Balint's earlier work, but from this point on it is explicit and central to her thinking; this and the next three chapters revolve around it. 'Mr. Smith', whose case forms the basis of this chapter, is also one of the patients described in Chapter 8. 'Unconscious Communication' (Chapter 9) explores in detail the topic which frames the present chapter (pp. 86, 96). This group of papers thus shares closely related themes.

The work with Mr. Smith is too complex to summarise. 'Memory and Consciousness' shows Balint following, without being prejudiced by her existing knowledge, the moment-by-moment movements, gestures, non-verbal utterances, and appearances of a patient through the very earliest stages of his history. The simple schema of stimulus and feed-back has developed into a subtle understanding of the communications of the unconscious between patient and analyst.

Mr. Smith had disavowed some unbearable reality, although he had developed another personality in an area that was bearable. The dis-avowed reality could not come to be acceptable or meaningful by the usual processes that are needed for internalising the bearable, that is to say, first by introjection and then by identification with the introject. Someone had to be there to recognise the patient who, on his own, was trying to look at what could not be looked at and to feel the unfeelable. If the baby cannot make sense of its world by finding enough similarities between things, or if the dissimilarities are too traumatic, then it cannot find a place for itself in this world. However, in the context of a truly present 'other', the imaginative perception of reality can emerge, and memory and consciousness become possible.

'Memory and Consciousness' was presented to the British Psycho-Analytical Society on 15 January 1986 and later published in the *International Journal of Psycho-Analysis 68* (1987), 475–483. Copyright 1987 by the Institute of Psycho-Analysis. Reprinted by permission.

Memory and Consciousness

Freud (1915b) said that the assumption of a consciousness in other people rests upon an inference and cannot share the direct certainty that we have of our own consciousness; and also that the unconscious of one human being can react upon that of another without passing through the conscious.

These inferences have been in my mind while treating a remarkable patient whose analysis I wish to bring alive in this paper, before confining it by theories. This is my aim during the analytic work itself. Not that I have sought to ignore our theories—they are constantly in my mind when working with this patient as when working with all others—but it has seemed more necessary than usual to do this analysis—and to write this paper—with an uncluttered mind. It will be obvious that the theories most relevant to my paper are those of Bion and Winnicott. I learnt about Bion's theories from reading his papers many times; about Winnicott's from the long personal contact I had with him, which gave me even more than his written papers.

So my patient is not an ordinary patient; to begin with, I judged him as 'not ordinary' mainly because of the 'not ordinary' feelings that he produced in me during the first three years of his analysis—feelings of frustration and confusion which I have never had to the same degree, even with perverse and psychotic patients. I felt, and was, more out of touch with him than I have been before, while realising there was a 'him' somewhere to be in touch with. In spite of this, my determination to work with him, and his determination to work with me, were never in doubt.

He is still in analysis and it is difficult to write about a patient whose treatment continues, because things are never static: already, since finishing this paper, other considerable changes have taken place in him, and in the analysis itself. I started writing the paper when changes had begun after about four years of treatment, but I did not realise how they would develop, or how the analytic work would change.

The patient, Mr. Smith, a tall, bulky, loosely put together man, was 48 when he came for treatment nearly five years ago. He is married but has no children. His wife and he spend week-ends together, but both have jobs which keep them apart during the week. Mr. Smith's parents came from the north of England and moved to London when the patient was about six, or perhaps younger. His father was a successful academic, who died when the patient was in his early twenties. His mother and eighteen-months-younger sister are alive and live together.

At the beginning of analysis—and I was his third analyst— Mr. Smith had no memories he could verbalise of any kind stemming from the time before he was at public school, where he did well, in his early teens. It was apparently only then that life started for him. He did not remember what had happened before, nor, indeed, what had happened at his last session, or any of the sessions, or in any of his analyses. But he remembered everything that happened at work. No loss of memory there. *He told me that it was no good making interpretations about his parents because he had none.* It felt as if it was not only that he had no memories, but no existence in childhood and infancy to refer back to. In his early twenties he had an operation on his testicles which resulted in his infertility. He said it was a relief: it solved all his problems. What problems, and what his associations were to them, were not then forthcoming, but were crucial later in his analysis. When he was at school, Mr. Smith began to read poetry, drama, and history, and he was enthralled by it. He learned about imagination and people, conflicts, paradoxes, and relationships. But these were created by the authors whose work he read, and were never linked with his own life, nor was he able to contemplate linking them. Just as there were no parents, so too there was no 'person', no 'one' to link them with. Nevertheless, they embellished his whole life, and could be used imaginatively, and perhaps even symbolically. These writings could be taken in by him and he began to build up a world of characters and events and places—a 'space' into which he could project. Projective mechanisms could, therefore, be used in relation to the kinds of literature that suited him; but this world was never linked with his own life.

Mr. Smith had no 'small talk'. He was lost in the world and did, in fact, get lost if he went out alone. Yet he could operate creatively at work and then go home (by chauffeur-driven car), dreading having to meet people for dinner or socially. He had to be in control and when he was, he was most sensitive and considerate, and highly successful in organising groups of people to work with him, in a research branch of industry. Presumably he used there what he knew about relationships from his books. On the whole he lived alone. I felt that he was 'outside' even when at work—not a true part of the business he owned.

Apart from the house, which they both seem to love, he and his wife have no mutual interest or friends. (In fact, although this is what I had been told repeatedly in the early years of analysis, their interests are not so different, only imaginatively so). Mr. Smith's wife is intelligent, cultured, and a good conversationalist, at the top of her profession, as is my patient, although their professions and thinking are totally dissimilar.

He spent much of his life trying to avoid close relationships with anyone, but seemed to have an easier relationship with men than with women; he was perhaps *with* a few of them. His mother did not exist at all: it was not so much that there was no mother as that there was a 'non-mother'. Mother was disavowed, non-present, in the sense used by Freud (1940a). This word is used by Freud to describe a subject who refuses to recognise the reality of a traumatic perception. (Anna Freud (1936) talks about 'undoing'.) My patient's father, however, was more real, and I imagined him sitting at a desk, working hard, with no face. He was, to some extent, *imaginatively perceived* by my patient and me. I will not define how I use this phrase 'imaginatively perceived', but will discuss it later; it is an idea which became alive for me during this analysis. Winnicott (1962, 1971a) talks about creative experience and creative living and says that a creative apperception of objects makes the individual feel that life is worth living. He says that, to some extent, objectivity is a relative term, because what is objectively perceived is by definition to some extent subjectively conceived of. I have chosen to use the expression 'imaginatively perceived' in this paper because for me it is a more direct way of saying what this patient demonstrated to me.

Mr. Smith solved the problem of how to think of women by dividing them into two categories: in one category were the girls, who were silly but lovable and were part of his fantasy life*; almost totally imaginary, although based on real people, and so were *imaginatively perceived*.

In the other category were mature women who were not part of his fantasy life, were sexually unexciting, nor were they *imaginatively perceived*, understood; they did not make sense. His wife did not belong entirely to the category either of silly girls or of mature women. He had married her when he was in his thirties and, perhaps because she did not belong to his childhood, she was not totally unreal. In fact, at the beginning of their marriage I think he did perceive her and she did perceive him; there was a relationship between them, but he now had no understanding of her nor she of him. An attempt had been made by both of them to include each other in their real lives and shared imaginative thinking, but whatever attempt each of them made ended in failure.

*For the significance of the spellings 'phantasy' and 'fantasy' see pages 94–95.

Mr. Smith was referred to me by a general practitioner who had sent me some very 'good' analysable patients before, and so I agreed to see him, although I had no vacancy. When he came to see me he arrived breathless and anxious, and sat down heavily in a chair. He told me that he made funny noises and conveyed that he was unusual, that I might not be able to stand him. He also conveyed urgently that he was desperate and that I must take him on, must put up with him; but he did not say so. I agreed to see him once a week, for a time, until I had more sessions free. During a part of the analysis also I was controlled by Mr. Smith in a way that is difficult to describe exactly. But I can think of it in connection with frustration. I did not feel that if he were frustrated, this would lead to memories of frustration and useful analytical work. On the contrary, I often felt that unless he could feel that he was in control, we would get nowhere at all. He did not, in fact, try to control me by leaving sessions late or arriving early, or refusing to pay his bills, or any of the more obvious methods used by some patients. Instead, he behaved as if I did not exist for him at all, for some years, except as a place where he could take control in the fifty minutes allotted to him, and where he would get my undivided attention. He made me feel that I wanted to help him; that it was not an impossible task; but I could not understand how the man who was in my room could be so successful in the business world. I could not, at this stage, *imaginatively perceive him.*

When Mr. Smith arrived for his sessions, he flung himself on the couch, half across it as if he had no time to lie straight (which he managed to do as the session went on) and urgently demanded attention. He made grunting, squeaky noises, loud or very loud, which differed a great deal. Until after about three years of analysis, when memory started to emerge, the sessions usually started like this, although sometime before that the noises had clearly become a greeting to me of one kind or another. At the beginning of the sessions, both he and I were there and met. That is to say, a baby (non-him) and an analyst (non-mother) met. I sometimes thought that I represented the nanny, but was aware of the non-existence of a mother and the non-existence of an 'I' or 'me' for much of this time. Sometimes, however, when we seemed more '*there*' I found myself saying 'hello' when I felt a verbal response to the noises was needed, and that no interpretation I could make would be right.

It was absurd to repeat what must have been the lack of response, or the faulty, inadequate response of his early childhood when he arrived in my room. He used the couch and the cushions—particularly the cushions—as a baby might, by putting his face into the cushions and holding on to a corner of one of them when he was in touch with his baby anxieties. His body was very much 'there' and he kicked and thrashed about with his feet and legs from time to time. He never used the rug. No verbal observations about me or my room, or memories emerged. After the grunts there was usually a rather agitated silence. If I interpreted what I thought his baby body was feeling—for instance, that he wanted something to hold on to but there was nothing, so that he could not find what he was looking for—he would listen and then, after a pause, would start to talk lucidly, coherently with well-chosen words, telling me about his life at work, or what happened in bed that morning. He usually did not speak of himself as 'I', but as 'he', and in the past tense. For instance, he could not work this morning. He woke up very early and so got up and tried to work. Then he went back to bed and masturbated. He then told me probably a rather complicated fantasy towards which he had mastur- bated. He always said 'towards', not 'with', when talking about the fantasy. It suggested to me that he was at a certain distance from the people in his fantasy, as he was from people in his life. He never said 'you' when speaking to me, but spoke about 'the analyst', and about himself as 'him'. The session was called the 'hour'.

I watched my own feelings and his feelings which he projected into me, with rather more than the usual attention. I needed to remain in touch with myself, as he did not seem to know about my existence. It was particularly important with this patient, although of course it is with all patients, that I should not project a false personality into him or try to understand the patient in the way he had been *mis*understood as an infant (Ferenczi, 1933) but there was less danger of this than in some analyses, because he appeared not to have any understanding of himself at all, except as a muddled, clumsy, incoherent body.

He made me feel this, and I had to live with this uncomfortable state without trying to make sense of it before he told me what it was like. Occasionally, there were changes in direction, there was a glimmer of clarity—a break in the clouds—and these were very important moments in the analysis, which he forgot, but I held on to.

At the end of the session there were at one time three of us present: a 'he'—probably the baby, an 'analyst', and *someone who spoke about him to the analyst*, who for a time was called 'the narrator'. During the sessions, then, and at the end, he (the baby) and the person who was called the narrator—one who made up sentences, who had a voice and not only a body—met. When he stood up I was myself; he looked at me and saw me briefly. He then rushed from the room.

To return to the sessions. When the narrator spoke about the grown man, the grown man and the baby came together to some extent, because the words were sometimes relished and quotations from poetry were made and at those times the baby's mouth seemed to be tasting words, eating words, and spitting them out of his mouth with pleasure.

At some stage I used the word 'babbling', perhaps as Bion (1963, p. 38) used 'doodling', and Mr. Smith liked this word very much. It was right for the baby on the couch, and for the narrator man (and these two became separate). The grown man could perceive himself as a baby when I used the words. The narrator disappeared soon after this, and there was a grown-up Mr. Smith who worked and read, and a baby whom he could perceive if I used the right words. This was after about three years' work. He told me that he ate a lot of fruit, at this stage, particularly pears which were lovely, but he hated apples. The implications for these preferences seemed fairly obvious, and I did make an interpretation about a memory of breasts and bottles which was not totally rejected. In this case, the words about what the baby had perceived were not denied, disavowed (Freud, 1923b); there was a memory of how he perceived the breast and the bottle, in his liking pears and dislike of apples. He sometimes put his fingers in his mouth, and his head searched round for something, as I have already said, and when I interpreted what he was looking for he usually fell asleep. When he woke up, no words came to him, although I sometimes asked him if he had had a dream. At times there were words like 'petrol pump', or 'tree', or 'corridor' which surfaced, but there were no ideas, no associations to them. No similarities or patterns emerged. I began to think of Mr. Smith as an autistic child and thought of Frances Tustin's (1972) observations about autistic children, which I saw as relevant to this patient, insofar as he had little awareness of being himself, had no inner presentation of his own reality, and could not recognise patterns.

At the time in Mr. Smith's life when he should have started speaking, his sister was born, and the connection between his difficulty with language and the birth of his sister was, I am sure, important; but apart from some associations, which I will now quote, I have no direct evidence of this, or that he was not confused and lost before, or that this trauma was not used by him as an organisation to prevent himself from getting in touch with previous disorganised states which were even harder to bear. He said he had never played with his sister. He then covered his eyes and said he had lost his second pair of spectacles. I thought this was telling me that he could not bear to see his sister, and could not deal with this by play. Things then came tumbling out of his pockets. I said he wanted me to see he was in a mess and that he did not want to see his sister. He reminded me of a fragment of a story he had written in which a princess, who was really a man brought up as a woman, was pleased that she was a woman (which she was not). I said that would avoid the conflicts that she would have if she were a man, when she would have to see things she did not want to see. So he had to live in a world which was not built up from his own perceptions. For instance, he thus did not have to see the difference between himself and his sister. I

referred here to his account about his feelings when he had his operation
on his testicles. He said it had solved all his problems. Everyone, or no
one, was castrated. There was no need to dread the loss of an object, or of
a subject. There was nothing to dread.

This material was worked with very slowly indeed. As in every
analysis, I had to wait for him to make the discovery for himself, but I
was surprised when he told me something which he had just discovered.
He did not remember that we had been talking about the same thing for
some time even then.

After about three years, the first word Mr. Smith told me which was
part of a chain of memory, and arose out of his own perceptions, was the
name of his Nanny—Do-Do. This memory was associated to a story he
was writing in which a nurse who brings up three princesses is disorderly
and chaotic and, in fact, is the Goddess of chaos and harmony. He said she
might be modelled on the analyst, whom he often saw as muddled and
incomprehensible. At other times he saw the analyst as wonderfully clear;
he held on to her sentences, and even sometimes wrote them down. After
he had told me about Do-Do, I was tempted to ask him what his younger
sister was called, as I wanted to find words and memory linked together. I
knew her name was Jennifer, but was she called Jennifer? He first said
yes; then corrected himself and said no, she was called Jen. He then told
me that I was called BAL in his diary, and he had been interested in
anagrams lately. He had played around with the three letters and thought
of balance, but he could not get very far with this. Later this changed.
This information was part of a friendly communication—the beginnings
of a relationship between myself and himself. There was a 'you' and a
'me', and an 'I'. This step forward was never quite lost and led to the
beginning of memories about what had happened at the previous session
yesterday, or even last week. It was a sudden change (after about three
and a half years of analysis). This sudden change could be described as the
beginning of consciousness; or as the patient waking up from a dreamless
sleep—a void—or being able to get in touch with his dreams and his
memories.

I soon discovered that the fragments of stories he had been telling me
had all been written down and put away in cupboards. He thought that
they would, in due course, turn into the most remarkable story in the
world, which would be unique or, if not, completely and utterly useless.
He spoke about jigsaw puzzles having clusters of pieces which went
together, but would not join up. We had spoken before about clusters of
associations. He then told me a story which was becoming more coherent
and was about princesses, dragons, giants, gnomes, dwarfs, and elves. The
elves were people who played; the gnomes did the work, and it was not

quite clear to either of us what the giants did. He thought that the elves broke up what the gnomes put together. He said there could be no story unless there was a narrative. He could not write if there were only ideas and thoughts. There had to be a plot. I interpreted his search for memory, which I equated with history (his-story). He said that analysis should be called synthesis—psychosynthesis. He repeated that in his story the elves broke down words until they were just sounds, and the gnomes had to work to put them together again. We spoke about the noises he made which he had tried to turn into words; they had needed to be broken down so that he could look at them and understand them and put them together again.

Following the Do-Do memories, when there was a 'he' and an 'I' and a 'you', a memory emerged connected with his second birthday when his mother had given a party with a Punch and Judy show. He had been absolutely terrified. He had hidden under a rug (which he did not do with me, but hid himself instead with clothes, papers, and sounds). This memory placed him in a family: on a stage where there were three people, and where the Punch and Judy show represented a primal scene and a battered baby accompanied by strange sounds. His imagination had, presumably, come into play at this time and the events of the Punch and Judy show were *imaginatively perceived* and linked with his fantasy life; this had been wiped out, together with what was associated with it. The two-year-old who had experienced this event—a two-year-old boy with an ego which could function—began to exist again.

My interpretations were not rejected and were followed by associations which were about where he should begin his story. Who starts everything? Where does it all start? This is the Oedipal question, and the first story. Where does *he* fit in? Can there be a baby with a mother and a father all alive? A story representing this, or attempting to solve this, came later, as I will report at the end of my paper, but this led to a part of a story which links back to the episode which I have spoken about, when the patient lost his spectacles, and which illustrated his fear of seeing, as well as his fear of castration. The story was again the one about the knight who was dressed as a girl: this time another knight came along, and told the first knight to take off his girl's clothing and to put on armour and fight. He agreed to do this, and was pleased, but when he put on the visor he was terrified and had to tear it off.

This story seemed to incorporate an actual memory, about the terrors of seeing his sister's body which represented fears and uncertainties which he could not tolerate and which made a focus for him. It also awoke in him the terrors of having to go into the world and to fight, to be in combat with other men, to be a man living in the real world. My interpretation about this led to a dream in which I, the analyst, was dreamt about for the first time as someone who was there, offering to feed him. In his dream he regressed to an earlier stage before he had lost the breast, or before he was anxious about the absent penis. He then spoke about the difficulty for the knight, because if someone else imposed things on him or dressed him up in clothes that were wrong, it was difficult for him to get rid of them. He then told me another story about a boy who had seen a nymph in the woods: the nymph was naked and the boy realised that she was different from him; the boy then had an erection. In this story, the boy's mother told him that this was wicked and that there were evil spirits working in him. I said the knight was misled by his mother, but it was he, the patient, too, who could not bear to look or have an erection. I said that he preferred to be a girl in order to avoid seeing dissimilarities, specifically the dissimilarity between himself and his sister. Mr. Smith insisted that in the story it was true. The knight had the clothes and armour imposed on him, whereas he, the patient, had certainly not. He had absolutely decided for himself. I interpreted that he thought he could decide to stop his mother and father from creating a sibling. This had confused him, so he pretended to see himself as the sibling, the baby girl, in order to avoid the knowledge that he was not in complete control and was still the baby—boy or girl.

I saw it as my main task for a time to use his myths and stories as one would dreams with other patients. He said that the people he invented were all parts of himself, of course, but he had not so far endowed them with feelings, or himself with feelings about them. The analysis, for a time, concentrated more on words and anagrams of words, than on narrative or story. So long as this was the case the patient avoided the need to feel, but playing around with words in the end led him to feelings. In finding his own words rather than using the words of the poets that he so often quoted, he knew what they meant to him. He gave me a vocabulary of signs which were endowed with feeling and linked directly with himself. The babbling baby and the articulate man grew closer.

He tried to find his own history and piece it together into sentences, so as to make a story about himself which he could tell in his own words. As he did this, Mr. Smith gradually became able to imagine with distress his own existence. His verbal and visual perceptions were more closely linked. The task was to help him to imagine and accept being himself— someone involved in imagining and accepting the existence of other people who had been seen in a lifeless way before.

If the ability to perceive is lacking because it is too traumatic or alien, can one then think of an individual as being truly conscious? Can he have unconscious phantasies or imagination and fantasy? I am distinguishing here between unconscious phantasy spelt with a 'ph' and fantasy spelt with an 'f' because fantasy spelt with an 'f' and imagination arise out of the ability to perceive external reality and identify with it, and play with it; and unconscious phantasy arises out of the instinctual life which needs to become conscious before it can be played with. Its contents in the unconscious are of course representatives of the instincts: they are a commentary, continually present in our unconscious minds, on our instinctual strivings. One certainly should influence the other, but it is possible for there to be an unconscious phantasy life, which is kept separate from external reality. The infant can remain in the 'area of creativity' (M. Balint, 1968).

In parenthesis, can we learn about unconscious phantasies except through the ego? Or is our method of free association a technique to outwit the ego? External reality can, in any case, only exist for the individual if it is introjected, identified with, and then *imaginatively perceived*. Identification alone is not enough. Mr. Smith disavowed external reality when he was young, and during the first few years of his analysis with me, but his unconscious phantasy life existed and became conscious only in fragments when he began to write his story. His instinctual life, one could say, was therefore active, but perverse insofar as it did not find satisfaction in external reality, in the external world, nor was it coherent to him. He could not build up a coherent phantasy life; nor could he be aware of external reality, because what he perceived was totally unacceptable to him, and he therefore postponed the learning about it and playing with it, which would have made him a part of it. He did not hallucinate, either positively or negatively, but he postponed reality, so to speak, and kept it on ice. One could, on the other hand, see Mr. Smith as not having been fully conscious at all when he was young, in the sense that he had no sense of himself in a place. He was an 'outsider' and still is in some respects.

A sense of being someone is needed for conscious thought. This is only possible if the someone belongs in an environment into which he can project, and whose projections he can use and later relate to. To be conscious there has to be an 'I' and a 'you': a relationship in a setting. Bion (1970) says that thought (i.e., consciousness) is required to solve frustration, and if a patient cannot tolerate frustration (in my terms, external reality) he does not get the relief from it that thought would give him if he could tolerate it. External reality, however awful, is better than nothing. Mr. Smith nevertheless seemed to be able to use projective mechanisms through books and plays which did not threaten him, and which seemed to respond to him imaginatively (Eigen, 1985). He could, indeed, play with their authors' imagination and would change the wording of some of the books that he read, to make them suit himself and to control them. He could play with their thoughts and change them in the ways he wanted to, and so the stories became his own, in a way that his early objects never did. The early objects, as well as the analyst early in the analysis, were not perceived, were not part of his world, could not be reached, altered, played with, or changed.

Mr. Smith had fragmentary ideas, fragmentary thoughts, and fragmentary phantasies, but could not turn them into usable thoughts, as they could not be put together—used dynamically—so they could not make a narrative. Sentences were made up, but they did not represent the thoughts which the patient was trying to form, or the ideas that he was trying to get at, or the fears which he was trying to avoid.

In trying to examine whether my work with this patient and my feelings with him are similar to my feelings with other patients, the closest parallel is some work I have done with perverse patients. In the counter-transference often a theme developed in the analyst which I *could* have communicated to the patient. The question, here, was: Is the thought that the analyst has at that time due to projection from the patient (who is having unconscious thoughts which he cannot put together, ideas which he cannot bear)? Should the analyst hold on to them, until the patient is able to tolerate the frustration and fear needed to have the thoughts himself? Can the patient, anyway, take in—hear—interpretations from the analyst about the projections from his unconscious mind? Sometimes the situation is clarified by some body action from the patient, or some physical pain which he is experiencing; and the interpretation can be made. Can the analyst's unconscious receive unconscious communications from the patient which then become conscious, so that the analyst can use these projections into his unconscious therapeutically? These are questions of technique.

Before my summary and conclusions, I will describe one more story which, after many recountings, led to feelings of anguish and despair in the patient at having only fifty minutes with the analyst, at having weekend breaks, and so on. These 'normal' reactions were felt for the first time. The story, which I had heard before with variations, and without feeling, was as follows: 'There was a banquet celebrating something. The knight was there, but could not enter the banqueting hall. He could look on from outside, through a window or door. There was loud music, and then somebody entered and bore aloft a newly born baby, a girl (the queen). There was great rejoicing. The mother of the baby had died—but there was no mourning. This did not matter. The knight could watch from outside, but never enter.' My patient then sobbed and groaned, but stayed conscious and remembered the episode at the next session. In later sessions the story changed again, but was told with increased feeling.

The sound of the mother screaming in childbirth, and then dying, was added to the story and the patient said that both birth and death must be accompanied by anguish, as was separation. Now Mr. Smith's own story—the day-to-day events of his life—emerged, including his anguish at not being able to give his wife a home or baby or anything she wanted, confusion about whether he is that baby, and the experience of frustration and dread.

CONCLUSIONS

I have had difficulty in deciding how I should describe his main defence: repression (Freud, 1909, 1915a) will not do—one cannot repress what is not taken in by the ego; nor scotomisation as in fetishism (Freud, 1927); nor splitting of the ego or personality into various autonomous currents (Freud, 1940b); nor is he a case of melancholia, where the ego is also split (Freud, 1917). These ideas, however, are not central to the question I approach in this paper, which is about consciousness. In Chapter 3, I used the concept of self, but in this analysis it was too vague a concept and not clinically useful to me.

The recognition of patterns and similarities is essential if a baby is to build up a world in which he can live and locate himself. Presumably—but not demonstrated in the analysis—the mother has to recognise her infant, make him feel he belongs.

If the baby cannot build up such a world, it may be because he cannot bear the dissimilarities he perceives (or the way he is perceived), so his perceptions are disavowed, as though the breast is there always, not sometimes absent; or it is not needed and there is no significance in the breast. The penis is there always, and, if not, there is no meaning in having a penis. All people are the same. But positive or negative hallucinations need not occur; instead, there is a disavowal of need and involvement and differences, and a postponement of consciousness and memory.

These disavowals may lead to complete loss of memory of the whole world in which unacceptable perceptions were made, including the perceptions of the 'one', the 'I' and the 'other', and to the absence of an imaginative world, a world with which the patient can play so as to be able to understand and own it; and find his way.

This does not necessarily prevent the individual from developing a personality in another setting, which is cut off from his family conflicts; but the disavowals remain, as does the absence of memories stemming from the environment in which he was brought up. The patient then lives in a state where, although going about his normal daily tasks and doing a good professional job, he is not fully conscious, or is in a state of consciousness unknown to himself. As Freud (1915b) said, there is a possibility of there being an infinite series of states of consciousness, and my patient still can only sometimes *perceive* in any environment which reminds him of, or is in danger of bringing to mind, the early anguish which he never mastered.

chapter 8

Using two potentially creative patients, Balint proposes a new theory of the psychic 'place' of creativity. An area of meaningless non-relationship, perhaps that described by Michael Balint (1968) as the Basic Fault, a primary crack or chasm in psychic communication which although inhabited is uncrossable, can, according to Enid Balint, be climbed out of, but only if it is explored. For the patient the analyst does not exist, yet some experience of his or her non-existent presence, or sense of a previous presence, enables the patient to search for something lost in this hitherto unnegotiable space. The consulting room with its contents, sounds, and interpretations becomes a space which is not a void. The search can take place only if the compliant modes, with which the patient may have had to operate in order to survive, are painfully but irreducibly rejected. Although the search is made alone, what is found has something of the other in it, so that a shared imaginative perception of the world can be born and the future artist can potentially communicate to others what he or she has found.

'Creative Life' has not been published before. Enid Balint presented it to the British Psycho-Analytical Society on 18 October 1989.

Creative Life

I start with some quotations. The first is not from an analyst but a priest (Drury, 1988):

> Between ourselves and reality we intersperse more or less ramshackle systems of images. Whether it is because real life is not enough for us, or whether it is that it is too much for us, or whether (as seems most likely) what happens in any day is both not enough and too much, we deal with this by making representations of it. . . . We are like Tennyson's Lady of Shalott, weaving away at our looms and seeing the world refracted through a mirror.
>
> The painter turns from the mirror to look at the world. . . . He can make marks which are not exact imitations but free parallels, real representations. . . . He has let his body, mind, heart, eye and hand included, be the passage through which nature's alien peculiarities are reborn into wide human meanings.

Van Gogh (1958, letter 531) wrote: 'I can very well do without God both in my life and in my painting, but I cannot, ill as I am, do without something which is greater than I, which is my life—the power to create'. Like other artists such as Cézanne, Van Gogh is saying he has to paint to work out his salvation, to exist. The threat is of not being. The need is to be, in order to avoid a chaos and passivity which is the equivalent of death.

One quotation only from Freud (1939, p. 71): 'Whenever [men] are dissatisfied with their present surroundings—and this happens often enough—they turn back to the past and hope that they will be able to prove the truth of the inextinguishable dream of a golden age'.

My last quotation is from the Russian film maker Andrei Tarkovsky (1989): 'Film directors can be divided into two main categories: those who strive to imitate the world they live in, recreating the world about them, and those who create their own world. Those who create their own world are usually the poets'.

These profound and thought-provoking words are a background to thinking about my work with patients who have trouble feeling alive in the world or, as I have described it in the previous chapter, in imaginatively perceiving it. In spite of this they may be potential artists. (Perhaps we all are, but that is another discussion.) These potential artists have a particularly traumatic and devastating difficulty in making contact with external reality. They do not die in infancy, however, but get seduced into feeding and living (Winnicott, 1988). Perhaps the parents of such patients had been so seduced themselves. We sometimes find out. These infants feed passively, although desire cannot be entirely absent. Winnicott thinks this involves a split in the personality and assumes that there is always, as he describes it, a silent relationship with a private world of subjective phenomena, which I call imaginatively perceived phenomena, as well as a false and compliant, uncreative relationship with the outside world. If later the infant becomes an artist, Winnicott (1945, 1965, 1988) thinks he will link these first 'real for him' perceptions with the perceptions he has related to in a compliant way.

Like Winnicott, I think the artist's, and infant's, first 'true for themselves' perceptions are the basis for living. Unlike Winnicott, however, I think that if the infant becomes an artist, struggling to overcome the barrier and make his imaginatively perceived phenomena available to other people, he will have to discard the perceptions from the compliant part of himself. People are enabled by artists, as they sometimes are by children's play, to make contact with an experience, an imaginative perception, which they have lost—a loss which has diminished their own awareness of living. It is true that in representing his imaginative perceptions the artist will portray himself, but his compliant world of pseudo-observations need not, and in fact must not, be integrated with the imaginative perceptions which are his own and real for himself. In his art the compliant self must be painfully cast aside.

Such work is creative as children's play is often creative. The infant's early imaginative perceptions remain unconscious, but they are not static. They develop as part of unconscious fantasy life, and when this is shown forth, either in analysis or in artistic creativity, it can produce agonising fear in the patient or artist in case the experience is lost. There is a dilemma whether or not to portray it, in case it is too overwhelming for the analyst, the audience, or the patient's or artist's own compliant self. Either way chaos, madness, or horror may threaten. The greatest fear, though, always seems to be that the experience cannot be repeated and will be lost. There is a search for words or movements that will represent the forgotten, but not lost, infantile imaginative perceptions; and simultaneously there is an attempt not to represent them. It is essential at these times for the analyst to be quiet and not intrusive, but also absolutely *there*. It is hard to describe this, but what matters is for the analyst simply to go on breathing. He must not put anything into the patient's mind; the patient is occupied in finding his own words or actions. At the end of the session, however, when the intensity is over, interpretation may be needed as the patient returns to his normal world. He usually thinks the experience has gone for good, and he is surprised when the process restarts in the next session.

This experience of perception can exist only in the atmosphere created for it by the artist, or when it happens in analysis. The artist is objectively alone, but must have had some imaginative perceptions as an infant to enable him to create such an atmosphere, while in analysis the atmosphere is re-created by analyst and patient together. In my view the infant cannot perceive reality unless it is perceived mutually with someone else. The mother, who can give complete attention to her infant, is normally the first person to provide this atmosphere, although it is not always possible for her to do so, nor can she always do it without resentment or fear. For the infant, even while there is as yet no other person or object, there is not a void. This absence of void is important, and I have written about it in Chapter 3. There is a space in which the infant lives (Winnicott, 1988), where he can perhaps smell, touch, hear, and hold on to something. It is an alive space, not the dead one so well described by Green (1986, chap. 7). This space can be refound in analysis. It is of paramount importance to the infant's first imaginative perception of the world that that space is partly filled with the content of the unconscious internal world: the other, as yet unperceived, person. It has so often been said that there can be no infant without a mother. We must add that there can be no live breast, either biologically or psychologically with milk in it, without a live infant. The one creates the other. Winnicott (1956, p. 311) says that 'the mother's meaning for the child depends on the child's creativity'. My idea is that the first imaginative perception can only arise out of a state of eager aliveness in two people, the infant with the potential for life and the mother alive inside herself and tuning in to the emerging infant.

As clinicians we are aware of this. We know the need to allow our patients to discover their own words and movements for representing what they feel, and not to have to be compliant and use ours. This is particularly important when the patient is in the very early, receptive, unintegrated state. As writers it is equally important for us who try to describe our analytic observations to use words that are right for ourselves, but that are right for the audience too. They must not be integrated into a concept before both writer and reader are ready, so that the concept does not seal off further creative work.

I use the phrase 'imaginative perception' to describe what happens when the patient imagines what he perceives and thus creates his own partly imagined, partly perceived, world. Drury's words are simple, brief, and right for me, that the artist can 'make marks which are not exact imitations but free parallels, real representations'. The writer cannot use words passively accepted from someone else, which to him are meaningless. He must create his own, but, again, they arise in relationship to another person.

I am going to describe briefly some work with two patients. Analysis always arises, of course, out of a relationship between two people, and so no two analyses can be the same. Attention is centred, however, on only one of the two, namely, on the imagination and perceptions of the patient. Both the infant and the patient in analysis will start to feel concern for the other, and then guilt, and a state of mutual concern soon develops. That depends, however, on being able to tolerate the existence of the other person; and in the phases of analysis I am about to describe such a state has not yet been reached. The patients were aware that they were not alone. I do not think anything can even start if the patient feels he is in a void. He may not be able to perceive any object which he desires or can imagine, but still he can feed, listen, and even take in what is said in a passive way, while sensing that there is something which he has lost or which is missing. He may try to find the missing object which had been imaginatively perceived, or he may repeat the trauma of his loss and feed passively throughout his life.

The danger in analysis is that the patient may try to repeat this passive, accepting 'feed' which the analyst offers by his being there as a person, as well as by providing couch, chair, an atmosphere of warmth, interpretations, and so on. It may take a long time, perhaps years, before the patient can take the risk of looking away from the mirror and rejecting the person behind the couch and what he stands for. Then a new phase is entered and new work can start.

Michael Balint (1968) describes work of this kind when investigating what he calls the Area of the Basic Fault. He speaks of how at some phases in the analysis words will have no settled meaning for the patient who can become silent, lifeless, and hopeless. In the same book he speaks of another area of the mind which he calls the Area of Creativity. In my view the Area of the Basic Fault is only overcome when this phase is worked through, that is, when the patient is no longer regressed to a stage where he has no mutual experience with his analyst but becomes silently hostile, disillusioned, and desperate and eventually appears to give up hope. He sometimes does this without reproaching the analyst, who may wonder what he is doing wrong. He realises, though, that he must not be passively overwhelmed by the patient's projections, which have to be followed even more minutely than usual, and he must also watch his own rigid expectations. This state is overcome only when the patient painfully allows himself to feel alone, in the analyst's presence but with no *person* being there. He may then begin to perceive for himself and to enter the Area of Creativity. The patient is alone with no other person present, but the space is not empty. There is no experience of a void, and the analytic hour is in fact a relief from the previous experience of compliance. Although bringing no apparent satisfaction, it comes to fill the patient's life. To escape from the state of passivity is satisfying in itself. In order, therefore, to get out of the Area of the Basic Fault, my view is that the Area of Creativity has to be entered.

Neither of the two patients I shall describe was a creative artist. I should rather say that neither had achieved or overcome the struggle with what prevented them from being creative artists. Their fear of being abandoned and alone, of having destroyed all that there is, was too great. They both went through periods, short and long, when nobody existed for them, when they could not communicate and words had no meaning; but they showed an immense struggle to create and live. They did not seem to be false personalities, although some traces of this did appear early in the analysis of the woman patient whom I shall describe first.

When she came to analysis she was forty years old, married, and with two children. For the first three or four years I had a real existence for her in the transference. She sometimes idealised me, but it was not long before she swept me off the pedestal. She got in touch with a depressed, almost melancholic part of herself where she felt she could do nothing for anybody, but only destroy those who were close to her. We could work on a period in her teens when two close members of her family died, one of them by suicide. The acceptance of these losses and the guilt and pain which arose out of them led to associations with earlier periods of her life. I thought all this would help her to become less anxious, to love and care for those near to her, and to feel more alive. Before her analysis she could not bear to be with people or to sleep in the same room as her husband, even if she drank and took sleeping pills.

She did get better, but only for about a year. Then she entered a long phase when she was in the Area of the Basic Fault. I was increasingly disappointing to her, and she wanted to do nothing at all. She gave up her previous activities; in particular, she stopped doing things for people she was fond of. Her dreams showed her wish to annihilate them and her fear that she had done so. She became depressed, angry, and disillusioned, with both herself and her analyst. She saw to it that her family and her analyst were worried and hurt. She felt she had lost what she had once had, and in return she rejected life.

This behaviour gradually intensified. There were silent periods in the analysis, and her disgust and disbelief in herself and her analyst grew. She would say that my words were true, but she could feel nothing. I seemed to be talking to her through a long tunnel. She could not perceive imaginatively. She tried to get away from analysis, although she never in fact missed a session. Then she started to paint. At first this was with great fear, and very formal, rather pretty pictures emerged. Slowly, however, and to her own pain and disgust, her paintings changed. Then they stopped. Her silences in the session became alive. She had entered the Area of Creativity.

The analyst then started to feel alive, and was felt by the patient to be alive, not at first as an analyst or even a person, but as a place to be in. Much later it was as a person, about whom the patient began spasmodically to be concerned and guilty because she was horrified at what she had done to the analyst. She resumed painting and it became increasingly important. It still took a long time before she could begin to imagine a good session, or even part of a session as a free and mutually satisfactory time. When she did, it was a blissful state of joy to her, but it did not last and she was afraid she would never get back to it again. She always wanted me to tell her what had happened and could take it in when I interpreted the similarity between her experience with me and the experience during the first few days of her life. This made sense to her, not intellectually but in strong feelings in her body. I should add that during the first weeks of this patient's life the patient's father was extremely ill and the mother who tried to feed her child must have been distracted and, therefore, ceased to exist, or became dead, for the patient. When the mother stopped being worried about the father, she was over-enthusiastic and overwhelmed her baby, who then shrank from her and came to prefer a life where there was no one to a life where there was someone who repeated the experience for her of those first few weeks. She had imagined and perceived a marvellous 'object' or atmosphere, which had gone and was apparently forgotten. She feared to refind it and so, as Drury says, saw life through a mirror. Her mother probably could not repeat the first few good days, but could only remind her of her failure, which the patient then experienced as her own.

Later in this patient's analysis her interest in painting and in looking at pictures enabled her to feel at home with at least part of the world. She could create it by her imaginative perception of it, and briefly and unexpectedly she would become blissfully alive, although there were still periods when she regressed again and the analyst ceased to exist for her.

In the transference, projective mechanisms were very active and had to be followed minutely. The ebb and flow of belief and disbelief, of illusion and disillusion, were felt by the analyst as well as the patient. I had to work hard to avoid passively accepting her projections. When I was accused, for example, of being jealous of her and destructive about her painter friends, I had to be sure I was not; but I could be made to feel I was and that they were getting between me, the real feeder, and the infant who needed real food. I have mentioned passivity in this patient as a contrast to imaginative perception, but I should say that even in the first few years of the analysis passivity never led to a completely worthless, lifeless state. It was always interspersed with periods of violent despair which were alive and in which she objected to what she saw as the life offered to her by the analyst. In the areas of the Basic Fault and of Creativity which I have described, there was no instinctual satisfaction for her, as there is with patients who imaginatively have a feed or orgasm and then are satisfied and replete. Here I am describing a state which precedes the instinctual satisfaction of a real feed, but which must be present if the feed is to be a real one and not just compliant sucking.

The second patient, who is the 'Mr. Smith' of Chapter 7, was in fact creative in a particular field; but his wish to write a story using his own words and thoughts, and not the thoughts and words of others, was so intense that he was virtually unable to write or perceive at all. When he was born, his mother had recently lost her brother and she called her baby after him. It seems that she could not relate to the baby himself or accept him as her son. Not being able to see a live baby boy, she denied him an existence. His response to the compliance this demanded of him was to deny his mother's and his father's existence, and he continued to do this in later life.

He started analysis with me in his late forties and was already working, or existing, in what I felt to be the Area of the Basic Fault. He had been to two analysts before me, and he warned me at the consultation that I would find him very difficult to understand. When he arrived for his first session, and for months or even years afterwards, I realised that what he was seeking was the analytic room, the couch, and the cushions, so that he could discover a thought and a language. I, as a person, did not exist for him. He often told me that he never thought about me when he was not 'in the hour', but in fact he never thought of me as a person at any time at all. In the first part of a session his movements and sounds were like an infant's, but when he came out of this state of infantile frustration, in which there were no acceptable objects and no words, he spoke lucidly and clearly. My interpretations were useless or even made him feel chaotic; and it was clear that the one thing he could not stand was for me to put into him words which should have meaning, but had no meaning for him. My job was to wait for him to find words, meaning, and thought. Gradually, after about two years, he began to do this. 'Thought' appeared in the form of myths and stories which represented his earliest experiences. A few memories also appeared. He struggled to create experiences or relationships which were truly his own. He had found words that suited him when he began to read good poetry and drama in his early teens, and he often recited bits of poetry to me. It was not the content or meaning but the words themselves, which he almost spat out at me, that he conveyed as his own and not mine. This patient's response to passive feeding did not lead to the construction of a false self or even to any particular rebelliousness or passivity. Instead, he rejected what was offered to him and was determined to create something for himself. In some parts of his life he did indeed manage to do this. Creation was, for him, the essence of his being, but there was only one person. The word 'we' did not exist.

My patient reminded me of an autistic child who accepts the words of others but does not comprehend or reply. He could come alive when he read poetry and drama of a certain kind, particularly where ideas of loss and separation were predominant. But what really enthralled him was the sound of words that were 'real for him'. Such words were not seen through a mirror or accepted passively, but were real perceptions. Sometimes in the analysis he could accept ideas or words from me, with great pleasure, but also with great care. It was essential for me not to make him take in my ideas and words unless they were part of his imaginatively perceived world. When they were right, however, he remembered them and told me later what I had said, usually saying that he had thought of it himself before.

In this paper I have described people whose struggle to communicate with and contribute to the world in which they live is difficult, but who try unceasingly to do so because otherwise they live as uneasy, bewildered acceptors of a world that is meaningless. As patients they may accept their analysis, and it may seem to them that they have found what they have been looking for; but after some normal analytic work of that sort, a phase is reached when the effort to continue is no longer worthwhile for either patient or analyst. They then reject the analyst but not the analysis, and painfully, as if alone in the session, they try to regain what they have lost or create what it is that they need. They try to regain a state where they can imaginatively perceive, or create, a sense of being alive and not dead, which they hope will arise in the analytic hour. The session itself is present and sought after. Periods of fear and terror become interspersed with feelings of being alive, although often this too is terrifying. Later they may feel that something is being created between themselves and the analyst, who does then exist, but it is not at all clear what that something is. The analyst is still not always a person for them, but he is certainly not absent.

These patients may all be potential artists. I think that is true of the ones I have analysed. They seem to have been forced as infants, at a very early stage, to look at and experience the world through the eyes of mothers or mother substitutes who could not look at them so as to reflect a live infant back to them, and who did not make the infant feel or know what he looked like or smelt like or was. These patients then had no mutual experience which enabled them to feel at home in the world, to get something from it, or to give something to it. The alternatives were passive acceptance or rebelliousness and rejection. Instead of live infants, they were seen, perhaps, as frightening objects who might easily die, and so they experienced their mothers and the world in which they were living as full of dread and fear. The effect of all this is to produce an intense desire and need to create their own words, images, sounds, and movements, a need which may be a driving force in all artists.

These patients are different from those described in Chapter 3, whom I saw as being empty of themselves. These patients are full of themselves but get no acceptable feed-back or reflection from the people in their world. It is therefore the world that appears empty, and they have no mutual relationship with it. Unlike the patients who are empty of themselves, they do not live in a void, because there is not a total absence of reflection from the external world. They have probably had, even if only briefly, some real experience at some stage of their lives, some acceptable feed-back which was not totally discarded or annihilated. This gives them something which they can struggle to recover, to refind or create, out of the memories which they have lost and which do not necessarily ever reach consciousness again.

chapter 9

The main theme of 'Unconscious Communication' is the idea, touched on in Chapter 7, of direct communication between the unconscious minds of two people. It also hinges, like Chapters 7 and 8, on the concept of imaginative perception.

The importance and originality of the clinical work and the theoretical understanding deriving from it will be evident, though possibly controversial. In brief, Balint proposes that an unconscious transmission can bypass one generation and appear compulsively and destructively in the psychic life of the next generation. Retrospectively its presence in the bypassed generation may be deduced from, for example, unacknowledged physical illness. Here, the history of the grandmother's relationship to her own baby lives on as a 'foreign body'—an idea that has already appeared in Chapter 6 (p. 79)—in the unconscious acts of the granddaughter. Something is taken in by the baby, but it cannot be identified with or recognised. Such processes are qualitatively different from the more familiar mechanisms of projection and projective identification which they predate both developmentally and historically.

'Unconscious Communication' has not been published previously. A version of it was presented on 2 November 1990 to the Academy of Medicine in New York City under the auspices of the Institute of Contemporary Psychotherapy.

Unconscious Communication

Thus a child's super-ego is in fact constructed on the
model not of its parents but of its parents' super-ego.
. . . mankind never lives entirely in the present. The
past, the tradition of the race and of the people, lives
on in the ideologies of the super-ego, and yields only
slowly to the influence of the present and to new
changes; and so long as it operates through the
super-ego it plays a powerful part in human life,
independently of economic conditions.
S. Freud (1933, p. 67)

It is a very remarkable thing that the unconscious of
one human being can react upon that of another
without passing through the conscious . . .
descriptively speaking, the fact is incontestable.
S. Freud (1915b, p. 194)

This paper concentrates on a particular aspect of the relationship
between a mother and her child: a relationship which Freud understood,
but which has subsequently been illustrated by clinical material arising
out of patients from the Holocaust (e.g., Pines, 1986). There have also
been empirical observations about the effect on babies of their mothers'
internal world, which the babies perceive before the external world has
any substance for them (Stern, 1985). In this connection the mother's
mood is more important than her actions, as has been noted by many
analysts, perhaps most convincingly by Green (1986, chap. 7). I have
found that much more than the mother's general mood is absorbed by the
very young infant, who reacts, for example, to her aliveness or deadness
and to her unconscious anxieties, which do not necessarily arise from the
relation between mother and baby. What can be perceived imaginatively
by the infant and internalised by him are aspects of the mother's uncon-

scious life, that is to say, aspects of her mental life of which she herself is unaware. An analyst then has to understand parts of the mother's unconscious mind which, because the mother is not the patient, are difficult to comprehend in a reliable way. One way of describing this is in terms of projective mechanisms. The essential point, however, is that in trying to understand a woman one has always to be in touch with three generations: the patient, the patient's parents, and the parents' parents, that is, the patient's grandparents.

I shall describe a phase of analysis where I found that I could only make progess by working on the hypothesis that the unconscious mind of the mother of my patient communicated very directly with her daughter's unconscious, without the communication passing through the conscious mind of either, and that the daughter's illness, and indeed her whole life, was governed by this.

First some background data: the mother of this patient lived the apparently sedate rural life of an intelligent, educated woman, married to a successful businessman and devoted to her two children. She was probably slightly depressed and capable of some anxiety of an appropriate kind. She showed, as far as I could see, no sign of the inner chaos which might be expected from a woman who had suffered severe traumata of loss and abandonment in her own infancy. Instead, her first child, my patient, behaved as if she had been subjected to severe traumata and disturbances, and her life was anything but calm and sedate. During the early years of analysis I did not grasp that the patient was living out, or demonstrating, her mother's catastrophes as well as her own. It was only when this became clear that real work started in the analysis and I understood both the day-to-day transference manifestations and my own feelings during the sessions, as well as the possible cause of them. I began to think that parts of the patient's unconscious mind had been reacting on mine without passing either through my conscious thoughts and feelings or through hers. I thought that something similar might have happened between mother and daughter, probably in early infancy, which could account for her intense way of living, her strivings, and her illness and also my feelings of being outside, but not useless. I had sensed danger but could not locate it in a rational way. The analysis seemed straightforward and easy, but everything of importance was bypassed; and I was left at the end of each session feeling uneasy and vaguely cheated. I made what I thought were appropriate interpretations about her relationship to me and its connections with the past, but they did not make any difference to the situation nor lead to any change to either her feelings or mine, or in her life of anxiety and over-activity.

When she first came to analysis, my patient, whom I shall call Kay, was a thirty-year-old married woman with one child of eighteen months.

Her mother, who was illegitimate, had been put into an orphanage soon after her birth. She was adopted when she was two and a half years old. All Kay's mother's memories were about her good, caring, adoptive parents who by then were dead. My patient spoke about her mother's childhood without anxiety or unease, and her mother herself spoke of it with affection and pleasure. When I questioned this, quite early in the analysis, she could not grasp what I was saying and moved away from it. It sounded to her like analytic theory, no more. It had nothing to do with her own family.

Kay is married to a professional man; she lives comfortably and enjoys her garden, her house, and her possessions. She was able to give up work before her child was born and has devoted herself to him ever since. She came to me because she had become extremely anxious and exhausted and was advised to have analysis. I had seen her husband for a single consultation some years before they got married, and it was he who suggested she should come and see me. I had no vacancy at that time, but I offered her one in a few months, which she at first refused but later accepted.

Kay's father comes from a prosperous middle-class family from the north of England. When at last Kay thought about the possibility that her mother had had a difficult time in her early infancy and childhood, she asked her about it. Her mother said her adoptive parents had told her that she cried for the first few months of her life with them. Even this, however, did not suggest to Kay that her mother had perhaps loved or missed or been attached to the first parents she knew in the children's home, nor what it meant to her that she and her mother, Kay's grandmother, had lost each other.

Kay's own dread of losing objects and of not being able to find them was shown from the beginning of her analysis. I had no impression of a mother who was living under a heavy burden of denial and depression connected with loss, but I soon knew my patient was living under such a burden. Early in the analysis I connected this with an episode when her mother had a brief illness and Kay was separated from her, being only a few weeks old at the time. I linked the experiences of the two babies, Kay and her mother, but I did not realize the enormous importance of the mother's catastrophe for Kay until much later; nor did I appreciate at this stage the crucial difference between the lives of the mother and the grandmother and the life of my patient. I saw rather the similarity that both mother–daughter couples had apparently lost each other and not found each other again. Objectively speaking, of course, Kay's mother did not disappear for ever, but for Kay, with her own sense of reality in her own world, the mother who came back after the brief illness was not imaginatively experienced as the mother she had first known. That mother was lost for ever. Or was it possible that she could be re-found? As the analysis went on, it appeared that Kay was compelled to live not only her own life but also her mother's and grandmother's lives. She was trying to resolve something for them, as well as to find her own 'first' mother.

When Kay came to analysis she was looking after her son twenty-four hours a day; she could not leave him. Both she and her baby were suffering, not from an experience of loss but from a fear of it. Whose loss was it that must be avoided at all costs?

The analysis started straightforwardly, and although Kay showed her terror of dependence and loss she coped with it well, using her relationship with her son, on whom she was totally dependent and whom she totally overshadowed, to overshadow and deny her dependence on me. She left her sessions hurriedly, usually with something humorous cropping up at the end, and rushed back to 'real life' at home with her son. Life with me did not feel real to her. She strove to find what she needed but was terrified of finding it.

After the first analytic break she came back one day late and told me that the previous day, the day she should have returned, she had lost a ring. She had searched for it everywhere, over and over again; she could not stop looking. The ring had no value; it was of no importance; it was bound to turn up anyway. In fact it was a valuable Georgian ring given to her by her husband, and it never did turn up. The horror and disbelief that this loss brought were intense. Interpretations about the holiday and the lost session brought no relief. In fact they did not feel relevant either to my patient or to myself, in spite of seeming so obvious. Acting out can be obvious but nonetheless distressing as long as it still hides what is being denied or disavowed.

This episode was followed by two others when objects were lost. One was found again after a frantic, disorganised period in which I could again see what it was like for Kay to lose something. Both lost objects were soft toys belonging to her baby, who seemed quite calm about their loss. His calmness, though, had no effect on his mother. Kay said it drove her mad, and so it appeared. Only later were the panic and pain experienced in identification with the lost, neglected object itself, not just with the person who had lost it, and linked to Kay's fear of being lost as well as her fear of losing. Even worse was that the lost object had no value to her, and she felt guilty for not valuing it, particularly in the case of the ring her husband had given her. Presumably this was based on the thought that her mother and grandmother had had no value for each other and nor did she and I.

Similar panic states occurred at other times, not only in connection with the loss of an object; but the panic itself was usually brief and was followed by a fairly severe attack of what the patient called 'depression'. These episodes seemed to be connected to Kay's birthday, and because of this her family took it for granted that no birthday celebrations were possible. The 'celebration' was, in fact, the depression. This was a lifeless, immobile, agonised state during which Kay could do nothing, looked distraught, and dressed in a particular way, in what might have been baby clothes. They were white, not soft and clinging, but starched. During the hopeless, empty depression she spoke about loss and the sensation of things being 'all gone'. This phrase described something terrible beyond belief. Sometimes even Kay herself had to appear 'all gone' so that I would know what it was like. It was important for her not to make me feel utterly lifeless, or 'all gone', myself, but she made sure that that was how I perceived her.

We gradually saw these bouts of illness as repetitions of her own and her mother's traumatic first weeks. Kay assumed that her birth had been so terrible that her mother had nearly died. This was not true. In fact, she had a good first few weeks with her mother, who 'recovered' her baby when she got over her illness just as in reality Kay recovered her. This was when I began to realise how different were the experiences of the two infants, Kay and her mother, because the grandmother never did recover her baby nor that baby her mother. I came to think, and to interpret, that in those states Kay was experiencing what her grandmother had felt when she lost touch with her baby and never found her again. The grandmother was lost and not found; Kay's mother was lost and not found. Analytic work succeeded only when Kay began to identify with the grandmother who lost her baby. Although Kay's mother lost her own mother and never found her, she did find a substitute home where she may have been well looked after; but when she was two and a half she lost that substitute home and remembered only how good the third home was, the home of her adoptive parents. Any feelings about these losses were disavowed or denied. But the mother handed on the disturbance, chaos, and confusion to her baby, who reacted to it without knowing to what she was reacting. She received it, but without making it part of the world she knew and had created for herself. It was not imaginatively perceived.

It was difficult to follow the repercussions of the unconscious burden which brought dread and depression to my patient and led to spontaneous, uncontrollable actions that were not linked with thought. The transference, too, was difficult to follow. I was seen principally as the grandmother or the baby who had no life and was alone. I now understood the little jokes before she left each day; they were to avoid the pain of knowing that she left me as a child who had no mother, or a mother without a child, while she went home to a child who did have a mother.

Kay's life became centred around her wishes to make life less terrible for her grandmother and her baby, to deal with her own and her mother's guilt, and to keep her 'dangerous' grandmother away from her own child. When I interpreted to Kay her pity for me because I had no child and my envy of her because she did have one, she agreed and later was able to link this to her grandmother's real experiences.

Freud (1900, p. 149) said that 'identification . . . enables [patients] to suffer on behalf of a whole crowd of people and to act all the parts in a play single-handed'. This describes well what Kay was doing; but, as I shall discuss later, in her case it was because she could *not* identify with what she had introjected from her mother.

After this work which took place during the third year of her analysis, Kay began to talk about having another child. Her mother had had a second child, Kay's younger brother, but it did not seem to be this that had so far prevented Kay from thinking of having another child herself. Her fear was that if she did so, her first child would be neglected and 'placed in a home', with the house no longer being neat, tidy, and absolutely right for him. Of course, Kay was also frightened of my envy. She conceived while I was on holiday but waited until I got back to have the abortion she had wanted from the moment she knew she was pregnant. She could not bear the idea of what would happen to her son or to me if she did have a baby. Her body, as always, reacted very strongly, and she became ill and exhausted.

During the year that followed, the analysis was occupied with panic states which expressed themselves through various physical illnesses. These were sometimes quite severe and could not be diagnosed medically. Various remedies were tried. Finally Kay made friends with a woman who had six children and came to feel at home in a house which was messy, yet where the children seemed to thrive. She had to force herself to love it. Her feelings and her ideas about such homes made it hard for her to perceive that the children did thrive and the home was good. Soon after this happened Kay became pregnant and had her second child without undue stress.

To sum up: some patients are affected by aspects of their parents' unassimilated unconscious life, which does not seem to affect their parents' activity or behaviour but does affect their own. In analysis it can be traced to the experience of grandparents which was bypassed by the parents, instead of being introjected and identified with, and handed on to the children. The children do introject it, but it is not identified with and therefore cannot become conscious. I have come to see this as a foreign body inside the grandchild, which remains unconscious but gives rise to affect and action, which did not occur in the parent. Whether to describe this as negation, disavowal, or in some other way needs further discussion. The patient acts compulsively, out of that part of his unconscious, when it is triggered or touched upon by certain happenings in the external world. This does not make him feel confused; that happens only when he is unable to act upon it. For instance, Kay was compelled to find lost objects and to look after and mend them. Provided she could do this, she was able to live a harmonious social life. She did not seem split into two separate people but rather as though she had two separate lives to live, which she could manage but only with some strain. If, for example, she could not find a piece of furniture she wanted to repair, then she became frantic.

As in all analyses, one is tempted to try to understand the associations and histories of such patients in relation to their own infancies. The transference usually appears to confirm such reconstructions and indicates that there was some trauma that could give rise to the patient's panic and distress. These emotions, however, are not usually felt by the analyst as they are with other patients. The analyst is not in touch, either, with the unconscious thought that underlies the patient's compulsive activity. The projective mechanisms by which one might expect the unconscious thoughts and feelings to communicate themselves to the analyst are not active in these patients. The analyst thus comes to feel more and more out of contact, and the reconstructions do not bring with them the appropriate conflict, anxiety, or sense of guilt. Nor do they have any effect on the panic. The patient continues to feel dread but has no idea what it is about. She is driven into activity. If she cannot be active, she becomes confused and finds an outlet by, for instance, 'freeing' some object by buying it and trying to mend it, an attempt which often fails.

When Kay began to tell me how she looked after her house, her clothes, and the objects around her, she showed me two things. On the one hand, there was a compulsive kind of caring. It was only as she started to connect this with her grandmother's (never her mother's) tragedy that she became less driven to such activity, and stopped watching films and reading books which illustrated the kind of suffering she was trying to prevent. On the other hand, she could also be very uncaring and unfeeling, and it surprised her when she recognised this. It was noticeable, for example, that she had to be allowed to do whatever she wanted with her objects; if anybody interfered, she would get rid of the objects quite ruthlessly. If anybody actively asked her to look after someone in need, she would not do so and she was, again, quite ruthless in her ability to get rid of whoever made such a request. She would not take care of her mother if she were ill, but she would find the right kind of fittings for her mother's curtains and if it were her mother's puppy that was ill, she would take care of it, in her own way, twenty-four hours a day.

We are familiar with the idea that the unconscious mind of one person can communicate through the unconscious mind of another. For instance, the choice of partner in a marriage can often be understood only by relating it to how the unconscious wishes of both partners interact, rather than to the conscious decisions involved (see Chapter 17). We are less familiar in analysis with a situation where part of one person's unconscious mind is taken over by the unconscious mind of another and becomes subject to experiences which are not related to memory or to any objective or imaginative perception. This resembles a psychosis where the patient has no thoughts but those which are implanted in him by another. Roustang (1982) has also commented on this phenomenon.

Presumably Kay's mother perceived the loss of her own mother and the loss of her first home, but the trauma of these perceptions was so great that instead of assimilating and acting upon them she disavowed them. When she had a baby she handed over to it, or projected into it, her unresolved history. The daughter, Kay, had no perception of this but acted nonetheless as though the problems were hers and strove to resolve them herself. She had no notion of why she was compelled to find damaged objects and mend, or fail to mend, them; nor of why she so ruthlessly had to get rid of people who interfered with this compulsion. The wounds which could not heal or be resolved in Kay were the wounds her mother had either not felt, or felt only briefly and then disavowed, and the wounds her grandmother had suffered when she lost her baby. The unhealed scars were not Kay's own but those of her mother and grandmother. Resolution was possible only when Kay's identification with her grandmother became conscious. Then Kay's guilt and her mother's guilt became accessible and Kay was able to contain the inevitability of her own and her mother's history.

When and under what conditions is an ego too weak to absorb the projections of another person's experience? Kay's mother became ill for the only time in her life soon after Kay's birth. This may have been the only time that she was in touch with the loss of her own mother and her guilt about that, and it was perhaps at this point that she handed her history to her baby. When such unconscious communications are transmitted from a mother to her baby's unconscious, they are not connected with the rest of the baby's life experiences. This need not be seen in terms of splitting or the breaking of links. Rather there is a set of experiences which, although introjected, cannot be identified with by the ego. Thus they are, from the beginning, alien to the other life experiences. They do not, therefore, give rise to the kind of illness that splitting of the ego produces. Instead they produce something like a foreign body inside the ego or superego. This foreign body may have to remain in place until it can be dealt with by its 'host' when he or she is strong enough to do what the original recipient of the trauma could not do. In theoretical terms this may be related to what is known as the Area of the Basic Fault (M. Balint, 1968).

Such a chain of events means that one generation has to resolve traumata that another generation has failed to. This may explain situations where characteristics appear to be inherited from one generation to the next in ways which are genetically inexplicable. From a clinical viewpoint it may also shed light on certain kinds of negative therapeutic reaction.

In this analysis work based on these hypotheses brought about a change in the patient's relationship to me. It became easier for her to know what she wanted from me, and the projective mechanisms which had been missing also became active. She was not frightened of being taken over by me. I existed for her. One might say that she was able to create me, or to let me into her creative space. She could, that is to say, imaginatively perceive me and parts of reality that had been closed to her.

chapter 10

In 'One Analyst's Technique', Balint draws out the main features of her psychoanalytic technique which have been implicit in her earlier work. The paper is itself a resumé of her way of working and need not be further summarised here. Balint's central area of concern is her continuing interest in developing techniques for understanding pre-verbal and bodily processes and the interface of the verbal and pre-verbal. When and how does an experience become a thought? A person may introject something, may psychically swallow it; but for an identification with this introject to become a thought it must be imaginatively perceived. Chapter 9 described a patient in whom this had not happened. Each patient will do this differently and so, as Balint concludes, one's task as an analyst is not to explain a patient, nor to take a journey through history, but to learn a language.

'Technique', in the fullest sense of the term, is perhaps Balint's most abiding concern. It is not to be understood in terms of mechanisms but of science: not as a skill learned but as a search for a way of learning.

'One Analyst's Technique' is a new paper, written for this book; it has not been published or presented anywhere before.

One Analyst's Technique

I do not venture to deny that a physician quite
differently constituted might find himself driven to
adopt a different attitude to his patients and to the task
before him.

S. Freud (1912, p. 111)

This final chapter of Part I describes briefly what I hope will already
be clear to readers of this book, namely, the aspects of psychoanalytic
technique which are now most important to me. This description of the
technique that I use when I analyse patients takes for granted familiarity
on the reader's part with basic analytic principles. The analyst learns the
theory and technique while he is a student; he continues to learn throughout his professional life. His necessary preoccupation with the continuous
processes in his and his patient's unconscious mind is paramount; but also
with the discrepancies, omissions, and contradictions, not forgetting the
periods in analysis when the exchange between the analyst and patient
appears to be sensible and coherent but is in fact flat and meaningless. To
list the conventions that have grown up during the past fifty years which
are implied when the term 'analytic technique' is used would require a
chapter in itself. I propose here only to touch on those aspects which may
need spelling out, in the light of what I have written about my work in
the consulting room and elsewhere.

The earliest recommendations about technique are to be found in
Freud. I quote two short passages, although when looking at them I am
tempted to quote much more. He says: 'It must not be forgotten that the
things one hears are for the most part things whose meaning is only
recognized later on' (Freud, 1912, p. 112). Shortly afterwards, when
discussing the psychoanalyst's need for memory, he says: 'He should
simply listen, and not bother about whether he is keeping anything in

mind', and 'a conscious determination to recollect the point would probably have resulted in failure' (Freud, 1912, pp. 112–113).

Students or therapists who are not familiar with Freud's basic discoveries which led to the technical conditions he laid down may, when
coming for supervision, be looking for something very different from
what the analyst can offer. But when I, as a trained psychoanalyst, am
asked to supervise their work, I can only imagine that they come to me
because I am a psychoanalyst; and anyway I can only work as a psychoanalyst. If I work in any other way, I am an amateur, like a friend.
Sometimes I can decide deliberately not to use my analytic way of
working or even of thinking, but I cannot altogether stop myself thinking
with my analyst's mind.

My basic training is now part of me. It is not used outside my
working times, but it is used in whatever setting I am working in. My
task is to observe when something is required of me which is not helped
by this basic training, or by what I am or what I know, in which case I
may give advice or act as a non-professional, but I must be aware of what
I am doing. That is to say, I am using myself as a non-professional,
perhaps somebody with considerable life experience, and I must make
this clear to the person I am supposed to help. Life's experience can be
useful, as can a novel, a poem, or a picture. The importance of keeping
this distinction in mind seems fundamental when I am working as an
analyst even more than when I am working as a supervisor.

For me analytic practice does not depend only on whether I see the
patient five times a week, but much more on my basic understanding of
the task of psychoanalysis. Freud said that an analyst has to study the
defences and be aware of transference phenomena. He also insisted that
each analyst would have his own particular style. For me the core of
psychoanalysis is, in brief, the understanding of intrapsychic processes
and states, and of their relationship, or lack of it, with external reality, or
perceived external reality. An analyst also has in mind that there is a state
which is neither the one nor the other, but what Winnicott (1971a) called
a transitional space between the two.

I hope my particular style will have emerged from earlier chapters
in the book. If I am asked, as sometimes I am, what I think is essential to
analytic work, I may answer, after I have stressed the need for a basic and
thorough training in psychoanalytic theory and practice, that it is important for the analyst not to be too intrusive. This may seem paradoxical
and puzzling, because the overt, accepted aim is to make what is unconscious conscious: to intrude and overcome the defences. However, it is
not the analyst, but the patient, who shows the way in which a particular
analysis has to be conducted and the defences overcome, or the area of the
unconscious which has to become conscious. The analyst must keep to the

rules which seem right to him, but not without a continual review of them. If he deviates from them, not only must he be aware of doing so, but he must understand why he has done so and learn from the experience, which may be of help to the understanding of the patient. The analyst must always try to follow what he is doing and if it seems, not necessarily to the patient but to himself, unsatisfactory or wrong or incoherent, he can learn something from the experience both about the patient and about himself in relation to the patient at that particular moment. I am not talking about counter-transference here, nor do I think the experience I am discussing shows pathology. The analyst must not be intrusive or lead the way, but he must be there, listening alertly; and he must sometimes remove obstacles which are blocking the patient's ability to get in touch with a thought or a dream, or an impulse which is holding him up. The analyst sometimes has to point out such obstacles, which prevent the patient from finding what he is looking for but which have been put there by the patient himself so as to avoid having to undertake this painful task.

The analyst himself may sometimes be tempted to follow an easier path without realising it, especially if he does not have in mind where he thinks the patient, in spite of his fears and conflicts, wants and needs to go. Usually, however, the analyst has to wait. In my experience this seems more and more necessary, not less so, as the analyst becomes more experienced and more able to listen for variations and contradictions. He can be alert and observant so that he can allow the patient to show him, and tell him, what he needs to say and remember, and how he wants to avoid knowing about himself and his relation to his analyst. Perhaps he is up against a void, or at the edge of a cliff, or just about to fall into a torrent of water. Pain of that kind cannot be suffered (Bion, 1970, p. 9; quoted later in this chapter). Perhaps the patient cannot move, or does not know who his analyst is. At these times the most important thing is that the analyst should not withdraw, find good solutions, comfort, or try to relieve anxiety. Nor must he think that he has an impossible task at the moment when the patient most needs him. When neither patient nor analyst can understand or verbalise, what then has to be endured by both of them is the not being able to be helped or to give help, to rescue or be rescued; and, instead, having to stay there and not be terrified and so pushed into activity, during the time when it is not possible to do anything useful. Regressive periods may be very brief, but they must be observed and respected. This experience is particularly illustrated in Chapters 3, 7, and 8.

This idea, which is based on experience at many times with many patients, assumes what I said at the beginning of this chapter, that the analyst is properly trained and knows the theory and techniques described by Freud and others. The analyst must endure the trauma of not being able to find an escape from the suffering he is encountering or a way into the patient's unconscious mind or memory which would help him to understand and move. He has to endure being in a place where it feels as if nobody has been before, even though this is probably not true. Nevertheless, for the first ten or twenty years of his analytic life, when such occasions occur, the analyst will, though perhaps only briefly, turn to papers and journals and books which touch on his problems because he feels sure that another analyst, certainly a senior one, would be able to help with the patient and his suffering without difficulty, would be able to show the way and to understand the terror. It might be true. Analysts do find help by reading about other analysts' experiences and theories. But the recognition of the uniqueness of each experience is what really matters, as well as the ability to endure it and allow the patient to feel he is unique, and yet not utterly different from any other person. It also has to be remembered that unless the patient has experienced something of the kind before in his life he would not be able to experience it in the analysis. In the process of analysis the analyst may well be involved in repeating early experiences, such as that of a mother with her baby whom she cannot feed, or a mother with a child who does not thrive. Such knowledge alone, though, is of little help to the analyst because the work depends on a shared ability to endure the unendurable. The patient's treatment, and perhaps sometimes his life, depends on the analyst's ability to endure not being helpful, without becoming rigid, closed, or shut in. This does not mean he has to be passive in a masochistic, humiliated way, but that he must be prepared to feel safe and relaxed, not paralysed and trapped. In the end this, together with his patient's determination to survive, will find what is missing or lost, probably in a symbolic or somatic way.

I am not suggesting that analysts do better when they feel like this or when they feel generally that they are not doing well. Very often, if they give enough attention, they can do good work without such regressive episodes, but they must be careful before acting on the idea that it would help to make an early interpretation about something obvious like castration anxiety or fear of week-end separation. That kind of interpretation may seem obvious, and tempting to make in order to relieve anxiety, but there is a danger that it will hold up work rather than encourage it. There is a danger, too, in the analyst's not giving this kind of interpretation, which on some level the patient will expect. But it might hold up a dream or a free association. One could say that there is a danger of a compliant reaction by the analyst or the patient, but the analyst must try to see why he and the patient should want such compliance. The patient cannot know the rules to start with, and neither does the analyst with this particular patient. Various thoughts go through the analyst's mind throughout the treatment. Why is he saying that now? Why do I feel the way I do? What does the patient expect from me today? All these and many more questions drift through the analyst's mind while he listens to the patient's voice and is aware of the patient's body movements and of whether the patient is looking or not looking with his eyes and with his mind.

There is always a conflict in the patient between his wish to raise something and his need to conceal it. Each analyst has to be aware of the multitude of conflicts which are present at all times in every session and must try to pick out the conflict which seems the most pressing, not necessarily the most obvious. For instance, one of my patients recently complained of being cold, wet, and frightened. I did not comment. Later she told me a dream which, when interpreted, was connected with disloyalty and being shut out from other people's lives, and with a sense of not belonging. Afterwards this could be seen as representing a time in her life when, perhaps only for a few minutes, perhaps for a few hours, she had been left cold and wet by her mother, who might have been talking to somebody else in the room, or have withdrawn for a variety of reasons, instead of attending to her baby by changing its wet clothes. The baby/patient might then feel lost, not knowing where she was, cut off from the world which did not want her. If I had made an interpretation about my cold, wet patient at the beginning of the session, before I heard the dream, I would not have followed her sufficiently to make the interpretation which I then did make, namely, that I thought she was re-living a traumatic experience, triggered off by what I had done earlier in the month when I missed a session, and this was followed by the patient doing the same thing to me. The dream about disloyalty reminded me of these absences, and then she told me that when she got back to analysis the day following my absence, she felt she had never known me before. I was a complete stranger to her, and if I had come near her she would have felt violated. She had not told me so at the time. It was this dream and the associations to it which brought alive the traumatic events of her earliest months and years, and gave meaning to what she had said earlier in the session. Failure to recognise this would have resulted in an interesting but rather useless session centred on the patient's feeling of coldness and wetness which represented her need to be attended to, and on her not knowing whether she or anybody else was there. It would not have led to the association about her feeling like a stranger and that her parents were strangers in what had been her home. In fact, she had felt like a stranger in the world for most of her life.

The analyst need not know what to say to a patient in some sessions, and he must never forget that uncertainties exist. If he interprets mechanically, it can be felt; and that is in reality as much a failure, neglect, and absence when he needed to be present as if he misses a session. The patient needs dry, warm clothing, but the reason she needs it and her anger at the failure to provide it are as important, or more so, than the feeling itself of coldness and wetness. This patient had had a body memory of feeling wet and cold, but there had never before been a thought accompanying it, nor had the next potential thought—namely, that she should 'get out' and withdraw from the family to which she no longer belonged, and that she no longer had a place where she did belong—ever occurred to her. All this had never been a thought but it had, nonetheless, influenced her life. Now, however, a thought on the one hand and a feeling on the other, of being wet, cold, and angry and of not belonging, came together. In earlier stages of the analysis there had been wet and cold thoughts, there had been anger and alienation, and there had been feelings of not being part of the world and not belonging anywhere; but none of these had come together.

When working with patients who are trying to recover, or refind, memories which have never before been thought nor existed in words (Bollas, 1987; Bion, 1970), time has to be given to make the discovery. Words give meaning to experiences which then become thoughts. They arise out of associations, dreams, and body feelings. The patient who is able to bring these experiences together can allow them to become conscious in words which change his experience of himself in relation to other people. This does not happen instantaneously but marks the beginning of a process. These episodes are often repeated but gradually they change, and the patient, instead of withdrawing from a world where he may feel he does not belong, makes attempts, perhaps by symbolising his experiences, perhaps through some form of art, to feel trust and safety. Then he may allow some space between himself and the analyst, and feel greater trust in people in the external world who are different and separate from himself.

Bion (1970, p. 9) said:

> People exist who are so intolerant of pain or frustration (or in whom pain or frustration is so intolerable) that they feel the pain but will not suffer it and so cannot be said to discover it. . . . The patient who will not suffer pain fails to 'suffer' pleasure and this denies the patient the encouragement he might otherwise receive from accidental or intrinsic relief.

One of my patients felt chaotic if he was not in control. He therefore thought he was in control most of the time, and invented words and a whole vocabulary for himself which was right for him. If I used the wrong words, he would get confused but would probably not tell me what I had said wrong. One day he came to a session in a very chaotic state and told me that when he came to my house, instead of seeing the number '7' on my door, he saw '*no 7.*' He thought my house had gone away, but then realised his mistake, pressed the bell, and came in. It was the first time he could show me that he knew of my existence and of my power to do things in a way which he could not understand.

My decision not to interpret in this particular instance seems arbitrary, and I cannot prove that I was right. Perhaps I could have eased my patient's suffering and filled in a gap that he was seeking to fill, if I had spelled out and put into words what bit of his jigsaw was missing. That was the piece representing his mother, who was not where he expected her to be, and his supreme need to find her which, as I discovered later, led him to look in the mirror, where he could find her, or else himself looking like her.

Words were of the greatest importance to this patient and were often used as a defence against feeling. Sometimes, however, they were needed because he had not been given the right words but the wrong ones. The way he was told about himself as an infant gave him an unacceptable reflection of himself. Much later, in his early teens, he had tried to find his own words, looking for sentences and phrases which suited him and reflected to himself his own thoughts, character, and image.

In my view the analyst has to be just as observant, perhaps even more so, about what he does not do as about what he does. What the analyst does not say must be remembered by him more carefully than what he does say, because the decision to leave it to the patient, or to wait for the right time, is a very important one. It is so much easier to say what comes to one's mind when a patient says something than to remember what one thought but did not say. This happens all the time in every session, but sometimes the omission of something seems as striking as the one I am describing; and then it is forgotten, just like the trauma the patient is trying to remember.

Finally another, simpler, example of a non-regressed patient: it illustrates, though, the same necessity for caution in making interpretations and the analyst's need to be in touch with his own mind as well as the patient's. A woman in her early thirties, who could make relationships and live in the world (in a world where there were children, at least) was about to embark on the idea of becoming pregnant. In the session the patient spoke about her husband, who did not make her feel she was a suitable person to have a baby but rather that she was not quite healthy, or perhaps not the right person to have a child as other people were. He was aware that he himself might not feel good enough to be a father. He was a doctor, a consultant in a teaching hospital. The patient talked about a dream which related to a neglected child who had a promiscuous mother. The patient then told me about a conference which she had recently attended where she had had a good time and had looked good. She looked better than she had since leaving university. People told her so. She linked this with her work with me and thus made me feel good—or so she hoped—about her looking good. But was she like her mother? Was she promiscuous and neglectful? Did I need reassurance, so that I could reassure her about her ability, or right, to have both a baby and a husband?

The patient had no mother who could be relied on to admire her daughter, but only one who had to be flattered and not competed with. I made interpretations of this kind, which upset the patient, who was silent and then associated to a child who lived near her whose brother had died recently and who therefore had lost her mother for the time being. The work that was useful in this session was when the patient could talk about the 'loss' of the mother and her feeling of inadequacy about being a mother, because she was not sure that her baby would have parents; she herself might want to run away and be private, and not relate to either her husband or her child. How could a baby trust her?

This quite simple piece of work illustrates the fact that all analytic work can be seen in a variety of ways at any time; and unless the analyst can keep in touch with his own unconscious and imaginative mind he will lose focus and deal only with the words the patient is using and not with the patient who has decided to use those words. He will emphasise the wrong conflict.

How significant are first impressions, first interviews, or even consultations? I have found that my first impression, my first imaginary perception of a patient, is of great importance to me as work goes on. I usually write up my first interviews with patients with some care. This is not so much in order to get the details right about their date of birth, marriage, number of siblings, and so on. Those things are certainly important, and if one does not get such facts down at the beginning the opportunity may not repeat itself later on. But more important is to get down one's first impression of the patient, which, if one takes the patient on, will change over time. Sometimes, however, one comes back to the original perception and finds that there is something right about it which has been missed as time has gone on. One may see to begin with what is wrong, and come to understand the reasons for the failure during later work. The important thing is for the analyst to be aware from the beginning how he perceives the patient, how the patient perceives him, and how the cross-currents, projections, and introjections which occur are there right from the start.

During consultations the same kind of thing occurs, but the analyst has to be careful not to allow these mechanisms freedom. It is possible for him to stop them from happening by making some intervention of a kind which he would not make if he thought he might become the patient's analyst. In consultations I make 'interpretations' about the relationship between myself and the patient, not in relation to the unconscious but more to the patient's conscious expectations and fears, and his difficulty in trusting the consultant. His reaction to these sorts of comments is a useful guide; they do not intrude, and they do not necessarily elicit a truthful answer.

If the patient wants to try to link the present with the past, this has to be listened to and respected, but not responded to, because the consultant has no real idea of whether there is actually any connection or whether attempting true transference interpretations would simply be playing into an analytic game.

CONCLUSIONS

No two analyses are the same. In addition, each analyst works in a way which suits him and is probably different from other analysts, although there are fundamental similarities. We are all familiar with the comforting feeling when we read a paper or meet a colleague who echoes our own uncertainties and certainties.

When I myself work as an analyst or am used as an analyst in some other setting, I am aware of early basic instructions which I internalised as a student. I discovered a sense of myself working on my own; this is one-person psychology. Working as an analyst implies another person, but whomever I was working with, I became aware of myself in my chair with a special identity of my own. I cannot take it for granted that all analysts have similar internalised structures, and I was particularly fortunate in having theoretical seminars once a week from Anna Freud for two years during the beginning of my training. The clarity of her mind and her ability to tolerate other people's confusion were unusual, so I cannot assume that everybody has the same inbuilt structure. I do tend to take for granted, though, that if somebody is trained then some kind of structure will exist inside them. I am referring not only to ideas arising from metapsychology, like the ego, superego, and id, the instincts and defences, object relations, and so on, but also to the way in which an analyst responds to a patient. He needs to be able to observe phenomena which are strange and not to obscure complexities and paradoxes in human relationships because they do not make sense, or perhaps at any one time do not seem to make sense in terms of the transference relationship between patient and analyst.

It is only gradually on this basis that mutuality can be observed: how one person grows and changes, as the result of a mutual experience where there is a development of two people together. In every treatment, however, patients have periods of regression. They come and go. In some analyses the patient may be regressed for years, while carrying on a life that seems to be normal outside the analytic hours.

For me it is particularly important to be aware of, and not to try to escape from, times when I feel I am not doing the work as I should be, when I feel that I am not being a 'proper' analyst. For instance, I may not be aware of defences, transference phenomena, or conflicts and paradoxes. My ability to have hunches or formulate hypotheses may seem deadened, so that I fall back entirely on the rules that I learned from Freud and other people, and I forget the uniqueness of each session. Instead I try to push myself into a mould: a mould which is quite useless and dead because it is not linked with imaginative processes in the mind of the patient or of myself; processes of mutual needs, mutual satisfactions, mutual frustrations. Imagination is a precondition of the creative life. It can be safely used only if the structure and training are there; but the structure and training are useless if the analyst's imagination, or the patient's, is imprisoned.

In order to release himself and the patient from prison, the analyst must exercise the ability to wait—to see analysis more like the process of learning a language than a joint journey of explanation or research. The analyst who can do this will continue to learn with every patient who comes to him for analysis throughout his professional life.

PART II

The Analyst's Work with General Medical Practitioners

The relationship between psychoanalysis and medicine has been different in different countries and can only be considered in terms of the particular context. In the United States, for example, psychoanalysis was widely, though ambivalently, accepted as part of the overall medical and psychiatric milieu, while in France its diffusion, and perhaps dilution, into the general intellectual culture means that any caring profession must take some account of it. In Great Britain there has been no comparable pattern and little interaction between psychoanalysis and medicine, with the work of Enid and Michael Balint as an outstanding exception. Balint comments here on the caution there has been on both sides of the divide. Psychoanalytic ideas may be rejected out of hand or else too facilely accepted. She also emphasises that psychoanalysts need to appreciate the specific skills and understanding of the physician. Her aim is not to turn doctors into pseudo-psychotherapists but to help free them to accept as natural all the diverse aspects, even those that seem strange and irrational, of their patients' humanity. What makes this possible is the ability to tolerate uncertainty and confusion, while still observing things we are not in the habit of looking for.

In the latter part of the chapter she describes the method which has come to be known as the 'Balint group', by which she uses her psychoanalytic awareness to help doctors towards that goal. This account also provides a context for the work considered in the following chapters.

The doctors for whom these groups were organised are known in the British medical system as 'general practitioners' or 'GPs', terms which occur throughout the papers of Part II and also in the interview 'Afterthoughts'. These are doctors who are not attached to a hospital and who

---

'The Psychoanalyst and Medicine' was given as a Freud Memorial Lecture at University College, London, on 10 March 1975. It has not previously been published in full, but an abridged version appeared in the *International Journal of Psychiatry in Medicine* 7 (1976–77), 35–46.

work in the community as primary care physicians. They have a specified list of patients for whom they are 'the doctor', and family members usually all go to the same general practitioner. They refer to specialists when appropriate, but whatever is wrong it is to them that their patients will come in the first instance. This gives their work a particular range and continuity, as they are involved over the years with all aspects of their patients' health. It is important to appreciate this as the background to the work of a Balint group.

Balint also emphasises that between psychoanalysis and medicine there needs to be a two-way traffic. Each discipline should be enriched by the other (p. 135), and there is no missing the importance she thinks medicine has for psychoanalysis as well as psychoanalysis for medicine.

The Psychoanalyst
and Medicine

I imagine that the reason I have been asked to speak about this topic is that I am a psychoanalyst who for the past twenty-five years has worked with general practitioners. There are various ways of approaching my subject and I group them under two main headings. One is the biological, which would lead us into a discussion of psychosomatic illness, of the functions of biological systems, or of the influence physiological phenomena have upon psychological processes. The other, which I will explore here, involves examining not the relationship between systems and processes, their expression in bodily or psychological terms, and the influence the one has upon the other, but instead the relationship and the influence on each other of two kinds of people. These are people in different disciplines, such as the psychoanalyst, and I mean the person, not his theory or clinical procedures, and the physician. Both of them treat not just processes, systems, and illnesses but whole people. So we must examine how someone trained to work in one discipline can contribute, or relate, to the work of someone trained in the other. In parenthesis I consider it essential to the development of both disciplines that they should continue to cross-fertilise each other. Analysts must study the effects that physiological phenomena have on mental processes, just as doctors need to study how mental processes affect the body.

In the past, medicine has been inclined to preserve its homogeneity by excluding psychological methods and ideas, even when their scientific and therapeutic values were acknowledged. This was due not only to the unreceptive attitude of medicine towards psychoanalysis but also to some caution on the side of the psychoanalysts themselves. Psychology, psychopathology, psychotherapy, and psychoanalysis have all been considered as disciplines possibly related to medicine, but outside its range. Gradually, however, in some places, the artificiality of separating mental and physical illness, and mental processes from physical ones, has been recognised and their interaction acknowledged. It has long been appreciated, in fact, that psychology is related to biology. The workings of the brain can be understood biologically, while the function of the mind, as in problems of relating to others and to oneself, or adaptation in one's relationship to the environment, must be understood in psychological terms. True, it is not always easy to decide whether a psychological or a physiological approach is indicated when a patient comes to a doctor and presents an illness. One thing, however, has long been recognised. For those occasions when a psychological approach is chosen, then if psychoanalysis is to be of use in medicine, modified techniques must be found. The technique of psychoanalysis itself is not suitable except for a limited number of cases treated by psychoanalysts.

The dangers of the application of psychoanalysis in the wider field were soon realised. Freud (1910) had sounded a warning about 'wild' analysis. Alexander, who wrote an important book on the relation of psychoanalysis to medicine (Alexander, 1932), also cautioned against the unsound application of partial knowledge and untried procedures. Nevertheless, it was already clear in the 1930s that the advance of psychodynamic knowledge would open up a vast territory, one which to this day has not been systematically explored, requiring the application of that knowledge in various forms of psychotherapy. At the Budapest Congress of 1918 Freud (1919) already predicted that society would have to accept that the individual had the same right for help in his emotional suffering as in his physical illnesses. It was left to later writers, my husband, Michael Balint (1957, 1961, 1965), in particular, to see if the theoretical knowledge gained by psychoanalysts could be applied in the whole field of medicine and be useful to physicians as well as psychotherapists, psychiatrists, and specialists in psychosomatic medicine. As I shall show, it was not in fact the theoretical knowledge but other aspects of the analyst's equipment which were found to be of most importance in the wider field of medicine. The 'mysterious leap into the organic' is one of the oldest concepts in psychoanalysis, dating back to Freud's own early work and that of such pioneers as Ferenczi, Jelliffe, and Groddeck, and it is still attractive and intriguing. But these interests may have remained restricted to selected cases, and in any event psychosomatic thinking has never entirely become an integral part of psychoanalytic theory.

For a long time the question has been whether analysts should accept responsibility in this wider field. If so, what sort of responsibility? Or should they keep out of it? Should they, for example, develop psychotherapeutic techniques to be used in medical practice? Any assumption that such techniques were already available was, of course, wide of the mark. If psychoanalysts do accept such responsibility, what roles are open to them? One danger, if we are not careful, is that we may underestimate the relevance of the physician's own knowledge and not help him to make use of it. That is in fact, as I see it, our main task. Many analysts are so concerned about the risk of exploiting the patient's unconscious that they make it their first duty to advise their non-analytic colleagues what *not* to do and are so anxious about this that they fail to hear or learn from them what they *can* do.

We psychoanalysts, who see very few people each day, still tend to live in a rather closed community and spend much of our spare time discussing our ideas with each other. Yet whenever I give a lecture to, or discuss theory with, a mixed audience they are very well informed and often think I am talking down to them, even though I myself have found the ideas I am putting forward fascinating but difficult, complex, and hard to comprehend. Perhaps, like other psychoanalysts, I have made them seem simpler than they are. I am tempted to borrow for my argument a passage from Josipovici (1971, pp. xii–xiii):

> Gone are the happy days (as they say) when the majority of the public rejected modernism [read 'psychoanalysis'] out of hand and only a few brave voices were raised in its defence. At least then the situation was clear. Now we have a situation where everyone writes and speaks as though they understood what modernism [psychoanalysis] was about but where in fact most of the old prejudices still prevail. . . . Few people seem to feel that the issues raised by these [psychoanalytic] writers really *matter* any more . . . they are the classics . . . and as far as most readers . . . are concerned, they are well and truly dead. Indeed their too easy assimilation into the curriculum suggests that they have not really been understood.

No honest psychoanalyst ever really feels that he fully understands, finally and for ever, the workings of even one aspect of the human mind or of our theory, although sometimes we do so in our work with a particular patient at a particular time; it is always hard work. After we have formed a concept we revise and add to it. Freud did this, in common with all other scientists, and we continue to do so. Of course we can, if we so wish, use a turn of phrase or present some theory so that our audience thinks we know the latent reasons for human thought and action more precisely than we do. But 'common knowledge' about psychoanalytic theory and the analyst's use of it in his clinical work are often at variance. We can talk about our theory with conviction, and we can use it to help us understand our patients' communications. It must be said, though, that knowledge of it can sometimes hinder rather than help our observations of our patients, and if we are not on the alert it can block us. I am opposed to the use of theory without reference to observations in a clinical setting, and I take for granted only the most basic theoretical assumptions.

Among those is, of course, the concept of there being unconscious mental processes. Although you are familiar with this, I expect it still raises questions in your mind, because we can never assume that everything there is to say about it has been said and no new developments in our understanding of it are possible. Especially outside the clinical setting of psychoanalysis, we may have only just begun to see its implications and have only the vaguest idea of how to use it. Its importance for medicine as a whole, as well as in the wider social and political scene, is obvious but very hard to specify, let alone to make use of. Common facile interpretations in terms of symbolic meanings stem from an oversimplified view of symbolism and are usually wide of the mark. Furthermore, they imply that man is ruled by his unconscious drives alone and omit the fact that the unconscious mind tolerates contradictions and paradoxes, that man is continually struggling with his strivings and wishes, and that he defends himself against them, partly because of his terror of hurting people who are important to him and also because of the repercussions should he do so.

My approach to the psychoanalyst's contribution to medicine seems not unlike Lionel Trilling's approach to the psychoanalyst's contribution to art. He quotes Charles Lamb to refute the idea that the exercise of the imagination is a kind of insanity, and he stresses that the whole tendency of the psychoanalyst is to establish the *naturalness* of artistic thought (Trilling, 1950, pp. 153–154). Although in some ways Freud seemed to denigrate the artist as if he were a neurotic, he clearly saw and stated that in fact the artist was much more than that, and showed how much he revered him. He established that unconscious conflict can produce not only destructiveness but also creativity, and is not only wasteful but can also be of value. Just as Trilling saw that psychoanalysis is concerned with the naturalness of artistic thought, so my aim is to show that the analyst's main contribution to medicine is in establishing the naturalness of man himself. This includes particularly those aspects of man which may seem the most irrational and unacceptable, but in which some not wholly defended part of the mind can just be perceived by a trained observer; a part of the mind through which, once it is perceived, each man's uniqueness can show itself. I speak deliberately here of the mind, not the unconscious.

Most people, by force of habit, do not even notice these aspects. Josipovici discusses the limitations imposed by habit, emphasising the modernist insistence 'that what previous generations had taken for *the world* was only *the world seen through the spectacles of habit*' (Josipovici, 1971, p. xvi). The psychoanalyst too has to guard against limiting his vision by force of habit. Ideally he should be aware when his habit prevents him from seeing what he is not accustomed to see. If, out of habit, we only see what already strikes a chord in us, we may miss what is unique about someone; if our vision can be focussed on many different areas of the mind, it will illuminate many different aspects of it. If doctors appreciate the uniqueness of their patients and if psychoanalysts can help them to do this, which means tolerating periods of confusion when there are no familiar roads to follow, then their contribution to medicine can be significant. Physicians can then, perhaps, even enjoy their patients more while diagnosing and treating their illnesses. In my view the psychoanalyst's aim is to establish that what is taken as natural in a human being, or in society, is not necessarily more natural and certainly not more useful than what seems perverse or strange. *Humani nihil a me alienum puto.*

Before developing my theme further, I shall briefly describe the setting in which I work with physicians. For the past twenty-five years I have taken part in what we call training-cum-research seminars in which a psychoanalyst leader works once weekly over a period of two or more years with a group of eight to twelve general practitioners. They are asked to talk about any patient with whom they are having difficulties or who particularly interests them, preferably not patients with obvious neurotic or psychotic illness, but 'ordinary' patients whom they have seen during surgery hours. The other doctors in the group are then asked to comment. It is the aim of the psychoanalyst leader to keep the work going, helping the doctors to share their observations and ideas and to notice the existence of overlooked or obscure problems and contradictions. The leader also sets some boundaries. For instance, no 'wild' interpretations about the doctor's private problems are encouraged or even allowed. Only his professional difficulties with the patient are discussed. Wild guesses about hidden psychopathology in the patient are also discouraged. The emphasis is: 'What is going on now (*is* there anything going on?) between the doctor and his patient which is of special interest and can throw light on the doctor's difficulties with the patient or on the patient's illness?' Naturally the discussions often include a discussion of symptoms, even so-called neurotic ones; and the doctors try to understand, sometimes in the early days by quoting psychoanalytic theory, why a particular patient has developed a particular symptom. The leader encourages the seminar to build up a trustworthy picture of the case, to see the difference between facts and fantasies about the patient, between observations and inferences; and encourages the doctor to tell the group as much as he knows about the patient, including the supposedly trivial thoughts that occur to him, and not to rush in quickly to find explanations. Often the discussion centres on the patient's early life and an attempt is made to link early events with the patient's current problems and symptoms. Sometimes this helps the doctor to tolerate difficult patients better, and this can help doctor and patient alike. But the picture that is built up is inevitably impressionistic, and even if the development of the symptoms and the patient's unconscious need for them have been understood correctly, it is seldom that this alone is sufficient to help the doctor with the patient.

One of our main interests in this work has been in observing the richness of the unnoticed happenings, which once seen become obvious, in the interchange between the patient and his doctor, and to put these alongside those events which *were* seen and taken as significant. The unnoticed happenings to which I refer are not the unconscious processes in the mind of either doctor or patient. These can indeed sometimes be guessed at by the trained psychoanalyst, even outside his own clinical setting, but they cannot be reliably observed and are therefore useless for therapy. I mean rather the less 'noisy', less obvious aspects of the doctor's and patient's thoughts and actions, at the particular moment which is under review. An increased respect has developed in us for the significance of these observations in understanding the patient, his illness, and the treatment.

Here is an example. Recently a doctor in a seminar discussed a patient, Mr. F, aged thirty-four. He was married and had a son eighteen months old. He was a fine toolmaker by trade. He had been off work for some months, and the doctor presented him at the seminar because he felt he was making no headway in getting him back to work. The patient appeared to be depressed, and the doctor was ready to be angry with his employers for making him do such exacting work. He talked with the patient and prescribed appropriate drugs.

In the discussion it was thought that the doctor had strong ambitions for his patient. He wanted him to feel free to leave his job and take on an easier one. Because of the picture the doctor had built up of a harassed, over-strained patient, he had not observed what the patient himself felt. Nobody really knew what the patient wanted, but in spite of this the seminar gave plentiful advice. Gradually the psychoanalyst leader suggested that it was not a question of how to get him back to work but of whether he really liked his work or preferred being at home with his managing but amiable wife. In short, what were his own aspirations? What kind of man was he?

At a follow-up three months later, the doctor said it turned out that the patient did not feel angry with his employers, but liked his job and his boss, perhaps even being over-attached to him. When the doctor listened again, the patient could talk, as he had not been able to before, about what he *could* do and what he wanted. It also emerged that he had not been able to throw his weight about and be dominant at work. After talking like this he had been able to go back to work and had been well, although he did have another spell off work three months later. He felt more able to tell people to wait for him to finish the job rather than rush him, and was able to be in charge of a situation and handle it his own way. Interestingly, Mr. F's wife could not cope with the new Mr. F, and the seminar's earlier thoughts about her dominance seemed to be confirmed. In the new relationship she seemed somewhat 'down' and complained that her husband now read library books, played with their son, and did not make things at home any more. A good relationship between father and son had developed as it had between employed and employer, and this was being paid for by the wife. All this was perhaps a result of the patient's being able to assert himself with his doctor; something had to be recognised with another person before the patient could accept and make use of it himself.

During the discussion of this case there was plenty of opportunity to make wild interpretations about the role of father-figures, the patient's fear of homosexuality, and so on. What actually seemed useful, however, were the more ordinary, seemingly obvious trivia about the home situation and the wife's dominance, and the patient's relationship with his boss. Through them one could discuss his desire to set his own pace and establish his independence. Once he could share with his doctor his 'uniqueness', the particular kind of person he was—skilled, rather bossy, but able to function well in his own way—then he could get on. This illustrates what I have said before: a certain degree of what sometimes seems, because it is strange, to be illness must be recognised by another person before it can be accepted by the individual himself.

In this case, an understanding of the patient's unconscious mind was irrelevant. True, some physicians who work with psychosomatic illness find that if they understand the unconscious reason for a symptom in cases, say, of anorexia nervosa or ulcerative colitis, they can cure it; and indeed if the symptom can be removed the life of a patient may be saved. Psychoanalytic theory, even if not therapy, has undoubtedly helped physicians understand the unconscious need their patients have for a symptom, and can also help them to convey this understanding in a way acceptable to their patients. But human beings are complex, as I have said, and we need a broader view of ill people, such as psychoanalytic discussions of literature can offer us. Alexander (1933), for example, shows how Shakespeare illuminates the character of Falstaff not with symbolic meanings in the text or by an understanding of Falstaff's unconscious motives or his conflicts, but by tracing the development of his character in its relation to the young Prince Hal who is later to become King Henry IV. Alexander explains why Falstaff is so appealing a character, because through him Shakespeare illuminates an aspect of all of us which normally, out of force of habit, we do not see.

As analysts or physicians one of our aims is not to try to *remove* our patients' conflicts, telling them to be less angry, less passionate, or less unreasonable, but to enable them to use these aspects of themselves in a positive way and not think of them as only negative. To take a second example, one doctor reported that he had been in difficulties with a woman patient in her early eighties because she would not take her medicine and had been a great nuisance to her sixty-year-old daughter for many years. The daughter complained about her mother and vice versa. The doctor tried to arrange some 'home help' for this family, but whoever came was treated very rudely and refused to return. Finally the doctor sent the eighty-year-old mother to hospital so as to make life easier for the daughter. To his astonishment the daughter became depressed and was even angrier when the doctor visited her. The case was discussed in a seminar meeting, and it was thought that perhaps the two women complained only when the doctor was there. The mother came home again and harmony, although not without conflict, was restored. Apparently mother and daughter needed each other in a special way, but also needed to complain. They hid their satisfaction. Their conflicts were not resolved by their being parted, nor did they want them to be.

Let me describe a third patient. A girl of twenty came with her father to see her doctor. She was unmarried and pregnant, and the father asked the doctor to arrange a termination. He was determined that his daughter should not have her baby. Quite a long discussion took place before it struck anyone that we knew nothing about the patient's mother, the father's relationship to his own wife, or even about the father of the baby. This led the seminar to begin speculating about the patient's relationship to her mother as well as to the father of her baby and why the doctor had not realised he did not know about any of that. At this interview when her father was present, the patient's passionate feelings about her own mother and her ambivalence about being a mother herself were overlooked. Strangely, nobody even thought of them as important. They were not there to be seen.

This takes us into deep waters, and we need to develop theories about why one individual can tolerate conflict and ambivalence while another cannot, and to examine whether analysts or physicians can help their patients to increase their tolerance. That would take us far afield, but I emphasise this point because many artists and writers, as well as others who seek our help, are frightened that rather than release and strengthen them, so that they can make use of their tensions in a freer and better way, we may simply remove their conflicts, which they feel are linked to the bad, perverse side of themselves but which also make life worth living.

It is my belief that by setting physicians free to use and respect their own imaginations in a broader, yet still disciplined way, they can be helped to make observations which enable them to tolerate what they see in their patients and thus recognise them for what they are. This is within their ordinary, routine work. They do not have to become psychotherapists, make symbolic interpretations, or let their imaginations run wild in a phoney 'Freudian' manner; quite the reverse. But there are certain kinds of observation which, in my view, doctors do need to make about patients which they cannot make if they are frightened of either their own or their patients' imagination and strengths. One of the ways in which the psychoanalyst should help the physician is to show him how to respect and understand his own limitations, his behaviour, and his imagination, which must continue to be disciplined as it has been during his training, and to notice and respect those things about his patients which are different from what he expects them to be: those things, in fact, which Hippocrates said should be 'the secrets at the centre of the doctor's attention'. In my experience such work can contribute to the doctor's satisfaction in his professional life with his patients as well as to the satisfaction of the patients under his care.

Before I conclude, I shall let some of the physicians who have been working with me in a seminar for the last two years speak for themselves. Our proceedings are taped and transcribed, so this quotation is verbatim:

Dr. A: We seem to be looking at what we are doing in a slightly different way. Here we have been discussing this case, this particular case we have been talking of, and it looks like digging around trying to find something which might be wrong somewhere so that we can treat it or something, and you put it in a different light and you say 'Really all we are trying to do is build up a picture'. I suppose it is.

Myself: One might find some pathology or one might not. You can't tell until you have a look.

Dr. B: You might find something you wouldn't do anything about even if you found it.

Myself: But you notice it. You notice things and you might do nothing. But next time you see the patient, what you notice might set off another question in your mind which might mean that you might do another examination, either a physical one or by asking yourself questions; or you might even ask the patient a question.

Dr. C: There is always the danger that when you find a little bit of pathology, having dug around very hard, you then say 'Ah! That's the cause of the illness' and you've got to treat that.

Myself: But you don't do that, apparently.

Dr. B: You don't study things. That's the wrong word. You just learn to notice them.

Dr. F: I don't think that was quite the point. I think the point is, here we are talking about a very ordinary, simple consultation in the surgery, and on the face of it it seems rather ludicrous to talk about the marital problems because of a sort of very minor situation where somebody has come up to the surgery in a perfectly justifiable way, and it looks as though we're muck-raking in that sense; and what's the point of having fantasies which are to do with a situation which seems perfectly all right anyway? But if one then turns it around and says in what way is that family working and dealing with the unanswered question of contraception and the next child, without having to say therefore that's why mother brought the child up today with a cold or some fairly simplistic relationship; you know we're taking this in a sense as a window on to the family rather than saying these problems within the family are what precipitated the consultation, which is rather the way round I've always tended to look at the thing.

Finally a quotation, not this time from a seminar, but from an interview I recently had with a doctor. (I usually see each doctor after we have been working together for two years to see what he thinks he has got out of the work, and in what ways it has disappointed him and why.) This doctor said, 'The group has given me a preparedness to be daft, to make irrational observations and then to try and make sense of them'. This process, I must add, is very hard work indeed. It would be good to think that psychoanalysts can free physicians, and physicians free psychoanalysts too, to feel 'daft' sometimes, to alter their habitual ways of looking at people, to 'change their spectacles' and bear the temporary loss of orientation and the bewilderment that may ensue; and then to work, not at finding easy, ready-made answers, but to see what is there to be seen and not to impose their own world on their patients.

If this can happen, then the relationship between the psychoanalyst and medicine will be richer and more creative and not only we, but our patients too, will benefit.

chapter 12

It is interesting to see how Balint approaches a general survey of her subject. Strikingly, 'Talking Treatments' contains nothing about how the doctor should talk to the patient. Instead Balint's emphasis is all on the quality of the doctor's or therapist's *listening*. This recalls the supervision experience mentioned in the Introduction. An essential provision for making this listening possible is the setting or framework of the treatment, which is partly a matter of externals like time and place, but more importantly an internal matter of the doctor's receptivity. The 'analytic framework' is fundamental to psychoanalytic technique. In this chapter Balint shows that the concept can be applied across various therapeutic settings, while still respecting the differences between them. (Her comments here on marital therapy are highly relevant, of course, to Part III of this book.) What characterises all these settings is a particular professional involvement which is 'both distant and intimate' (p. 155). (There is a link here to the discussion of distance and closeness in Chapter 4, and a further connection is noted in the introduction to the next chapter.) In spite of this common factor, Balint resists the use of 'psychotherapy' as a general label for these talking treatments, because this way of 'talking-cum-listening' should be integral to medicine as a whole. She emphasises, nonetheless, that specific training is required to do this work. 'No one suggests that doctors should undertake any other kind of work without a thorough knowledge of the subject and the skills appropriate to the disturbance they are treating' (p. 158).

The clinical example of Mr. F, which appears in the previous chapter, was also given at length in the original version of this one. To

---

'Talking Treatments' was written as a review chapter in *Psychiatry in Medical Practice* (ed. R. G. Priest, Macdonald and Evans, 1982). Copyright 1982 by Pitman Publishing. Reprinted by permission.

avoid unnecessary repetition, it is omitted here in favour of a reference back to the earlier account.

The comments on outcome research (p. 152) reflect the original date of writing. Holmes and Lindley (1989, pp. 29–43) may be consulted for a current survey of the field.

Talking Treatments

INTRODUCTION: THE NATURE OF TALKING TREATMENTS

What are the facts about talking treatments? Have they a right to a place in medicine? Have any so-called psychotherapeutic methods a scientific basis and, if so, can they be taught? What are the methods and who should teach and practise them? This chapter can only briefly examine some of these questions, all of which aim to help doctors decide on the right treatment for some of their patients.

We can start our discussion of these questions with the work of a well-known physician, Breuer, in the 1880s. Breuer, a doctor with a high reputation, was treating hysterical patients; Freud was a friend of his, although much younger and only just qualifying as a doctor. Breuer described to Freud the treatment of a particular hysterical patient known as Fräulein Anna O., a treatment involving listening to her talk and described more fully below, so that later when Freud became interested in the study of hysteria and found the currently recommended methods of treatment, such as hydrotherapy, massage, rest cures, and so on were not very effective, his thoughts gradually turned to the remarkable success which Breuer had reported with Fräulein Anna O. Later Breuer, together with Freud, described this work in *Studies on Hysteria* (Breuer and Freud, 1893–95). This book is usually regarded as the starting point of psycho-analysis. It is interesting to ask ourselves to what extent, and in what ways, the procedures and findings described in these studies paved the way to the practice of all talking treatments as they exist today and influence medicine as a whole.

Perhaps one of Freud's most outstanding achievements was his in-vention of the first instrument for the examination of the human mind—a systematic method for exploring the unconscious. One could say that Breuer came across it, but Freud started systematically examining it and continued to do so, together with his colleagues, all his life. He was not the first to explore the nature of the human mind, or realise the existence of the unconscious, but he did discover a means of investigating it which he described, and he proposed a structure of the mind based on his findings which is still used. His work enables us to trace the development of the method he found for this exploration, and the structure and dynamics of the mind which he discovered, and on which his theories are based. At that time, what he described was primarily a one-person psychology but gradually psychoanalysts have, on the basis of his findings, developed theories of two- and three- and multi-person psychology and nowadays many analysts think of their work as a basis for the study of human relationships, and not just as a study of the human mind and its structure.

Breuer's patient, Anna O., herself demonstrated how to overcome some of the obstacles in the way of doctors who wished to undertake this work, and she herself invented the title of her cure. She referred to it as a 'talking cure' and also as 'chimney-sweeping' (Breuer and Freud, 1893–95, p. 30).

Breuer and Freud had both experimented with hypnosis and hypnotic suggestion, but with Anna O. only very slight use of these methods was necessary. This patient produced streams of verbal material and all Breuer had to do, he said, was to sit by and listen to them without interrupting her. Freud describes how he, too, gradually gave up hypnosis and contented himself with listening and occasionally putting his patient into a state of concentration with the use of pressure on her forehead. Many of us now find that if we learn to wait and to listen, the patient, if he wants us to do so, will concentrate without any encouragement and will talk in a way which is important to him, even if we ourselves do not understand the meaning of what he says right at the beginning. We have also found that patients will do so in many different professional settings.

A talking treatment should perhaps also be called a listening treatment, because listening—or a certain kind of listening—is necessary before a patient is able to embark on talking in a way that would be likely to be useful to him. In my view, this kind of talking-cum-listening should not be labelled psychotherapy (although it is difficult to avoid doing so when writing about it) as this suggests to the reader that it is a speciality and not an integral part of medicine, which I consider it to be.

In medicine as a whole, patients have to learn how much, and what sort of, help they may expect from their doctors and how much anxiety and suffering they must bear on their own. Doctors, too, need to know how much they must bear on their own and how much help they can expect from their colleagues, from specialists and others, and how much increased understanding of their patients' illnesses, or their patients as whole people with or without illnesses, they can acquire by listening. In my view, the acquisition of the skill to listen can in some cases ease the doctor's load of suffering and make his responsibility for the patient less arduous. This only applies to doctors who feel dissatisfaction with their work with particular kinds of patients, and who look around for ways of easing that dissatisfaction.

There seems little doubt that a considerable proportion of the complaints about which patients consult their doctors are not solely related to physical illnesses, but originate also from emotional problems and conflicts. For our purpose, it is irrelevant to establish the exact proportion of those patients who have emotional as well as, or rather than, organic illnesses. The figures vary in the literature available. It may be worth recording that as far as I know the lowest figure given speaks of about ten per cent of all patients. It is interesting here to quote from an article in *Pravda* (Vel'vovskii, 1973), where it is stated that on an average twenty per cent of those that were admitted to a clinic by doctors of different specialities would not have received much help unless they had also consulted a 'psychotherapist doctor': and a further thirty per cent were in need of his advice in the course of treatment. This was a result of a study of a sample of patients carried out in a poly-clinic which serves the workers in a factory in Russia. It is a rather surprising source of information and it would seem that, if it is true, there cannot possibly be enough psychotherapists or psychiatrists to meet the need and that perhaps other doctors must develop skills, so as to be able to listen in the right way in order to diagnose where an emotional problem exists as well as, or rather than, an organic one in a patient who shows that he is suffering, but finds it difficult to say exactly where his pain comes from. Even if treatment cannot follow, the skill to make a diagnosis alone is a considerable one which is largely based on a skill to listen and to talk with the patient; the diagnostic stage can be therapeutic in itself.

Before going further, I want now to consider a particular use of talking treatments in medicine, that used in Balint groups, as described by Loch (Loch and Dantigraber, 1976). Following this it should be possible to examine the different settings in which the treatments can take place.

Loch says that the aim of Balint groups—where doctors are helped to rethink their ways of relating to their patients and to listen to them in a different way—is to enable a suffering individual (the patient) to understand part of the situation in which he finds himself. By helping patients to understand the situation in which they are 'imprisoned', which is caused by the simultaneous activity of contradictory tendencies in themselves, they can regain a basic feeling of well-being or of 'at one-ness with themselves'. Loch quotes Hampshire (1972) as saying that man has to understand himself and be understood in order to be free, in order to extend his active life. Loch thinks that the kind of work that is done in talking treatments enables a patient to become active again, to find his way.

The case of Mr. F, described in the previous chapter (pp. 140–141), shows such a patient, who had to say something and be understood before he himself knew, and could accept, one aspect of himself about which he had been only vaguely aware; he was then able to act upon it. The patient's conflicts and contradictions were not discussed but all that seemed to be necessary at that time was for him to find out, by talking, what kind of activity he was capable of and what he enjoyed. Some patients need more. They may seek psychoanalytic or other forms of treatment; or else trained general practitioners may be able to provide the 'more'.

Another patient, a woman in her fifties, had to say and then to know that she could be loved and loving. This was a patient who had visited her doctor for some years, principally with minor complaints like tension headaches. One day she came in complaining once more of headaches and said that she thought she had better leave her job because the noise in the factory was so great and this was what she thought caused her headaches; she added that she could not leave because her husband and she needed the money. The doctor knew that this was not quite true, and went a bit further with his enquiries into why she had to work. The patient then quite unexpectedly began to talk about her childhood. She had been brought up in an orphanage and remembered watching the parents and friends of other children when they came to visit them. She had spoken about this before—but never, as then, with emotion. The patient was never visited in the orphanage and was extremely surprised when anyone ever wanted her and astonished that her husband had offered to marry her, because she did not expect to be loved or wanted by anyone. She had never believed that her husband loved her, but at the interview, with the help of the doctor, she suddenly realised that she need not earn so much money: perhaps they did not need it. She still did not think that she was loved.

A few weeks later the patient visited the doctor again, this time with a sore throat. She told him that she was doing less work and that she had realised, on the way to the bus to see her doctor, that perhaps her husband did love her, and on telling the doctor this, to her surprise she burst into tears. Something apparently had happened in the previous interview to make her reconsider some of the things that she had assumed about herself, which had led her to realise also that perhaps she could be wanted and was lovable. But it was not until she verbalised this in the interview with the doctor on the second occasion that she burst into tears, and really felt cared for. Gradually, after this, her feelings about herself changed and she stayed at home more and she and her husband did more together. This, put as briefly as I have described it, sounds a bit simple and naive, but we have a long follow-up record to show that the changes were stable. It is important to know that the patient herself never connected the interviews with her doctor to the changes in her life which followed them. However, the doctor seemed to be a key person for her; a necessary link enabling her to change.

The doctors' aims in this case and that of Mr. F seem very different, but the similarity between the two is that in both cases the patients verbalised a problem—which then led the doctors to be active in a different kind of way. It is my view that it was this verbalisation in a particular kind of atmosphere, in a particular kind of setting at a time which suited them, which was needed.

Before proceeding, I must refer to the astonishing paucity of early writings on technique—particularly by Freud. This suggests that there were in him, as there are in most of us today, some feelings of reluctance about publishing this kind of material. In fact he was highly sceptical as to the value of 'lessons in technique'. He never ceased to insist that the proper mastery of the subject could only be acquired from clinical experience and not from books.

In spite of being well aware of this danger, I am writing this chapter, which I hope will be seen more as a signpost to treatment, and an introduction to the art of listening, than as a lesson on how to conduct it. I, too, still think that one can learn to listen and to talk with patients only by trying to do so on the job, but I will add that one should, if possible, be able to discuss one's experience with colleagues; otherwise one may be unaware of what has taken place during the talk: it is important to have another person listen to oneself.

One of the difficulties of examining patients with emotional problems is that the doctor's own emotions have to be taken into account. They are very often involved and it is only natural, and certainly not unusual, for the doctor to feel angry or impatient, or sympathetic or protective, towards the patient and sometimes these feelings cannot be controlled. If the doctor is aware of them, however, they are much less likely to interfere with the communication with his patient than if they are unconscious. They can even be helpful if understood.

As Ferenczi wrote (1919, pp. 186–187), apparently referring to a discussion he had with Freud:

> As the doctor . . . is always a human being and as such liable to moods, sympathies and antipathies, as well as impulses—without such susceptibilities he would of course have no understanding for the patient's psychic

conflicts—he has constantly to perform a double task during the analysis: [we should say during any encounter with his patient where talking is important] on the one hand, he must observe the patient, scrutinise what he relates, and construct his unconscious from his information and his behaviour; on the other hand, he must at the same time consistently control his own attitude towards the patient, and when necessary correct it; this is the mastery of the counter-transference.

This is asking a great deal of all of us, even for analysts who have plenty of time during their training to learn to use their feelings (counter-transference) in an appropriate way; still more for general practitioners in their surgeries, although from my experience it is not impossible. We still have very scant theories of personal relationships, and many about the structure of the mind. Freud himself had profound intuitive understanding of his patients and this gave him a therapeutic personal relationship with them. They got better partly because Freud understood them and they could understand some aspects of themselves which were preventing their development or their activities. Freud himself saw his cures, in the earlier years, as due to the removal of conflicts and anxiety due to the dammed-up tension of repressed instincts and the recovery of infantile memories related to primitive sexual fantasies. We tend nowadays to think that help is also given by the professional understanding a patient gets in the relationship with a trusted person, however brief it is.

Clinical experiences with therapeutic techniques are not necessarily reliable. Malan (1963, 1976) and others have said that psychotherapy is one of the subjects least amenable to scientific study. Most writers have been unable to demonstrate from controlled studies that psychotherapy itself brings about any greater improvements than life experience alone, although it has been shown that dynamic psychotherapy can be more or less validated for psychosomatic conditions (Luborsky, Singer, and Luborsky, 1975). Malan, however, is hopeful about the outcome of studies and says that 'all that is needed is . . . the objective handling by researchers of subjective judgments made by trained clinicians'. His findings are very important and merit careful study by anyone wishing to brush talking treatments to one side.

SETTINGS IN WHICH TALKING TREATMENTS TAKE PLACE

Before proceeding to study in detail the settings in which talking treatments take place, I will give an example of one case which was studied in two different settings, to show how difficult it is to know the reason *why* the outcome was so different on the two occasions. Was it because of the settings in which they occurred; or because of the ways in which the doctors were able to listen; or the timing? We shall see how difficult it is to answer these questions.

The case was first reported by a general practitioner in a training seminar. It was taped and transcribed and I can quote some of the discussion verbatim. The doctor started to describe his case and said:

One case I have got is a thirty-five-year-old man, married, one child, who generally has an anxious personality. One day he jumped into the shallow end of a swimming pool and hit his head. After being X-rayed he suddenly said he couldn't feel the right half of his body, head, arms and legs. I think he finished up in various teaching hospitals. He had E.M.I. scans. He tends to be pushed to the psychiatrists who call him an anxiety depression. He has been put on various drugs; he's been reassured that there is no serious abnormality, yet he insists he can't feel the right side of his body, so you can prick him and he feels nothing. They say there is nothing wrong with him so he says, 'Well why is it I can't feel the right half of my body?' When you ask him whether he has got problems and why he has got this terrible anxiety state he says, 'Why is it when I am eating I can't feel the food on the right side of my cheek?' You say, 'Well, that's all in the mind'. 'Well, why is it when I am on the lavatory I can't feel the right side of my cheek?' And this goes on forever and we are not just getting anywhere. He keeps saying he can't feel, and we keep saying it is in the mind. Various psychiatrists have suggested putting him on antidepressives but others are against it and he is awfully tense and he has got himself so that he just can't do anything or say anything but that he can't feel the right side of his body. And he says, 'Why can't you give me some other tablets and make me better?'

Some of the doctors in the group asked about the patient's family life and the doctor said he had not found out anything; there had been masses of neurological examinations and the doctor said he just had to reassure him, that is all they could possibly do, but whatever they say, he just answers, 'Why can't I feel the right side of my body?' The group tried to find out more about the patient but the doctor could only say how frustrating a case it was (and the group agreed). He had therefore passed him back to make another appointment with another teaching hospital.

It so happened that another general practitioner in the same group, who was working at the psychiatric department of this teaching hospital as part of his training course, saw the same patient. I will quote from the beginning of his report.

I have got a follow-up on last week's case—the chap with the hemi-anaesthesia. He came along full of the same problems. He's got quite a lot of guilt feeling. When he was nine his sister died in a motorbike accident; she was seventeen and she was admitted to hospital with multiple head injuries and he said at the time they had just had a row before she had gone out. 'I hope she never comes back,' he had said at the time, and of course she didn't come back. She died. Last September he and his wife had a row and she said, 'Drop dead' and he went and banged his head in a swimming pool. His troubles all started from then and he reacts very strongly from the fact that his wife said 'Drop dead' so he is going to die because of his sister.

The group asked the doctor how he got the patient to talk like this but he did not answer but continued, saying:

He is quite forthcoming. He has got a son of six and he resents the relationship between the mother and son. I think they are quite close together. He is a bit of an outsider. His wife works at the same school as the son goes to. They are there together all day. He is a bit resentful about that, but I have got to talk to him separately about that.

The discussion continued.

I quote the case rather fully because it is important to see the different way the patient used the two doctors and the different ways in which he talked. We cannot know whether this was because on one occasion he was in a general practitioner's surgery and on the other in the psychiatric department of a teaching hospital, or whether he was ready to talk on one occasion and not on the other. We must remember that he had been in the psychiatric departments of many teaching hospitals before. From years of experience with general practitioners we do know that patients can talk to their general practitioners in both ways demonstrated by these reports. The relevant factor may be that they perhaps can talk when the time is ripe *and* when the doctor offers to listen, that is, when the setting in which he works makes it possible for him to tune in to his patients. I must state that the general practitioner who reported this case had very little time indeed in his surgery and was hampered by this factor, which some general practitioners might be able to overcome. If the doctor feels he has no time, the right kind of trusting atmosphere certainly cannot develop even if the patient is ready to talk.

We have a follow-up on this patient and it is interesting to note that, when our second doctor returned to the ward after the seminar meeting, the patient had abandoned his symptom and was playing ping-pong. One must ask why was he doing this; why at that particular time, and also why was he not able to do so on other occasions. His treatment continued, although there were few long interviews, and at the time of writing the patient is at home but visits his doctor regularly once a week in the out-patient clinic.

Let us now try to describe in general terms the kind of atmosphere that is needed for talking cures. How is the atmosphere created and what does it consist of? It is a setting in which the doctor can observe freely, not behave automatically, convey his observations so they mean something to the patient, and not turn his back on unpleasant facts or confessions or asides. It would make it much easier for beginners if a kind of guide-book could be provided for doctors, with a plan of how to start the journey with the patient, pointing out the ways to look and where to go, and perhaps giving some hints about how to respond to various communications. Unfortunately, this is impossible, because no two patients are alike and no two doctor–patient relationships are the same. But if the right atmosphere is created, and the patient feels he can say what he wants and that he may be understood, he may feel less alone and even feel that he is more related and similar to other people outside the surgery or consulting room than he previously felt. He may begin to feel that part of him corresponds with parts of other people, and ideas which he was only partly aware of, because of a feeling of shame or guilt or oddity, can be acknowledged by him, even though only in a half-understood way. In the case we have just discussed this seemed to happen and it enabled him to say he felt he was treated as an outsider by his wife and his son.

The setting in which the doctor sees the patient, then, is not made up entirely of the physical setting in which the treatment takes place, or the training or lack of it in the doctor. It does not matter so much, perhaps, whether it is in a hospital ward, or the general practitioner's surgery, or in the psychiatric department of a hospital, but what does matter most is the doctor's personality, the way he behaves and thinks and the way he relates to and thinks about people. Words, it is true, bridge the gulf between the two people, the doctor and the patient, but more than words are exchanged between them; they are in a way emotionally involved with each other, in a special, professional way, both distant and intimate. I have already made it clear that I do not think that all patients want to be understood and listened to all of the time. It is sometimes difficult for doctors to know when a patient does *not* want to be understood or listened to, and it is important that he should take the timing of the patient's request for help into account. If doctors can leave patients alone when they want to be left alone on one occasion, it often seems to follow that patients will come back to their doctor when they do wish to talk and to be understood.

We recently had an example of this in a case mentioned by a woman doctor at a seminar.

The doctor reported that she was seeing a twelve-year-old boy complaining of tummy aches. Various medicines had been tried, but the boy still went on complaining and stayed away from school. The doctor had spoken to the school and they had said that the boy seemed to be in some trouble, but he was not performing too badly and they wished that he would come back and attend school and not be kept away by his tummy aches. The doctor felt that the boy was troubled and told the seminar that his mother had died a short time before and he was being looked after by an older stepsister. No one could talk to this boy about his mother's death or about his feelings for her, or about her long terminal illness, which the boy had witnessed in their home. The members of the group sympathised and felt too that it was impossible to talk to the boy about such a painful subject. They offered advice, suggesting various other remedies that should be tried for the tummy aches. Gradually, however, somebody ventured to say that perhaps the boy would like to talk, otherwise why did he come to his doctor? The doctor who was looking after him was delighted and said that, in fact, after a long silence at the last interview, the doctor had asked the patient what he was thinking about, and the patient had said, 'I was wondering what question you were next going to ask me'. The doctor said she would like to talk to the boy about his mother or to try to get him to talk about her. At a follow-up interview later on, it seemed she had been able to do so and that the boy wanted to come back weekly.

This patient therefore did want to be listened to, but it was difficult for anybody to think that something as painful as one's mother's death could be spoken about, even in the trusting atmosphere which this particular doctor clearly provided.

A professional relationship exists usually only in the setting in which it takes place and it stops abruptly when the two people concerned leave it. Thus a kind of frame is put around the work and the patient need not leave the doctor feeling totally vulnerable because of what has passed between them.

Whatever the technique, the therapist's attitude to the patient will be as important as any verbal communication that takes place between them. This involves the therapist in having the courage to be himself (his professional self, that is) and in being willing to accept his own peculiarities, weaknesses, strengths, and limitations as a doctor, as well as those of his patients. He will certainly not be the same with every patient, because different people call for different responses, but he must certainly not 'put on an act' with the patient and be, for instance, very friendly, very loving or very aloof and 'professional'. It is often only too easy for the doctor to present himself as a strong, dependable father-figure who may have some magic cure. This, however, is not very useful and it is easier for the patient if the doctor is relaxed and quiet and on the same level as his patient, not above him or beneath him, particularly in difficult cases and when the patient feels that only a miracle can help him. It is very tempting for a doctor to think that his patient needs more love and for him to try to give it, but this is not his task; he cannot, for example, make up for early deprivations. What he can do is to listen attentively to what is said and understand it in a professional capacity and, in particular, never to forget that there is always something new to understand. He may have to wait, but it is often not the facts about the patient's past, or misunderstandings about his relation with, for instance, his parents which have to be understood, but odd trivialities which the doctor would never guess might be told him, so that he cannot prepare himself to hear them. It is very difficult indeed for the doctor to be attentive in this way, but if he does not feel in a hurry—even if he has only 'six minutes' (Balint and Norell, 1973)—his attitude may enable the patient to say something quite quickly. We have found, in studying short interviews, that the capacity to waste, perhaps two out of six minutes of an interview, is well worth the time. If the doctor feels in a hurry and therefore rushes in with ideas, the whole of the six minutes will be wasted and not only the first two or three.

CLASSIFICATION OF TALKING TREATMENTS

Talking cures vary according to the training of the doctor, and one way of classifying them is according to that training; or they can be classified according to the therapeutic goals. In the case I discussed about the man who was seen by the two doctors (pp. 153–154), the training of the doctors was the same, as was their goal, which seemed to be only to remove the patient's symptoms: it was expanded later, as it often is.

We cannot discuss goals, of course, without discussing diagnosis, as our first task must always be to make a diagnosis, and not one that consists only of labels; on the basis of that diagnosis we decide on the goal. It quite often happens that the goal is to leave the patient alone with his symptoms, or to see what happens for a time before deciding on what kind of therapy to try; it can be to keep in touch with the patient, or at other times to leave him alone and to let him get in touch with the doctor himself, if he wishes to do so. Some 'talking' of course will have taken place between the doctor and the patient before any of this is decided. When I talk about diagnosis in this chapter I mean not only what is traditionally called a diagnosis in medicine, but what we have called, over the years, an overall diagnosis, which can be described as an appraisal of the ways in which a patient sees himself, how he relates to and sees the people who are close to him, and how his illness or disturbance is shown in his life (E. Balint, 1969; see also Chapter 14). This overall diagnosis includes a description of the patient's physical illness or disturbance as well, but not seen in isolation.

Many doctors, and others who act as leaders of therapeutic groups, do so with apparently little specialised training in this field, and some of them learn 'on the job'. I think that training is needed, as in other branches of medicine. No one suggests that doctors should undertake any other kind of work without a thorough knowledge of the subject and the skills appropriate to the disturbance they are treating.

There are, however, many therapeutic groups in existence run by only partly trained workers, who aim, for instance, to enhance the freedom of expression of the individual or the removal of some inhibition which is preventing him from being active. These are concepts similar to those which I have talked about earlier (Loch and Dantigraber, 1976) but the techniques used are different. They remind one of the early work by Alexander and French, who developed a therapy which aimed to provide a 'corrective emotional experience' for the patient, in order to do away with the necessity of long-term psychoanalytic treatment (Alexander and French, 1946).

I must now briefly describe some differences in psychotherapeutic techniques in the different settings used by doctors where talking treatments are the main instruments they use. I will not go over the general points I have already made but will dwell upon the differences between one setting and another. I can only describe a few of the settings in which I myself have worked, or with which at least I am very familiar. I will start with the psychoanalytic setting.

The Psychoanalytic Setting

Classical psychoanalysis starts when a patient, after one or more preliminary consultations with the psychoanalyst, decides that he would like to, and is able to, spend years, rather than months, weeks or days, exploring the relationship between his unconscious mind and the world in which he lives. The work is based on the acceptance of the idea that there is an unconscious part of the mind which, although unconscious, influences the thoughts and behaviour of each one of us.

Analysts nowadays vary in their opinion about the frequency of sessions they offer their patients. Most work three to five times a week with each patient, and Freud himself sometimes saw his patients six times a week. Some analysts consider that they can do analytic work even when they see their patients infrequently. They presumably accept Freud's idea that anyone whose work includes an ability to use 'transference' phenomena and is aware of the 'resistances' can call his work psychoanalysis, thus leaving the frequency of interviews open (Freud, 1914, p. 16).

It is difficult briefly to describe transference and resistance. I will refer to the definitions of Laplanche and Pontalis (1973). Transference is 'a process of actualisation of unconscious wishes. Transference uses specific objects and operates in the framework of a specific relationship established with these objects. Its context, *par excellence*, is the analytic situation' (p. 455). Resistance is defined as 'everything in the words and actions of the analysand that obstructs his gaining access to his unconscious' (p. 394).

At the beginning of the work the analyst makes a diagnosis, trying to arrive at some idea of the patient's basic conflicts and of the way that these are interfering with his development and activity and feeling of contentment. The analyst must always be prepared to reassess his ideas and his diagnosis as the work proceeds. The normal technique is to ask the patient to say what comes into his mind, no matter how irrelevant or inconsequential this may seem. The analyst listens carefully, not only to the content of what the patient says, but even more to the association of ideas—how one idea follows another. It is by following the association of ideas, including those given in dreams, that the analyst can get into touch with the unconscious part of the patient's mind. The work is based on the idea that unconscious conflicts, both within the patient and with people in his environment, are largely responsible for his difficulties and for his suffering.

The Psychotherapist's Setting

Psychotherapy varies from simple advice and reassurance to very elaborate and well-studied methods of helping patients to change in their attitudes by talking to their doctor. I have had very limited personal experience of these methods, and will only describe one kind of psychotherapy which can be used in the setting of the hospital or in the doctor's consulting room.

Michael Balint describes how he had been interested for many years in the possibilities of a therapy which would not last so long as the classical psychoanalysis (Balint, Ornstein, and Balint, 1972; Malan, 1963). He saw that there might be disadvantages in this, but he thought that there were also advantages. He thought that if such work was to be undertaken, the results of the therapy must be comparable to those of an analytic treatment and must be stable in about the same degree. Fewer patients might be suitable for this sort of therapy, the chances of failure might be greater, and the work perhaps so difficult that it could only be undertaken by trained psychoanalysts. Balint decided that those trying to work in this way should concentrate on the interaction between patient and therapist and on the elaborate processes and techniques that developed as a result. It was felt that unless a focus could be found early in the work, this type of therapy was impossible. But it was important that if the focus proved to be wrong, and did not persist during psychotherapy, it should not be adhered to and a longer form of treatment might prove to be necessary. A great deal of work has been done to validate these theories (see list of references, p. 92, in Balint, Ornstein, and Balint, 1972). It is very difficult to make the kind of diagnosis required to arrive at a focus, and the work can best be undertaken by psychotherapists and psychoanalysts working in a team or workshop.

The General Practitioner's Setting

I have already reported some cases which have been treated by general practitioners either in their surgery or in hospital. I will therefore only enlarge on general practitioner treatments by describing work arising out of a study of ordinary short interviews during surgery hours. (For fuller discussion of the general practitioner's setting, see Balint and Norell, 1973.)

In this study, our aim was not to try to find short cuts in order to avoid longer psychotherapeutic interviews, but to measure, as precisely as possible, the therapeutic potential of the doctor–patient relationship in the general practitioner's everyday setting. In the work, which lasted more than five years with a group of seasoned general practitioners, we came to realise that, instead of solving exciting puzzles and problems, the doctor was expected to 'tune in' to his patients' wavelength of communication, so that he could respond to them. The traditional aim of pinpointing the seeds of the trouble or the suffering is not always appropriate. As an alternative, it was suggested that the aim of this kind of therapy should be to provide the patient with the opportunity to communicate whatever it is he wants, in a brief time. We found that this resulted in a brief, intense, and close contact, which was then followed usually by less intense and less taxing meetings between the doctor and the patient. What comes up during the intense interview can be explored in subsequent interviews. The task of the doctor is to give a great deal of attention to what the patient is saying, or is trying to say or to convey, at that particular time, rather than to study the underlying causes of his illness, though of course the latter may engage his attention on subsequent occasions.

This still seems to me to be the most suitable technique in general practice, but it is one in which experienced listening is more important perhaps than in any other setting. I am repeating what I said when I was talking in general abut the nature of talking treatments. The aim in the general practitioner setting is, from time to time, to meet a patient's need in a short interchange without any guidelines and without any theoretical ideas present in the doctor's mind at the time of doing so. If he has theoretical concepts in his mind when he listens to his patient, it may block his ability to hear and he may not have the time to correct it during the short interview with the patient.

The Setting of the General Medical Ward

A patient in hospital medical wards may also need to be listened to and to talk. All the general observations I made earlier apply here too, but there is one striking difference, which is that no one doctor is in sole charge of the patient. In fact, each doctor is a member of a team, with a senior doctor at the head. Nurses, aides, consultants, registrars, and housemen are all working for a patient and it sometimes seems a matter of chance who the patient decides to talk to, or who decides to listen to the patient. This could quite easily be a nurse, and the nurse may not think it worthwhile reporting some of her observations to the doctor, or the doctor may not think it worth listening to some of the observations of the nurse. However, it does seem that such discussions between the team looking after a patient, who is causing anxiety because he does not get well in the expected manner, can be rewarding. The variation here seems to be the communication between professional staff. In other settings it can be extremely important that the doctor should not tell anybody else what his patient has said; the need for *privacy* can be one of the most important needs that a patient has. He may feel that he has to be certain that what he says will be regarded as secret before he can trust his doctor at all.

The Setting for Marital Therapy

It is not infrequent that patients approach their doctors with trivial problems which later turn out to be based on difficulties in the marriage. The doctor then has to decide whether to discuss the problem with the patient who comes to him, whether he should send for the spouse, whether he should see the two partners together, or whether he should refer them to another doctor. In some settings, for instance at the Institute of Marital Studies, two workers see the two partners, either together or separately, and some aspect of the marriage itself, rather than the problems of either one of the partners is taken as the focus for work. *In general practice* the partner who comes to the doctor first to complain should be seen as the patient and should be worked with before the spouse is sent for, even if the spouse is thought to be the sicker of the two. It has been our experience that unless some work can be done with the patient who comes first, then very little help can be given at all. It is also our experience that it is rare, if ever, that only one member of a family is to blame. However tempting it is to think that one person is the 'guilty' party, it seldom turns out to be so at the end. It is common experience to note, for instance, that the wives of alcoholic husbands, or the husbands of alcoholic wives, are seldom without problems themselves. These do not arise out of, but dove-tail into, the spouse's alcoholism and it can be very helpful if, at the outset of the treatment, this is borne in mind. This is difficult work because the interactions that take place between marital partners are often hidden and complicated, and because of the difficulty in discovering these interactions the work cannot be undertaken in the normal 'six minutes', not at any rate in the early stages of the work.

A case will illustrate the difficulties involved.

Recently a wife, who brought her baby with a cough, complained that her husband was angry with her because he said that she no longer looked after him properly. She was not interested in sleeping with him, as she had a baby. She said that her husband never left her alone, was very demanding, and since her baby was born a year ago she did not like having him in bed with her, and often anyway she had to get up in the night and look after her baby when it cried and she then took the baby into bed to comfort it. The doctor wondered who needed comfort. There was a complicated interaction here between a woman who resented the demands her husband made, and preferred to respond to the demands of her baby; and a husband who was jealous of the baby which comforted his wife, and who would have liked to have been able to care for both wife and baby. His greatest need was to feel he could look after someone rather than to be looked after, and hers was a need to manage alone. The wife had usurped his role and it was hard for the husband to bear it, or to realise he wished to care, and not be cared for. Once the couple understood this, it was easier for them to readjust. The couple were seen together after the second interview.

Other Kinds of Psychotherapy in Various Settings

Before concluding, I must state once more that I am well aware that there are very many kinds of psychotherapy. I have concentrated on a very few with which I am familiar, which will perhaps illustrate some of the general points I have tried to make earlier in this chapter. Most doctors give reassurance, and we have often asked the question whether the reassurance they give is for the patient or for themselves. If one examines the results of reassurance, we usually find that the patient gets addicted to it and asks for more and more. Simple reassurance may be what some patients want, but if it does not work it is no good repeating it, and it may be based on a faulty diagnosis.

Finally, when talking and listening to patients, much more goes on than the content of the talk itself: it is the way it is said, the order of the ideas that are talked about, the manner of the therapist, and the relationship between therapist and patient which count.

The object of this chapter is not so much, therefore, to confuse the doctor with advice about the dangers of this or that treatment, and the advantages of the other; what I want to do is to make it clear that, although there are variations in technique which can be described and arise out of the settings and goals and training of the doctor, *the same kind of two-way trusting atmosphere is needed in all of them*, and so long as the doctor does not work in ways which he may have been taught but which he does not fully understand, only good can come of it.

chapter 13

It was stressed in Chapter 11 that the training experience for doctors in Balint groups is not aimed at turning them into psychotherapists. That realisation was arrived at through experience, and 'Research, Changes, and Development in Balint Groups' documents the change from the early days of Balint groups, when an assumption did hold that a scaled-down version of psychotherapy was the object of the exercise. This implied a search for the unconscious cause of patients' problems, often with a focus on their personal history and the symbolic meaning of their complaints. Balint describes the move away from this position towards cultivating a certain kind of attentiveness to the patient's present situation. This involves the ability to identify with the patient's own experience, but also to draw back from the identification and view the problem from outside. It is the doctor's biphasic oscillation between these two standpoints which makes a difference to the patient, and towards which Balint groups now direct their work. This biphasic stance is central to Chapter 4, and the introduction to Chapter 12 also refers back to that paper. It is clear that the handling of closeness and distance is a crucial element throughout Balint's work.

A second change in the groups has been in whether the doctor actually tells the patient what he has understood. For certain kinds of understanding it has, surprisingly on the face of it, turned out to be more effective when he does not. Balint suggests reasons for this on pages 171–172, but it might also be seen in the light of Chapter 8. Is the patient unconsciously picking up the doctor's perception after all, without the doctor's being conscious of communicating it?

'Research, Changes, and Development in Balint Groups' was originally published in *While I'm Here, Doctor: A Study of the Doctor–Patient Relationship* (ed. A. Elder and O. Samuel, Tavistock, 1987). Copyright 1987 by Enid Balint.

Research, Changes, and Development in Balint Groups

T he aim of Balint groups has changed very little, if at all, over the last twenty years. Changes, however, have occurred in the techniques which the general practitioners study in the groups. It may be more of a surprise to find how little our thinking has changed than the way in which it has changed. I do not think this is due to our inflexibility.

What is general practice like? Andrew Elder describes it as a world where:

> The doctor is frequently in the dark, getting glimpses of his patients from time to time, being careful not to find out too much, being content to find the right distance for the patient and himself; sometimes taking the initiative and at other times needing to be more restrained. (Elder, 1987, p. 54)

If a doctor thinks that this task is one that he would like to undertake and that it is not too far from his ideas about general practice, a Balint group should be able to provide the means by which he can learn to do so.

I am assuming, of course, that such a doctor would be well trained and continue to be interested in traditional medicine all of his professional life, because without that none of our ideas has its place in medicine, or can be used reliably.

I will explain briefly how we started. In 1949 Michael Balint led a group of non-medical professional workers at the Tavistock Clinic—a mixed group I had started in 1948 with the aim of trying to understand and work with people with marital difficulties. We then decided to start working with general practitioners using the same techniques we had developed during the previous work.

Our method of work and our research method were stable and consisted of discussion, in a structured setting, of a doctor's difficulties with a patient, one particular relationship at one particular time. The same leader, the same doctors, discussed patients together in the same place over a longish period. Verbatim transcripts were made of each meeting.

We found the use of the doctor's own notes distracting during the discussion itself, and we soon adopted a method based on the method of supervision used by Hungarian psychoanalysts. This was to encourage students to speak freely without notes, contradict themselves if necessary, have second thoughts, remember things they thought they had forgotten; so that a complete picture emerged in which the feelings of the doctor himself were evident alongside the facts he was reporting.

If you have never worked like this with a leader trained to observe in a particular way, who can tolerate the absence of a consistent story for a time, and use the muddle rather than try to discard it, this method may sound very strange and unscientific. It consists of amassing facts and the feelings about the facts at the same time. Our work is based on the idea that human beings, whether doctors or patients, unconsciously defend themselves against certain thoughts and ideas. They try to get things in order and this often involves leaving out facts and the feelings about them. The story seems clear and the doctor when reporting is unaware that it is incorrect. In our kind of discussion and reporting, such omissions and falsifications come to light without embarrassment.

A trained observer, possibly a psychoanalyst or someone who has worked with one for a long time, is needed to help piece the data together. Hunches, fantasies, and feelings should be expressed without embarrassment but not treated as sacred. The work of the group and of the doctor in charge of the patient is to see if what is said is true—to examine on what such fantasies and hunches are based—so that the doctor can, if appropriate, change his ideas about his patient. This is all done in a stable setting, and each doctor gets accustomed to looking at his and his colleagues' work, with the same strictness and freedom.

We still use the same method. But do we listen in the 1980s in a different way for different things? Have we changed? We are, perhaps, even less anxious to make a coherent story, to make 'sense' early on in our work. We still make a working diagnosis, but we are now more observant of changes, however minute, which take place in the doctor–patient relationship, as shown in the doctor's feelings about his patients and in the patients' complaints—even changes which take place during one consultation. We are particularly careful not to fit new observations into old patterns where they are inappropriate.

Early in our work we sometimes spoke about our ability to train general practitioners to do some form of psychotherapy, and we blamed unsuccessful results on the fact that our doctors did not have much experience in this field. It was assumed then that had the 'psychotherapy' been better the patient would have been cured. The most common basis of any form of psychotherapy, it was said at the time, is an understanding of the patient's real problems. It was, therefore, thought that had these been understood the patient would have been helped. By 'real problems' was meant the underlying cause of the patient's illness. I now often think it is unnecessary and can be unhelpful at any given time to try to discover what a patient thinks is the cause of his present symptom or unhappiness. In general practice work the patient's feelings in the present, and the changes in them, seem more important and more reliable.

All our work is based on one human being—a professional, understanding not only intellectually but in other ways as well; medically, based on traditional medical teaching, and by identification. Intellectual understanding alone is not enough. To understand, one must listen to what one does not understand, watch, and notice the human being one is talking to and one's self at the same time; noticing and watching changes in one's ways of reacting to the other person. Identification depends more on a willingness, or even a desire to understand, than an ability to sympathise. However, once an observer has identified himself with someone or something, he will find it difficult to feel objectively about that person or thing again. So he must first identify and then he must withdraw from that identification and become an objective professional observer again. The identification must have a biphasic structure. In addition, a doctor must be able to respond correctly, without too much delay.

Scientists in other fields describe how difficult, or even impossible, it is to observe anything without influencing the object observed. No two observers will see exactly the same thing. The value of Balint groups is to facilitate observations.

I will describe a case.

It is a follow-up of a woman patient who had been seen and reported on almost a year before, soon after her first child was born: the baby, a girl, was suffering from a severe cough. The doctor had the cough 'investigated' but it continued. The patient continued to come to see the doctor, complaining that she could not stand being kept awake at night any more. She must get back to work because she was no good at being a mother anyway, and she wanted to carry on with her career. Her husband was no help, either. The group had discussed this case the year before and had thought the patient was a rather overdominant, masculine woman, although there was no real evidence of her being masculine, other than her not being able to cope with her first child and wanting to go back to work. The working diagnosis was of a dominant woman with a weak husband who was presenting her child with a cough and who bullied her doctor. At the follow-up, however, the question of whether the woman was dominant came under review. Could it be taken for granted on the grounds that the doctor fitted in with her requests for frequent examinations of the child and anyway, the group asked this time, was this diagnosis of any help to the doctor or the patient? Most of the group were doubtful, but did not know where to turn, and then slowly began to look at the interview itself, which the doctor was asked to report in greater detail. The doctor then told us that he thought the patient was very lonely. She had moved quite far from her home when she got married two years before, and the picture of the dominant, unattractive woman disappeared and we seemed to have somebody else as a patient. The doctor began to feel more at ease when he talked about her and said how lonely it must be for her. How awful it was for her to have a child and to have no one to share it with. He got in touch with feelings in himself and identified with the patient.

But there had been no biphasic structure in his identification with the patient, so he was not able to help her, only feel sorry for her. After the discussion in the group he could see how to help. The patient was then able to feel less alone with her husband, less lonely, and to let her husband share more.

I will give another case to illustrate this point.

A doctor reported on the case of an old patient of his, one he had known for several years, who, at the age of thirty-six, was dying of cancer. She had had all the possible treatments and was now so distressed and so unwilling to go back into hospital that her general practitioner had advised that she be left at home until she died. The hospital had agreed to this. The doctor, however, then found it was very difficult for him to visit his patient and reported this case to the seminar because of his difficulty in visiting his dying patient. The seminar was very subdued and made all sorts of excuses for the doctor. They could well understand how, because he could do nothing for her, he could not bring himself to visit her; that he was very busy, and so on, and so on. The case was discussed for quite a long time before someone said he was sure the doctor wanted to visit the patient but was so identified with her he could not face it. The doctor agreed: yes, he wanted to go but he could not face the way she looked, although when he saw her he did not mind at all. In fact when he got into her bedroom he was very pleased to sit on her bed and hold her hand, which she put out towards him when he entered the room. He began to see her as a separate person whom he could be with and relate to. This doctor needed to realise that the patient was a separate person, and one who did not expect anything of him he could not give; a person who was glad to have somebody with her who could accept the fact that she was dying, and that she did not look too frightening. There was no need for him to say anything special. We will come back to this.

When did we begin to observe the changes in our focus of interest, changes in the techniques we were trying to devise for general practitioners? It is difficult to say, but a new appraisal started in January 1966, when a research team consisting of ten general practitioners and two, sometimes three, psychoanalytic leaders met at University College Hospital under the leadership of Michael Balint and myself. The group ended in 1971, a year after Michael Balint died. A book, *Six Minutes for the Patient* (Balint and Norell, 1973), based on the research in the group, was published in 1973.

The new techniques that we were aiming at had to be based on a reliable understanding of the patient's individuality and particularly of the developing relationship between the patient and the doctor, that is to say, on processes rather than states. The time needed for these techniques had to be compatible with the routine ten minutes or so that the average patient gets in a medical practice. We encountered severe difficulties in this group; the principal one was caused perhaps by the realisation that their old well-proven methods had to be given up, or at any rate considerably modified. This was partly because of the new conditions and partly because we were not sure whether the results in the long run gave the doctor, and therefore the patient, sufficient satisfaction. In the old method which we were giving up, the doctor had responsibility for understanding not only what the patient tried to convey to him, but why the patient had become the way he was. Although he was as interested as we still were to recognise omissions and distortions in the patient's story, his aim then was to solve something, which is, after all, the traditional role of the doctor. But in the new technique the therapist's role was to tune in to the patient and to see what it was like both for himself and for the patient and what changes occurred and how varied and inconsistent his feelings and the stories that he got were. The need here to identify and then withdraw from the identification is paramount. The technique which arose out of these ideas was called the 'flash' and consisted of a moment of mutual understanding between a doctor and his patient which was *communicated by the doctor to his patient*. It was not an understanding about the patient's past about which the doctor was very likely completely aware, but was usually about something in the patient's current life and which was reflected in the relationship with the doctor for a brief time. These episodes were very hard to follow up reliably, but when they have been followed up changes do seem to persist in the doctor's feelings about the patient, but we have not been able to observe reliably in what way the patient responded to them. It appeared that they were sometimes brushed aside, not referred to again.

In the research reported in this book and in research being undertaken at the present time, the focus is on a technique similar, in some ways, to the *flash* technique, but different in important ways. We are now more concerned with making observations about changes that take place in a doctor's feelings about his patient and a patient's feelings about his doctor, changes which *are not communicated at the time by the doctor to the patient*. This is crucial.

In the *flash* technique, when a flash occurred the doctor communicated his thoughts and feelings to the patient. Nowadays we prefer to wait and see what happens to a patient when a doctor's feelings change—sometimes suddenly—about him.

Here is another case.

A woman in her late sixties, married to a man eight years younger than herself, had come complaining of depression for many years, for which she had been given pills which she said had always helped her. The doctor had changed the medication from time to time and each time the patient seemed satisfied, although she came back again with the same symptom. One day, however, the patient came as usual—or so it seemed—and the doctor found himself asking her whether there was something that was particularly wrong. The patient said her husband had a mistress, but this kind of thing had happened so often before she did not think it had any particular significance, and she spoke in a way that did not make the doctor feel that she was particularly troubled by it. But at that time the doctor found himself seeing the patient as an old woman with a deaf-aid (which he himself had given her some years before); a woman who felt that her life was over with her husband who would never want her any more; that there could be no more sexual relationship between them; and that she was finished. Actually, it was the doctor who felt all of this and who reported these feelings at some length to the group. We did not know what the patient felt. In this interview the doctor had not said anything about this to his patient, but he was shocked. He did not suppose that the patient was aware of any of this at the time, but the group felt that probably the patient had felt old and useless many times and that it was the doctor who had only just picked it up. Perhaps the patient felt better because of this. The patient returned in three weeks' time and said that she was depressed, but for the first time said that the pills were no good and that there was no point in her having any more. She had come because she was going on holiday with her husband and she wanted to talk to the doctor first about it, but she did not want to use pills. The patient said she was terrified that she was going to spoil the holiday. Her husband had planned it after giving up his relationship with his girlfriend and this made the patient particularly anxious that she should not spoil it; that the better relationship which seemed to be growing between her and her husband should not be spoiled by her being so awful and depressed and useless.

In this interview the patient showed something which could have been caused by the doctor's feelings in the interview before, when he had felt despair for her and fear for her future but had said nothing. We could say that the patient had 'unloaded' her feelings into the doctor and in consequence she had become partially free of them and was able, instead of being passive about them, to become active, as if free for the time being and not simply having to accept her fate. If this was so, it was a major change. The idea is that what the doctor 'took in' during that interview had afterwards enabled the patient to be free enough to take the initiative at the next interview by not accepting the pills as usual; and also to behave differently, more actively, less like a victim with her husband in the meantime. The doctor, having had insight into the patient's ideas about herself, not, that is, into what she was actually like, but into what she felt she was like, enabled her to come alive and to rid herself, temporarily at any rate, of her heavy, passive depression. The doctor had, so to speak, taken in what the patient projected into him and had held onto it for a time without immediately handing it back to the patient in the form of an interpretation. At the next interview, however, when she came saying she did not want the pills but did not want to be depressed, he was able to respond appropriately, having by that time got rid of the patient's depression. He did not, of course, say 'you are an old, deaf woman and there is no hope for you', but spoke about the holiday and the processes that were going on inside the patient, at that time.

There have been other cases, as I have already shown in this chapter, which confirm our ideas about this particular kind of tuning in. One could talk about it in terms of the doctor being willing to accept and to hold on to feelings given him by a patient during a consultation, and examining these feelings before withdrawing from them, or isolating himself from them. We then have to examine the effect this has on the patient, namely, when the doctor does not interpret but holds on to feelings which a patient has aroused in him, and with which, for a short time, he totally identifies but which he is able to distance himself from later. He knows what it is like to be the patient but also is able to see that that is not all the patient has inside him. The doctor must become aware of the feelings the patient has, and be ready to hear what the patient says at the next consultation as well. The patient can then become the active one and is not deflated by accepting something about herself passively; or, if that is too threatening, by having to fail to take it seriously at all. The patient can change once the doctor knows what it is like to feel the way she does. She can then tune in to other parts of herself. But she cannot change, sometimes, by being told that she should change, or being told what she is like. She is given the freedom to change in this way.

This brings me back to another reason why we run our groups the way we do. It is so that the doctors in the groups can be active, not passively receptive, either of their own feelings or to what the leader says. They can talk freely about their patients and their feelings about them, at one particular moment, in one particular session, bearing in mind that this is almost certain to change. In so doing they can get in touch with feelings in themselves of which they were not aware. This may enable them in due course to understand something about their patients which they would not have been able to, had they been out of touch with their own feelings and the seriousness of them.

To take the responsibility for their own feelings and thoughts, to realise how hard it is to observe them reliably, how easy it is to miss what other people say: these are some of the things that doctors in Balint groups get to know about. Balint groups allow such processes to occur, allow doctors to realise how hard it is to observe, particularly when the observations are not stable. In this work, activity of a special kind is released in the doctors, a kind of psychic activity: liveliness, not passive acceptance; observations, not instructions.

chapter 14

This chapter describes a research project which examined the effect of a Balint group on the doctor–patient relationship, not only in cases which a doctor had chosen to bring to the group, but on randomly selected ones. It shows, in one particular context, the systematic attention to detail and the discipline of method which underpin what may appear as spontaneous insight and intuition. It describes the classification scheme adopted to cover both the traditional medical approach to a patient and the particular concerns of the seminar group. This involves the idea of the 'overall diagnosis', already mentioned in Chapter 11: a general view of the patient's whole life and personality, together with his important relationships. The emphasis here on this concept corresponds to Balint's statement in Chapter 11 of the analyst's role in helping doctors to appreciate the unique individuality of their patients as well as the phenomena of their illnesses.

Working with this dimension showed that in spite of a thorough medical knowledge of their patients the doctors might know little of what went on in their minds. Developing this awareness brought new flexibility into the relationship between doctor and patient, which let the doctor see fresh ways of helping the patient and gave better access to the purely medical problems.

The point emphasised in the Introduction, that the seminar leader is working as a psychoanalyst but is not teaching psychoanalysis, is elegantly illustrated. The doctor treating Janice, 'although knowing a very great deal about her patient, still at each interview was not necessarily in touch with what was her most pressing need of the moment. She had to be alerted to allow the crucial anxiety to appear' (p. 183). Compare that

'A Study of the Doctor–Patient Relationship Using Randomly Selected Cases' was originally published in the *Journal of the College of General Practitioners 13* (1967), 163–173. Copyright 1967 by The Royal College of General Practitioners. Reprinted by permission.

with: 'Each analyst has to be aware of the multitude of conflicts which are present at all times in every session and must try to pick out the conflict which seems the most pressing, not necessarily the most obvious' (p. 124). The work seems identical. Yet a few lines further on Balint comments that there were Oedipal issues, which would be highly important with regard to Janice's relationships with boyfriends, but in view of this doctor's particular style of work, it seemed appropriate not to explore them. For the doctors themselves, just as for their patients, like Mr. F in Chapters 11 and 12, it is important to emphasise what they *can* do. The point is made again in Chapter 15.

A Study of the
Doctor–Patient Relationship
Using Randomly Selected Cases

T he research on which this paper was based started when I was asked by the Tavistock Clinic to form and lead a group of general practitioners who had already had several years of experience in the Tavistock Training Scheme. Early in our work this group decided to study the ordinary run of cases in general practice.

The first stimulus for the research arose as a logical sequence out of the work done during the training of general practitioners which was started by Michael Balint at the Tavistock Clinic in 1949. In those seminars general practitioners met with Balint and later with other psychiatrists to discuss cases which were presenting them and their patients with problems, usually of an overt emotional kind. The aim of these seminars was to study the causation and handling of the emotional disturbances, chiefly by studying the doctor–patient relationship. In this way it was hoped to enable the doctors to become more flexible observers of themselves and thus to achieve some skill in treating their patients. From time to time, however, it was decided to review not only those patients who were chosen by the doctors because they were difficult or interesting, and so forth, but to study an unselected sample. The first idea was to have reported at a seminar all those patients who had visited one particular doctor at one particular surgery. Thus, from the beginning of his work with general practitioners Balint sought to understand the nature of general practice as a whole and not only to understand those patients who presented their doctors with problems.

While studying these unselected cases it was found that the usual diagnostic thinking was unsatisfactory for the description of what the doctor knew about the patient. In order to help this shortcoming, we gradually developed the idea of describing the diagnostic findings in two dimensions. One dimension was the familiar one which has been developed by medical men during the past centuries. This, the traditional diagnosis, is not sufficient to do justice to the richness of material which the doctor can observe and must understand, so the second dimension comprised everything that the doctor knew and understood of the patient's whole life and whole personality and his relationship to the important people around him, in which the illness described in terms of the traditional diagnosis is perhaps only an incident or a part which made better sense if understood in terms of the whole. This dimension he called the overall diagnosis. It is nearly always about one person within a family; an overall diagnosis of one patient; but it can also be an overall diagnosis of the whole family.

It was soon recognized that general practitioners with their vast store of knowledge of their patients and their patients' families over time, and with their easy access to their patients, are in a somewhat better position to formulate this new kind of diagnosis than consultants who are only in touch with their patients for brief periods. This new kind of diagnosis, then, was based partly on the patient's presenting complaints and on the results of the examinations, but mainly on his way of relating to people, including his doctor.

The second stimulus for the study came from research undertaken in Frankfurt under the leadership of Professor Mitscherlich. Here seminars similar to those at the Tavistock Clinic and based upon them were started some years ago. Mitscherlich too in the early 1960s made an attempt to get hold of an unselected sample of the problems with which general practitioners are faced. His method was to study the tenth patient who visited the surgery of one particular doctor on a prearranged day. More recently in London, Dr. Alexis Brook at the Cassel Hospital and Dr. J. L. Wilson at the Tavistock Clinic have undertaken a similar type of research. These researches were chiefly focussed on the psychological aetiology of illnesses. Their main aim was to determine whether the symptom presented by the randomly selected patient was purely organic in origin, purely psychological, or a mixture of the two.

The work which I am about to describe has a somewhat different aim. We have tried to study a relatively small number of randomly selected patients—fifty in all—and to follow them up over a period of time. Our aim, broadly speaking, was to study the value of the overall diagnosis for the patients' therapy and the role of the group in this work, or, more specifically:

1. To study the doctor–patient relationship at the time of the first report (that is, before the research could influence it).

2. To study the effect of the seminar discussion both on the doctor-patient relationship and on the traditional and overall diagnoses.
3. To observe in what circumstances it is rewarding for the doctor to deepen or intensify his relationship with his patients.
4. To study the correctness of the predictions made by the seminar in the discussion at the first report of the patient and in every subsequent report.

Our hypotheses were:

1. If the doctor decides not to change his handling of the case, no major change will occur, even though he understands the situation better.
2. In cases in which the doctor decides to change his handling on the basis of the better understanding of his patient—provided that he has the requisite skills—substantial changes in the doctor–patient relationship and in the course of the illness will follow.
3. That these changes can be predicted in terms of the overall diagnosis.

In this paper I hope to demonstrate the value of the overall diagnosis for the patients' therapy only. I will start by describing our method of work.

METHOD

The method of selection of cases is as follows. One doctor was asked to bring to the next meeting the notes of all the patients he had seen at one prearranged surgery. The doctor announces how many patients he has seen at that surgery and then, using a random table, it was decided which of them is to be presented. The discussion was taken down verbatim and the results of the discussion were summarised under nine headings. Later I will report a case using the nine headings on what we came to call our Initial Interview Cards. But, before doing so, I will describe some aspects of the doctor–patient relationship as they emerged at the first interview when the relationship was unaffected by the seminar discussion, or by our way of looking at cases.

We found that the doctors' knowledge of their patients was concentrated on what was needed to fulfil two requirements:

1. In order to understand the patient's illness, or illnesses, which in the doctor's judgement should be taken seriously: that is to say,

the illnesses which merited medical attention. In these areas their knowledge was considerable and it was very rare to find in the seminar discussion that some detail had been overlooked, or some gap had been left uninvestigated.

2. In order to maintain the kind of relationship which had been implicitly decided upon and accepted by both doctor and patient, but which was not overtly stated or understood by either party.

It was discovered, therefore, that very often there were wide gaps in the doctor's knowledge of his *patient* (although not in connection with the traditional diagnosis) which had to be filled in before the overall picture, the overall diagnosis, could be confirmed. In spite of these gaps we found that the overall diagnosis made at the first report was often valid, or only needed slight amendments, because in our discussion our way of looking at the material presented gave us an overall dynamic picture. The relevant facts outweighed the irrelevant inaccuracies and the omissions.

When, however, the patient was discussed in the seminar, it often surprised the reporting doctor as much as the rest of the seminar members how many gaps there were in his knowledge of his patient's life. Although these gaps did not hinder the proper medical care of the patient, they were surprising to everybody, including the doctor in charge. The doctor knew as much as he needed to treat the illness which in his judgement should be treated. But he knew very little else. One could say, why indeed should he? However, some of the doctors seemed to feel rather guilty about this state of affairs and felt, for some reason which I will try to discuss later, that they should know more.

After a case had been discussed in the seminar and an overall diagnosis had been made, it was quite likely that the doctor would change his mind about the areas of the patient's life which he should treat, take seriously, or be interested in. He might, therefore, want at the next interview with the patient to fill in some of the gaps in his knowledge which were relevant to these new aspects of the patient's diagnosis. He would also probably have learnt something new about his own approach to his patient. He would have learnt things which were encouraging as well as discouraging, but this new understanding would very likely only have a limited effect on his continuing relationship with his patient. He would understand more about the therapeutic nature of his relationship, but he would not necessarily change his therapy, even if pressed to do so by his colleagues. We have in fact discussed cases where the new understanding of the patient led the doctor to change in his relationship with the patient. For instance, in one case a dying man was followed up during his terminal illness. Here the traditional medical treatment of the patient would have been the same without the seminar discussion, but the effect of the seminar discussion did bring about considerable changes in the doctor's understanding of his patient and of his own reaction to the dying man, and, in consequence, allowed an increase in the intimacy of their relationship which reduced the strain for the doctor and perhaps relieved the suffering of the patient during the last months of his life.

However, this was not always the case and the changes that took place as a result of the discussion were at times difficult to understand and in consequence could just as easily be under- as over-estimated. I will need to give a rather full example to show what I mean and I hope that it will demonstrate an everyday doctor–patient relationship and the effect of the seminar discussion on it.

The case which I want to report to you in detail is of a young girl, Janice, aged fourteen, reported by Dr. J, a woman doctor. I will use our Initial Interview Card with its nine headings as it was devised when the case was first reported.

1. *Date reported to the seminar:* 25 October, 1963.
2. *Date seen by the doctor:* 24 October, 1963.

These two headings, as you see, are objective facts.

3. *Apparent reason for coming:* swollen ankle, hurt playing netball yesterday.

For this heading the patient's actual words are used where possible; if this is not possible the seminar attempts by discussion to arrive at the patient's own motives and conscious reasons for visiting her doctor and tries to exclude the doctor's idea about why the patient came. In this case we have not the patient's words, but it was easy to see what her conscious reasons for coming were.

4. *Examinations:*
    (*a*) *Done previously:* many minor physical examinations done by the doctor.
    (*b*) *At this interview:* ankle examined and x-ray arranged.
5. *Traditional diagnosis as made by the reporting doctor:* sprained ankle? ? fracture.

As you will see, headings 4 and 5 also concern objective facts and some conclusions drawn from them. The traditional diagnosis is always given by the reporting doctor. Sometimes the discussion of it extends

over to the field of the overall diagnosis and occasionally the presenting
doctor changes his mind and then this is also recorded. In this case the
traditional diagnosis was unequivocal and did not lead to a discussion.

The following headings—6, 7, and 9 (not 8)—are the most difficult
items and most of the time of the seminar is spent in clarifying and
formulating them. The difficulty all along in filling up the cards is because of our new way of thinking. We have to separate the wheat from
the irrelevant chaff and put the right emphasis on each piece of information according to its importance. Differences of opinion, of course, often
occur in our seminar and our usual practice is to record both the majority
and minority views. In this case, however, there were no such differences
in our diagnosis. Now, let us go back to the card.

6. *Information leading to overall diagnosis:*
   (a) *from information already known:* a scatty, anxious family centred
       on an over-anxious, depressed, inadequate mother who had
       difficulties with her femininity, who was overweight and
       whose depression lifted when her weight was reduced and
       after she attended her doctor weekly. Patient (Janice), the
       younger of two children, had a long history of childhood
       ailments clearing miraculously when the family moved and
       joined Dr. J's practice area only two years ago. Janice had
       been complaining recently about loss of weight —she comes
       alone—she has shaky biological knowledge—she is readily
       reassured—accident prone—nervous, jumpy like a little bird.
   (b) *Information from this interview:* patient comes alone as usual with
       minor complaint.
   (c) *Information derived from seminar discussion:* Dr. J contains the
       family's anxieties and the doctor's relationship to patient's
       family can be described as a non-panicky, practical one where
       the doctor does not invoke consultant or community help, yet
       needs to prevent the family from submerging her. Janice is
       forced, perhaps, to mature too soon; she keeps tugging at her
       mother and her doctor with her minor ailments, to remind
       them that she exists and she is failing to thrive. When mother
       loses weight and her depression, Janice also loses weight but
       becomes anxious about her failure to thrive. Janice is unaware
       of her emerging sexuality. Father's identity is shadowy.
7. *Overall diagnosis:* an emotionally immature girl of fourteen with
   doubts about her capacity to mature.

This last heading, No. 7, the overall diagnosis, can, of course, only
be filled in if we are confident that our understanding of the material adds

up to something sensible. Perhaps I ought to say here that psychiatric formulations like 'depressive reaction in an inadequate personality', or a 'schizoid paranoid withdrawal' belong to the traditional diagnosis just as much as an upper respiratory infection or allergic conditions of the skin.

8. *Prognosis in terms of the traditional diagnosis:* (This is not very difficult!) Excellent.
9. *Prognosis in terms of overall diagnosis:*

This, of course, can only be filled in if we are able to make an overall diagnosis at all, a point that can easily be forgotten. The real difficulty is to arrive at the overall diagnosis, and the prognosis as a rule follows from it. Surprisingly the situation here seems very similar to that about traditional diagnoses. Here, then, is the prognosis in terms of the overall diagnosis.

> The doctor–patient relationship is good, although the doctor is frightened of being submerged and does not go into Janice's emotional difficulties. Patient's emotional progress is uncertain without adequate mother for identification, but she is seeking a substitute in her doctor and may find it.

This is the end of the Initial Interview Card. I must say here that the filling in of the card followed a very free discussion and no attempt was made to keep to the headings one by one. By the end of the meeting, though, an attempt was made by the seminar to fill in the headings, which were then put on a card by our project officer, one of the associate psychiatrists. The cards were then carefully examined at another meeting of the seminar and an agreement was reached as to whether the formulations present a correct summary of their original discussion.

The card that I have just given you is a typical one. It shows a fairly close relationship between the doctor and her patient. Although the doctor has not discussed this patient's emotional difficulties with her, she knows the mother well and is aware of the daughter's potential difficulties with the mother and is on the look-out for any real sign of distress. During the discussion many doctors felt that the doctor should give Janice an opportunity of voicing her doubts about her ability to thrive and mature, and the doctor agreed. She had been aware of them but had felt that she was coping with them well enough by dealing with her minor physical symptoms. The patient clearly has confidence in her doctor. The doctor's emotional tie to her patient emerges from the description on the card. She likes her patient, thinks she can look after her by her manner and behaviour rather than by asking questions and doing work which would involve a closer relationship between the two. The seminar thought, though, that after the discussion it was likely that a greater intimacy would develop between the doctor and patient.

I have three follow-ups to this case. The first was given on 19 February 1964, five months, the second on 24 June 1964, nine months, and the third on 20 January 1965, fifteen months after the original presentation. In the follow-ups our discussions are summarised under nine headings similar to those for the initial interview card. We note the dates and reasons for the return visits and the examinations done since the last report. The main headings, however, are those giving new information leading to changes in the overall diagnosis, the changes themselves in the overall diagnosis, and changes in the prognosis.

Now to summarise these three follow-up reports:

> At the first it was reported that the patient had been seen several times since the first presentation with trivial complaints: the ankle did not mend as quickly as was expected and during these visits the doctor gave Janice an opportunity to talk. Then on 14 January 1964 (three months after the original report) Janice complained of a pain under her right bosom. Nothing was found wrong, but a discussion ensued about brassières. The patient apparently wanted her doctor to examine her breasts. It seemed that the girl was growing up and the doctor remarked that she was 'anxious not to invade her privacy more than she wants me to'. Clearly the two were getting on well and the doctor was less frightened of getting submerged if she let the girl talk.
>
> At the second follow-up, nine months after the first report, Janice had been seen on five more occasions. At one of them she complained about increased weight (note not decreased weight this time). She chatted with her doctor about her future occupation and seemed relaxed. There were still recurring minor ailments concerning her limbs; again her ankle had been painful, she had had warts, but nothing serious. On the follow-up card, under the heading 'New information leading to overall diagnosis', we noted that the patient had filled out and was now a normal dumpy teenager, had developed adequate breasts, and lost her birdlike jumpiness over the past six months. She had a boyfriend with whom she went dancing and it seemed probable that the doctor–patient relationship was becoming less important to the patient. It even seemed that perhaps the patient was becoming rather depressingly normal for our doctor, who rather liked adolescents who had difficulties, or were rebellious, and who did not find it too easy to assume their femininity.

In the discussion the seminar laughed at our doctor for being bored with her successful patients and she was able to see that perhaps she was likely to be rejecting and less interested now that the girl was more feminine and, as was reported, a normal, dumpy adolescent with boyfriends. It was thought that perhaps the doctor would push this patient away unless she was aware of her new attitude to her.

At the third follow-up it was reported that this patient, who was now fifteen, had not been to see her doctor for four months after the last follow-up. Then she appeared in the surgery with trouble with her fingers which seemed bent backwards. She then had trouble with her ankle again. She was seen several times during this period between November and January and once she said to her doctor: 'Don't you like my hair colour better now?' The doctor then realised that she had not noticed any change in the colour of the girl's hair and saw that the patient was, so to speak, tugging at her sleeve to make her notice her and be interested in her development. She therefore responded and the girl began talking about her boyfriend and raised anxieties about her menstruation and her appearance. It seemed at this follow-up, therefore, that the doctor–patient relationship was still important to this patient although it was less interesting to the doctor than it had been in the beginning.

This case shows several things:

1. It demonstrates the multitude of possibilities open to a doctor in general practice. He can vary his proximity and distance with his patient, not only in response to periods of diagnosable, 'traditional' illness, but also in response to 'offers' of a much less obvious and tangible kind, such as Janice's half-spoken requests. As long as he understands what he is doing and realises that either he or his patient can change this distance, no rigid unalterable relationship need be fixed once and for all between them. The doctor knows that his patient is likely to come back again for some minor or major complaint and that he can change his relationship to suit the current illness or the current needs, provided that there is not too much strain either for patient or doctor.

2. It demonstrates how much general practitioners know, but also how little they know about what goes on in their patients' minds. Our doctor here, although knowing a very great deal about her patient, still at each interview was not necessarily in touch with what was her most pressing need of the moment. She had to be alerted to allow the crucial anxiety to appear. The patient's remark about the colour of her hair might have been left and might not have been taken as a sign that the girl wanted to go further unless our doctor had been coming to our seminars and had realised the importance of such signs and signals. Further, in this case we know very little about our patient's relationship to her father, which certainly some doctors will think is highly important and should have been investigated as it might throw light on her relationship with

her boyfriends. But our doctor felt that as things were going well with her patient she would leave an examination of this topic to a time when the patient obviously wanted to talk about it, or to such a time as when it became clear to her that the relationship with the father was, in fact, proving an obstacle to the girl's development.

To summarise, our doctor had succeeded in helping the patient over a difficult period and then surprisingly had become disappointed. The girl became less interesting to her; the seminar, but not the doctor, was happy about the result. The doctor was then shown by the seminar her preference for rather rebellious girls and her dislike of unaggressive and accepting femininity. The doctor seemed to accept this new insight and we thought that there was now, perhaps, a better chance for her to be able to accept this sort of patient and to be able to understand, hear, and notice this sort of patient's communications.

Our optimistic expectations, however, proved unrealistic. Since first reading this paper we have had another follow-up on Janice. On 27 October 1965, nine months after our last follow-up and almost exactly two years since the first report, Dr. J reported that she had been notified by the local executive council that Janice's family had left her list with an N (transfer to another doctor in the practice area). It had followed a series of visits by various members of the family when they had been seen—we do not know whether by accident or on purpose—by Dr. J's part-time assistant. Soon after this Dr. J went on holiday and was not available for a few weeks. The last member of the family to be seen before the notification arrived was Janice herself, who came complaining of boils on her face and was seen by the assistant.

Very naturally a good deal of time was spent in the seminar trying to decide the reason for this surprising event. Various very strong comments were voiced, but roughly the seminar was divided into those who thought that the reasons why the family changed to another doctor were linked with the predictions made, and that the event should not be thought of as so surprising in view of the predictions. Others in the seminar thought that the family had just reverted to their previous unstable pattern and had taken the opportunity of Dr. J's absence on holiday to change, as had been their wont in the past; we do not know.

There have been cases where the doctor had changed his relationship with his patient for a time following the seminar discussion, and then had deliberately and not only because of the patient's pressure, gone back to his old relationship. For instance, one doctor reported on a woman patient of sixty who for many years had come to the surgery regularly once a month for a prescription for sodium amytal. She was given six grains at night and that seemed to satisfy her. The doctor described her as a rather masculine-looking woman presenting a wooden appearance, who had needed sedatives all her life. She was not a burden to the doctor, but the seminar thought the doctor was careful not to get involved with her in case she became a millstone around his neck. Following the seminar discussion the doctor encouraged the patient to talk. She spoke about her husband who had died a few months ago and said she was depressed. She had lost interest in life and never joked any more. After this she became friendly and smiled. About a week later she lost her amytal capsules and came in in a rather excited, agitated way to ask for more. The doctor gave her more without fuss and she was grateful and made fun of the event. A week later she came again complaining of depression. Usually, remember, she only came once a month. The doctor was busy and did not go into the reason for her depression, but gave her some dexamphetamine. Then, for the first time she volunteered some more information. In spite of these new offers the doctor did not feel that he could respond. First he said it was because he was too busy and then he said, no, of course it was not that. He had not had a satisfactory interview with the patient either from his point of view, or from hers. He had decided that therapeutically it was a waste of time to go on with this additional treatment and quite readily the woman returned to her old pattern of visiting her doctor once a month for her sodium amytal capsules. The seminar thought that he might not only have felt threatened by our patient, who had for the past forty years been in need of regular sedation, but had also been pushed by the seminar to intervene in the first place against his own inclinations. Later, however, we heard that a compromise solution had been found, and a livelier relationship had been established between doctor and patient which was not felt by our doctor to be a waste of time.

I would like to stress that there is always in any doctor–patient relationship, in addition to the ordinary transactions that occur, an emotional component which affects the doctor in his work. The doctor cannot help but be affected by his *and* by the patient's wishes. He may react to his patient's wishes by withdrawing, or he may react to them by playing into them, or by understanding and working with them, but the areas of knowledge that he has about his patient and the distance that he keeps from him not only depend on the doctor's wishes, but on the patient's wishes as well.

This brings me back to the point I raised earlier to do with the doctors' feelings of guilt about their incomplete knowledge of their patients. I think this is because they feel that if they were really good doctors they would know everything, and there is an unwillingness to realise that the patient has something to do with the way he is treated and the medicine he is given. Doctors are, of course, trained to make diagnoses and they are horrified to find that these diagnoses can prove incomplete in ways which they may never have considered. Although the overall diagnosis is a new idea, our doctors already feel towards it as if it belonged to the field of the traditional diagnosis.

A good doctor, after examining his patient, may decide that in this particular case nothing need be done. This may be a correct decision, but he must be able to feel that he has reached this decision after a proper and reliable diagnostic assessment of the case. Our introduction of the overall diagnosis threw a further burden of responsibility on the already overburdened doctors because every new piece of knowledge, or understanding, seems also a further demand to do something, even though the doctor may not be prompted by a *furor therapeuticus*.

Conclusion

You may wonder, if the discussion in the seminar does not invariably alter the doctor–patient relationship, or help the doctor to treat his patients differently, what the point is of having such discussions, or what the value is of the work that we do. This is a difficult question to answer precisely and when I gave my group of doctors the first draft of this paper, they thought I ought to try to answer it, otherwise my audience would think that neither they nor their patients had benefitted from our work. They thought that you would think that the kind of work that we are trying to do was work that all good general practitioners do anyway and which was done by general practitioners in England in the 'good old days before the health service'. One of our doctors said that he had thought this too at one time and told us how when he came to his practice his senior partner, who was now dead, was thought to be the perfect country doctor and was certainly one of the best diagnosticians our doctor had ever met. He then went on to say, and I now quote: 'For years after he died I kept on finding shattering things that had gone wrong with families in the practice where he had completely failed them with the very best intentions'. By this he meant that he had found emotional upheavals, strain, and severe unhappiness, which they had kept hidden from the old doctor.

Our doctors felt that they were very much less likely to fail in this way as a result of our way of looking at our patients and of formulating our overall diagnoses, and that even where their understanding of their patients appeared not to alter the therapy, they thought there were certainly many fewer 'shattering things' that had gone wrong with families in their practice without their knowing it than would have happened before our work started.

chapter 15

This chapter complements the previous one. As the opening paragraph and the later examples indicate, it is based largely on the same research project using randomly selected cases. This time, however, the focus is not the patients but the changes brought about in the doctors. These seminars are not therapy groups. On the contrary, Balint emphasises that 'The individual is not spared or protected in relation to the work he reports, but is spared and protected in relation to his personal unconscious motives' (p. 196). Change occurs, nonetheless, in the 'professional self' (p. 156) of at least some of the doctors, and Balint outlines the evolution that can be observed in the participants' responses to the group experience. Balint's emphasis throughout is on the truth of experience: true reactions to the group and its leader, a true relationship to the patient, and an appreciation of the doctor's true capacities; as opposed to the imposition of a false experience, relationship, and identity by purporting to teach something which the doctor cannot do. Characteristically, Balint appreciates that if a participant is hiding his real identity, it may not be out of aggression but in self-protection so as not to lose it.

It is interesting to compare this chapter with Chapter 9. Apparently having little in common, they both revolve around the question of whether one is a passive recipient of another person's experience—Kay and her mother, the group member and the group leader—or whether one can make it one's own by identifying with it, and thus use it for one's development.

In the last part of the paper Balint asks how far what appears in the groups may also be a feature of the psychoanalytic training process. Analytic students need to be open to regression in their analyses while exercising an adult, professional responsibility in their work, particularly

'Training as an Impetus to Ego Development' was originally published, together with a discussion of it, in *The Psychoanalytic Forum 2* (1967), 56–70. Copyright 1967 by International Universities Press, Inc. Reprinted by permission.

in treating their analytic training cases. The conflict may be hard to handle, and Balint suggests that trainees might benefit from 'a group which entertains both similar and dissimilar ideas from theirs, and which nevertheless accepts them while criticising their professional work' (p. 197). These reflections would seem still to be relevant for training committees in analytic institutes.

When this paper was first presented it was followed by a discussion in which, interestingly, the speakers tended to regard the compliance and rebellion noted by Balint as obstacles to learning which needed to be overcome, rather than as the evolutionary phases through which learning took place. What was clearly picked up, however, was the temptation which Balint warns against for the group leader to retreat into being an expert teacher, so as not to be required to have the courage of his or her own stupidity (p. 192).

In the clinical vignettes, Example 4 is a case which was also described in the previous chapter. It is left in place, however, because it is considered here from a different perspective, that of the doctor's capacities rather than the effect on the patient.

Training as an Impetus
to Ego Development

I am going to put some questions before you which have been going through my mind during the past fifteen years while I have been participating in a training programme for general practitioners, particularly during the past two years while undertaking research into a sample of randomly chosen cases with a group of experienced general practitioners who have attended our seminars for many years. My inquiries are also relevant to psychoanalytic training, and I will discuss them in that context later in this paper. But it was the changes in the doctors and their reactions to the strains of examining and reconsidering their relationships with their patients during the training that led me to formulate the questions: (1) What happens in a seminar to bring about changes in some of the doctors and not in others? (2) In what kind of doctors can changes occur, and what kind of changes are they? (3) What activity on the part of the seminar leader facilitates change?

To discuss these questions, I must first describe the general practitioners' seminars in which our principal aim is to study the doctor–patient relationship, rather than the interactions among the seminar members.

We do not attempt to teach theory but to help the doctors become more flexible observers of themselves and their patients to the end that their therapy is more efficient and reliable. Our discussions emphasise the relationship of a given doctor to a given patient during one particular course of treatment; how the understanding of this relationship helps the doctor understand the patient's illness and the patient himself, and how it may clarify difficulties in the therapy as well as in other relationships in the patient's life. (I might mention here that the varying responses to the considerable strains imposed by such observations parallel those of psychoanalytic candidates.)

Certainly, every course of medical treatment is determined by the patient's illness and personality and by the doctor's knowledge and skill and only secondarily by the doctor's personality. But each doctor's way of practising medicine is an expression of his personality, which, in turn, determines his attitudes and approaches toward the practice of his profession.

Our doctors report—only when and if they choose to do so—usually those cases with overt emotional or psychological problems with which they seek help and discussion in the stable setting of the seminar. The understanding of the problems presented for discussion is limited, so far as possible, to the reporting doctor's observations of the patient's life, his illness and ideas about it, his fears and hopes, the interaction between the doctor and the patient in the surgery, and the doctor's own emotional participation in all these. The doctor learns to observe and to report on such items as the patient's arrival, how he enters the office, where he sits, what he starts talking about, and how the doctor himself feels when he sees the patient. Through observing and reporting, the doctor makes his own discoveries, which are more meaningful to him than sterile and mechanically used theoretical knowledge. Thus, in little ways, bit by bit, an understanding of the patient's life can be built up. Michael Balint (1965) calls this the 'overall diagnosis'.

In our training scheme the doctors are given an opportunity in a special kind of environment, the training seminar, to study and increase their awareness of these important events, and particularly of their interaction with their patients. Just as in infancy certain ego functions develop in a stunted way if there is not a proper interaction between the growing individual and the environment, so throughout life, and particularly perhaps in professional or work relationships, stunted professional ego functions develop; the individual then tends to feel exploited and wooden, and what he does in the world gives him little satisfaction if his relationship to his environment is fundamentally unsatisfactory. In Chapter 3 I have shown how the environment has to reflect back to the individual his activities in a reliable way. If, despite setbacks, he continues to seek new ways to achieve satisfactory experience, it is essential that the environment not fail him again.

Accordingly, our seminar environment must avoid forcing false relationships and consequent false identities upon its members. It must avoid presumptions of making him agree to do work which he feels does not suit him, and it must recognise the kind of work he *does*. To maintain and increase his self-awareness, each doctor has to be recognised and understood as he is in the setting of the seminar. When our method of training is used (and we use the word 'training' rather than 'teaching'), the doctor does not risk losing his feeling of control in his own practice. The maintenance of this sense of control and power in his professional life is crucial. True, it may take each doctor some time to become properly self-assertive in the seminar setting, where it is most necessary to avoid a teacher–pupil relationship. The doctors want to be constantly educated by the seminar even less than children do by their parents. They learn in other ways.

The doctor's own conflicts, which may be echoed by those of his patient, are never discussed. The seminar concentrates on observations of the patient's problem and of the doctor's way of reacting to and dealing with it. Emphasis is on the doctors difficulties in handling the case and sometimes on the reason he chose to report it. There is tacit agreement that the doctor can deal with his own problems intrapsychically. If he cannot and asks, or shows need, for help, he is referred for consultation.

Applying Erikson's (1950, chap. 7) concept, the seminar can be thought of as providing a phase-specific psychosocial crisis in which new identity and opportunity for ego development can occur. These dynamics are observable in the following phases which occur fairly regularly during the life of any one training seminar:

1. *Over-Idealisation Phase:* The members of a new group tend to admire the ideas thrown up by the seminar and its leader. Some doctors imitate the leader or other members of the group with varying results, some of which seem effective and impressive—for a time. It seems that the doctors' introjected seminar ideas are superego introjects, unassimilated and not really identified with.

2. *Compliance and Rebellion Phase:* Now the doctor feels threatened in his professional identity and sets up various defences—mainly compliance or rebelliousness or other false solutions such as pretence or an attempt to remain perpetually in the first admiring phase. During this time no real use can be made of the ideas of the seminar and no real changes occur. I will discuss this more fully later.

3. *Temporary Withdrawal Phase:* The doctors who enter this phase seem to ponder the ideas of the seminar for varying lengths of time. They attend, talk very little, and rarely present cases. Their own and the group's acceptance of their reticence reinforces the feeling of membership. The seminar, so to speak, merges, and all members make use of this freedom to merge without having any need to participate actively. They seem to identify as part of the attending professional family but not with the work of the seminar.

4. *Assimilation Phase:* Some of the doctors become more active, and it is clear from their diffident reporting that they have changed in their self-

awareness. They are freer and more sensitive in response to their patients' needs and to the ideas of the seminar. They assimilate their introjects at their own pace and with caution.

5. *Swings from Compliance to Rebellion Phase:* Doctors who have experienced the previous phases and have changed in their attitudes toward work and patients may revert to periods of compliance, as they again become over-impressed by what they have learnt. These disturbing swings often lead to rebelliousness and seeming rejection of the seminar and its leader, as if to prove that the learning is useless, burdensome, and time-consuming. There are two ways to explain this: (*a*) the ego identifies with bits of the new superego introjects; (*b*) the ego assimilates bits of the new superego introjects. The result in both versions is an ego change, but perhaps its structure is different.

6. *Self-Awareness Phase:* In this phase the doctor is aware of the changes in him. He feels he is one with the group and is tolerant of the other seminar members. He is able to become self-assertive and work out his own individual way of relating to patients and practicing medicine. Perhaps fifteen to twenty per cent of our doctors achieve this, and although the gains are never lost, there is always more to learn and each doctor will probably repeat some of the phases of growth again and again: thus the 'better' doctors—those who change most often—may report in a teasing way; the leader is not an equal but the parent and is treated as such.

Of all these phases, I think that of compliance and rebellion is one of the most interesting—and the most dangerous—in our training programme. Compliance can be described as rebellion gone underground and is deliberately resorted to when the doctor wishes to hide his real identity in order not to lose it. He may ignore the seminar's ideas or else use them to ensure bad results when he next sees his patient.

Another form of compliance can be resorted to without intention by the doctor who is capable of change. Confused by the seminar, he senses he will be submerged if he cannot go along with ideas other doctors seem to understand and which make no sense to him. He does not feel he is not under*stood*. He feels he does not under*stand*. He may lose touch with himself but does not know how to regain his equilibrium without admitting to what he feels is unique stupidity. If he has what Michael Balint (1957) calls 'the courage of his own stupidity' and admits to his confusion, the whole seminar—and he, too—may become alive. Then a sigh of relief is breathed by one and all, and a step forward is made.

At such times, it is often the ideas of the seminar leader himself which are shown to be stupid and confused and not the doctor's. But to have this courage, the doctor must possess enough ego strength to risk a serious threat: at this stage, if he is not understood, or is ignored, he may resort to further compliance which serves to make him even more befogged, and separate still more his real ego function or self from his compliant self.

To overcome the feeling of confusion from loss of ego identity, the doctor may then introject the ideas of the seminar, set them up inside himself as superego introjects to be faithfully obeyed and imitated but not to be assimilated or identified with. Then a vicious circle of rebellion against them, followed by compliance, can continue without the hope of reality testing, or of making another attempt.

Such patterns are, of course, well known in childhood and adolescence. I think they are most likely to recur when adults are faced with new experiences which demand almost as much from them in the way of change as is expected from the adolescent entering into the world of adults. The egos of our doctors, though, being stronger than those of adolescents, are capable of sustaining brief regressive periods of rebellion and compliance, and the changes do not upset their identity overmuch.

In this connection, I must emphasise how important it is that the group leader avoid imposing a false identity on his group or on individual doctors and that he reflect back to them correctly. If he succeeds, the group settles down to a more realistic, receptive relationship with their patients and with the seminar, and the doctors feel more comfortable and effective in their professional work. They enter subsequent phases becoming self-assertive and making adaptations without resorting to meaningless rebellion and compliance.

These processes may be repeated over and over again in any one individual doctor, during the life of the seminar, or they may also affect the whole group simultaneously. They reflect the development of new ego functions and demonstrate the rate at which these can be gained both by individual doctors and by the group. *They may perhaps be inherent in the development of ego function.*

I will try to illustrate my ideas with examples taken from our research into random sample cases for which the doctors had not sought help and which, therefore, they considered unproblematic.*

Example 1. A doctor told of the physical and mental deterioration of an elderly couple who were long-time patients of his. He reported that he had interviewed them at length and had inquired whether they were depressed and whether they were getting along together. He offered no

---

*Using a random sample table as a control, a case was selected for presentation to the seminar from notes of all patients a doctor had seen at one prearranged surgery (see Chapter 14).

other information to help the seminar contribute to clarification of the problem, and the ensuing discussion was short and unproductive. When the reporting doctor 'supposed that nothing could be done,' there was no comment.

In reporting the case a month later, the doctor noted that when the couple came together, they always sat down so that the husband was behind his wife. The doctor wondered whether the wife sat in front of her husband to shield him, to look after and protect him from the doctor, or whether she wanted to be in front so that she could get her say in first.

These observations were useful and led to more information and to a better understanding of the case. The doctor's apparently compliant—but really rebellious—attitude had changed. He now agreed to help and be helped.

Because he had wanted to be let alone, he had preferred to think for a time that nothing could be done.

Example 2. A doctor had been able to overcome the rather provocative, flirtatious manner of a young married woman so that she was able to weep and show her loneliness when she visited the surgery for minor ailments. At one seminar, however, the doctor reported that his patient had come along 'all dressed up looking like a dog's dinner.' She was concerned about her mother who was ill in hospital and who might be needing money. The doctor thought the patient was getting too demanding and gave her logical explanations as to why nothing need be done, and sent her on her way.

The seminar set to work to learn why he had both behaved and reported in this brusque and offhand way, unlike his usual manner.

In the next report, the doctor indicated again his unkindness to his unhappy patient and teased the seminar leader for her sympathy for the hysterical girl. Ensuing discussion revealed that he had not been unkind to his patient as he had reported but had actually been understanding and had done good work with her.

In the seminar—though not outside it in his surgery—he was rejecting the identification with the seminar and its leader.

Example 3. Before presenting his case, a doctor had referred his patient to a psychiatrist who felt he could not help but who agreed that the woman was depressed and had grave marital difficulties. The doctor then continued seeing the patient for long interviews. In one of his follow-up reports, the doctor described her improvement: intercourse had been successful for the first time, and she seemed less depressed. Yet our doctor was dissatisfied and unwilling to recognise the very progress he had reported.

He had been unable to 'hear' or accept what his patient had told him because he did not want to believe at that time that his 'skill' was useful. He had to be told so by the seminar. He then had permission, so to speak, to accept his identification.

Example 4. A doctor reported on a woman patient of sixty who for many years had come to his surgery regularly once a month for a prescription of sodium amytal. She was given six grains a night, which seemed to satisfy her. The doctor described her as a masculine-looking woman who presented a wooden appearance and who had needed sedatives all her life, but he could offer little else about her. The seminar thought the doctor had carefully refrained from involvement with her lest she become a millstone round his neck.

Following the seminar discussion, the doctor encouraged the patient to talk. He learned that her husband had died a few months ago and that she was depressed; that she used to joke with people but now had lost interest in life. She became friendlier and smiled before leaving.

A week later she lost her amytal capsules and came in, excited and agitated, to request more, which he gave her without fuss. She was grateful and rather humorous about the whole event. Another week later she came again (usually, remember, she came only once a month), complaining of depression. The doctor was busy and prescribed dexamphetamine but did not inquire into the reason for her depression. Then—for the first time—she volunteered some information about herself: she felt as if she did not care about anything and she kept on dropping things. Despite this 'offer,' the doctor could not respond. He still did not ask why she felt depressed and dropped things, and he admitted in the seminar that 'it was a very unsatisfactory interview, from my point of view and probably from hers'.

After this, the patient returned to visit the doctor once a month, asking only for the amytal. They settled down to their old pattern, and when we heard about her for the fourth or fifth time in our follow-ups, she seemed the quiet, unexcited, and unresponsive depressive she had been before. Clearly, she could talk to her doctor up to a point. Clearly, the doctor felt he would be overburdened if he encouraged her further. Interestingly, this doctor often reported cases with which he wanted help, and he was eager to try new approaches involving longer interviews with his patients.

The doctor could not change enough to make full use of the seminar's demonstrable help.

DISCUSSION

The primary aim of our seminars is to help the doctors acquire better skills in understanding their patients and to use the understanding for better therapy. I contend that the acquisition of these skills is tantamount to changes in the ego.

Our seminars provide a setting in which it is possible to observe change in individual doctors under the impact of a training process. Where cases are presented and discussed with particular reference to the doctor–patient relationship and where verbatim records are kept so that the processes may be reliably followed, it may be easier to observe these developments than in other training programmes.

My observations and experiences suggest, then, that ego development, seen in the acquisition of new skills, may occur in doctors attending training seminars under the following conditions:

1. When the individual doctor can, without loss of personal privacy or professional authority, become a member of and identify with, a small working group or team, the aims of which are limited to a discussion of the doctors' professional activity.

2. When the team, and the leader in particular, can accept the individual doctor whether he actively works in the seminar or not and whether he openly identifies with the ideas current in the seminar or not.

3. When the team, and the leader in particular, recognises and respects the individual's professional activity and reflects it back to him in a selective, reliable way—which I have not yet managed to clarify—but which enables him to gain some new professional self-awareness. *The individual is not spared or protected in relation to the work he reports, but is spared and protected in relation to his personal unconscious motives.*

It is obvious that the conditions needed for ego development in a training seminar and those needed by children and adolescents for ego development in a family setting are similar. I wonder, then, whether such conditions may be integral to the training of psychoanalytic candidates, too. It is my conviction that seminars of our kind do give an opportunity for ego changes in certain doctors and that the seminars, therefore, are good and valid examples on which to base a study of some aspects of psychoanalytic training, mainly of changes in the ego.

To discuss finally the bearing of these observations on analytic training, I will reintroduce the questions I formulated at the start of this paper: 1. What happens in the seminar to bring about a change in some doctors? 2. In what kind of doctors do changes occur? 3. What activity on the part of the leader facilitates change? I have attempted here to answer questions 1 and 3 only. Question 2 would take me too far afield and recently Michael Balint, Robert Gosling, Peter Hildebrand, and I have completed a book on it (1966).

It seems that compliance, rebellion, and false solutions occur during analytic training, too. During certain periods of the training analysis, the candidate's ego is weak, and therefore he resorts to introjecting the analyst and to using him as an auxiliary ego. Thus, the dangers of a false solution are present. The standard remedy for this is that these problems, along with all the others, should and can be dealt with within the training analysis.

Is this absolutely true? And to the extent to which it is not true, can—or should—anything be done about it?

Two processes occur at about the same time during the analytic training: (*a*) the candidate's personal analysis; (*b*) his clinical and theoretical training as an analyst. The personal analysis may demand at times regressive or withdrawn behaviour, while the rest of the training, especially while the candidate is treating patients under supervision, requires full adult responsibility which must be respected and encouraged. Certainly, in some cases, these demands conflict, whether for brief or for prolonged periods, and it is not always possible in the analytic treatment itself to keep a balance between the work of ego strengthening and the highly disturbing regressive work in certain phases of the transference neurosis. It may not even be desirable that too much emphasis be placed on maintaining this balance.

My impression is that many candidates, just before or after qualification, have considerable problems in these respects. Some candidates seem to be rather compliant, they do not wish to criticise anything vaguely resembling the ideas they have come to respect, and they feel irritated and upset if anyone else does so. Others appear to acquire a superior smugness towards anyone who has differing opinions from theirs; they can entertain no thoughtful scientific discussion. Yet others are definitely rebellious; nothing is safe, nothing is reliable, everything must be attacked.

In my experience, some candidates need a long time to overcome and free themselves from these attitudes, partially during their training analyses or in continued personal analysis after qualification, but also, I think, haphazardly. To my mind, this problem seems particularly difficult to resolve because the candidates do not have the opportunity to identify with a group which entertains both similar and dissimilar ideas from theirs, and which nevertheless accepts them while criticising their professional work.

Rather apprehensively, I would like to put forward for discussion the idea that seminars of the kind here described might help the candidate over some difficult periods. The difficulties, as I have pointed out, are because the candidates are compelled to function simultaneously in two utterly different worlds: (*a*) in the primitive privacy of the analytic setting, and (b) in the public professional worlds of their practices. The fact that many of the problems are common to—and that the candidates must function in—both worlds further complicates their resolution.

Our seminars could perhaps help because: (a) each member's ideas and contributions would always be considered seriously and listened to; (b) every criticism made in our seminars must be directed to an actual case, that is, to a particular doctor–patient relationship, the development of which automatically shows whether the criticism is helpful and justified or unhelpful and invalid; and (c) since personal problems and motives are never discussed, the seminars might offer the candidates an in-between world without infringing on the analytic, inner world.

The difficulties of being compelled to function simultaneously in two different worlds might, to some extent, be diminished, and the dangers of candidates developing false solutions and resorting to rebellion and compliance might therefore be considerably reduced.

All this ideally should—and I am sure often can—be done in the training analysis alone. However, the problems encountered in most training schemes in this area of ego development are serious enough to warrant rethinking of the situation and to justify consideration of these propositions.

PART III

The Analyst's Work
with Marital Therapists

chapter 16

'Marital Conflicts and Their Treatment' is an apparently simple introduction to marital therapy. In fact, this straightforward-looking paper
repays reading sentence by sentence, and perhaps the most important
sentences come at the end: 'no decision need ever be taken about what
should happen in a marriage. Our aim is only to try to understand what *is*
happening' (p. 206).

Balint starts by saying that a marriage cannot be considered in terms
of two individuals; the partnership must be the focus. She immediately
turns, however, to the importance of each individual's developmental
history. Compatibility is not a matter of rational evaluation; the question
is how well the irrational, unconscious needs and satisfactions which
derive from those histories match up on either side. The country girl may
marry the townee, and quarrelling may be a pleasure, provided 'our
partners in marriage [are] able to participate in, or at least not be
antagonistic to, various kinds of irrational demands and behaviour'
(p. 203). Marital therapy is to do with helping the partners with their
responses, which are largely at an unconscious level, to each other's
particular forms of desire, again often unconscious and irrational, for
pleasure and satisfaction. So the theme of shared unconscious communication appears again, as it has done in Parts I and II.

There is a striking open-mindedness about the possible results of
marital therapy. Both partners may change in step together; one may
change to follow the other's development; the only change needed may be
in their becoming able to enjoy their pathology; or the conflict may have to
be resolved by separation, as in the case of Mrs. Y in Chapter 6.

'Marital Conflicts and Their Treatment' was published in *Comprehensive Psychiatry* 7
(1966), 403–407. Copyright 1966 by W. B. Saunders Co. Reprinted by permission.

Marital Conflicts
and Their Treatment

The theme of this paper is a familiar one. It is that, in trying to understand marriages, it is of little value to start by trying only to understand the two individual partners separately. My idea is that you have to start by trying to understand the marriage in itself. The marriage has to be taken as ill and a diagnosis made of where the illness lies.

As we all know, marriages between two people with similar tastes, pleasures, and ways of life often do not work, and we have learned not to be surprised when we find that what looks as if it ought to be a very good marriage turns out to be a bad one, and vice versa. Positive pleasures in many marriages are hidden from the world and only the negative ones are shown, or the reverse. Each person's way of seeing the world is different and each person is, to some extent, unaware of this and also of what his expectations are; but in spite of this he will probably be unhappy if his expectations cannot, at any rate to some extent, be gratified. Sometimes, in fact, the more obvious and rational requirements one person might have of another in marriage are ignored, and we are not surprised to find that a woman who loves the country marries the man who detests it; or that a couple who never stopped quarrelling had no idea at all of separating. Quarrelling may be a necessary pleasure to them which may be made public, and their more positive pleasures may be hidden from the world.

Why is it so difficult to make a realistic decision about the right marriage partner? The implicit fantasy in all of us is that there is a right partner for everybody, and though we know, as a matter of fact, that this fantasy proves true for some of us, it certainly does not for all. There are many bachelors and spinsters as well as unhappily married people. Apparently, quite a number of people cannot solve, or perhaps even face, the task of finding a suitable partner. Many methods have been tried during history for solving the problem of how marriage partners should be chosen, and each method can show an acceptable number of successes and quite a number of failures, with a majority in between the two. Nowadays, although it might appear that people are completely free to choose their own partners, they are not entirely free, because even in our present-day society certain traditions and social customs limit people's choice. But still, by and large, there is a greater freedom than there used to be, and one would think that this should lead to greater harmony and satisfaction. Why is this not true?

If we go back to examine what happens in early childhood, we find that young children have strong likes and dislikes, and right from the beginning they have to learn to adapt to their parents, who also have likes and dislikes. The children gradually learn to adapt, but this means curbing their own desires and urges; they make endless compromise solutions in order to satisfy their own wishes without sacrificing their parents' love. Some of these urges are curbed or diverted, or may be repressed. Repression may be total and permanent, in which case they are never allowed direct satisfaction, or it may be partial and temporary, or the original urge is turned approximately into its opposite; or, again, it may become dormant, emerging periodically from the repression, and this emergence may even be a kind of explosion. In other cases, the original urge may emerge only if certain strict conditions obtain.

Out of these elements a world is built in which some things are allowed and others are not; some are good and others bad. The child himself, as well as the adult, is largely unaware of this, and throughout life the difference between one person's inner model and another remains basically unchanged. As the child grows up, he is able more and more to perceive the world, and he can change his inner model to some extent, but he cannot altogether correct, by his perceptions, the picture he built up of it when he was young and when his fantasies were very strong and his ability to perceive rather weak. By the time he is adult and ready to marry, although his perceptions of the world will be capable of change, it will be very difficult for him to perceive it through somebody else's eyes. Certain things will be good and acceptable, others bad; certain things wholesome and desirable, others shameful and even disgusting. A further complication arises because these model worlds are only partly openly accepted; they are partly enjoyed in secret, and most people are only vaguely aware of them. In spite of this, it is essential that our partners in marriage should be able to participate in, or at least not be antagonistic to, various kinds of irrational demands and behavior. Our pleasures which, of course, do not make sense to any outsider, have got to make sense to our partners, and it is partly because of the fact that they are so 'nonsensical' that it is very difficult for any outsider to understand what is

right or what is wrong with any particular marriage, or even to know if
one partner is a suitable one for the other.

Before starting to work with patients who come to us with marital
difficulties, we therefore have to try to understand where the satisfactions lie and where the dissatisfactions are intolerable. We have, in fact,
to make a diagnosis of the illness in the marriage. We then have to
discover what has to change in the marriage relationship (not, of course,
in the so-called guilty party only) at the moment of time when the
partners come to us for help; we have to make what is, at the moment, an
intolerable fit which creates tensions into a tolerable one which gives
satisfaction.

In trying to understand marriages we have then to bear in mind that
past (and perhaps only half-realised) satisfactions and the prospect of
future ones can be strong enough to influence each of the two parties to
make necessary changes *together*, or, if the one deviates from this parallel
development, to encourage the other to change so as to remain the same
satisfactory partner that he was before. Sometimes we even have to help
one partner realise the 'unsatisfactory' part of his marriage really suits
him (if it does, of course) and that he could not manage without it unless
he himself changed profoundly.

It often happens that the difficulty of one partner dovetails into the
difficulty of the other but that each partner can only see the difficulty in
the other one and fails to realise that he himself is colluding with it. Basic
changes in the character of the two partners of a marriage may be needed
in some cases if a marriage is to succeed, but often the relationship itself
can be seen as a container for very powerful feelings and can satisfy needs
which are unconscious to both partners. Symptoms can then be seen to be
part of a positive process in the marriage, rather than a liability. Hence,
even if people are rather ill, the marriage can sometimes be worked with.
The two people *need* one another.

In working with people with marriage difficulties, I try to keep five
questions at the back of my mind, in order to make a diagnosis about the
marriage and to plan treatment. The questions are:

First, how does the patient see himself? (How does he feel about
himself? What kind of person does he think he is?) And how does he see
other important people in his life, not only his father and his mother, but
anybody else whom he mentions in his interviews (or perhaps even avoids
mentioning)? And, in contrast, how do I see the patient and his family?
How differently do I see them in this diagnostic stage of the work?
Gradually I compare the picture I build up with the picture that the
patient presents. Also, gradually things begin to change. Patients are, of
course, never consistent, and often, as time goes on, the two pictures

(mine and theirs) become more alike. We both get a more realistic picture.

The second question is: How does the patient see his problems? In what light does he see them, and, parallel again with this, how do I see them?

The third question (perhaps the central one) is: What brought these two people together originally? Why did they marry? What gratification did they seek and expect, both consciously and unconsciously, from their marriage? One can sometimes begin to answer this question quite early in the work; sometimes it takes a long time, but it is always important and can never be left on one side, and if it cannot be answered, then this kind of approach has to be abandoned and individual therapy considered.

The fourth question is: What has gone wrong with the marriage? That is, what happened to the expected gratifications and pleasures that started the marriage off, and what sort of unexpected frustrations arose?

The fifth and last question is: What brings the patient now? It usually turns out that there has been trouble for some time, but the crisis that actually brings the patient is important, and very often if the therapist can understand and answer this question, he may enable the patient to see things, and his role in them, in a different light, and even to take this understanding back into the marriage, in which case some slight but important change might take place right at the beginning of treatment.

If the insight that a patient gains can be fed back straight away into the marriage relationship, it may elicit a satisfactory response from the partner, since it is possible that it will re-establish or fit in with the earlier mutual attraction which brought the two partners together. On the whole, in fact, one might say that this kind of positive response is more likely to take place in therapy where the focus is on marital difficulties, than in other kinds of psychotherapy. In the latter there may be no immediate possibility for testing the insight gained in a real setting. Where the work is focussed on a marital difficulty, the patient can gain insight into his own activities without too much guilt and shame, particularly if his partner is in treatment too, and therefore can participate in and share some of the strain which otherwise he would have to bear on his own.

I will now illustrate what I have been saying by reporting briefly on a married couple who sought help after ten years of marriage. The husband, who first asked for help, was about thirty-five when he finally realised that he was doing nothing with his life and that his marriage was deteriorating. This was a man who had arranged both his professional and his personal life so that he would not be deeply involved in either, and up to this time it had seemed as if this was all that he could manage, and his wife fitted in with this very well. Neither of them could contemplate lovemaking or having a child, and the wife spent her whole time cleaning the house and arranging her clothes and hair. In this treatment the patient did not wish to be helped back to the previous balance where the lack of contact was satisfactory, but to change so that he could make contacts and involve himself with people and have feelings about people and events.

Although at the outset it seemed as if this would be a very long-term treatment, after less than a year quite definite changes were brought about in both partners, who were seen by separate therapists, and they were able to start making a relationship with each other at a pace which suited both of them.

One other example: A woman of forty came to her doctor complaining of headaches and depression. Soon her complaints changed and she confessed that she could only enjoy lovemaking when she was angry with her husband and often felt contempt for him when he was making love to her. During treatment it emerged that her husband unconsciously sought this atmosphere and encouraged it in his wife. This pattern suited them both for a time, but both needed help at one point before they could continue to enjoy sharing this sort of lovemaking and getting the most out of it.

The point here is that the neurotic form of satisfaction did not have to change, but both needed to be made aware of some unconscious feelings before they could enjoy it. In other cases, this kind of therapeutic approach will not be effective, and even in this case, at another point, a different approach may be needed. The therapist has to make a difficult decision after the diagnostic stage about the aims of his treatment.

To sum up, I have tried to show our approach, in a therapeutic setting, to the understanding of marriages. I have pointed out that our aim is to try to understand the interaction between two people and, on the basis of this, to decide whether the interaction can be made satisfactory without basic changes in the two partners, or whether, and in what direction, one or the other or both of them need to change to make the marriage work. As in other forms of psychotherapy, no decision need ever be taken about what *should* happen in a marriage. Our aim is only to try to understand what *is* happening and to enable the couple to see what is satisfactory and unsatisfactory at the moment that they seek help.

chapter 17

'Unconscious Communications between Husband and Wife' draws on Balint's work at the Family Discussion Bureau, later to become the Institute of Marital Studies. She was instrumental in setting up the Bureau in 1947–48, with the specific purpose of undertaking research into marital breakdown and developing a therapeutic approach to it. She has remained closely involved with the Institute of Marital Studies ever since.

Like the previous chapter, this is an introduction to the subject, but behind its accessibility are complex and subtle ideas. It goes into some detail about how the individual's developmental history is related to the unconscious expectations and defences which he or she brings to the marriage; and the theme of shared unconscious communication now occupies centre stage. The intrinsic connection between psychoanalysis and family dynamics is stressed at the beginning, and Balint shows that, like the analytic partnership of patient and analyst, the marriage partnership is an arena of transference. We can see clearly here how Balint's roles as individual psychoanalyst, trainer of family doctors, and marital therapist are organically connected. Another theme, prominent in the later papers of Part I, which can be recognised here in a different context and in a paper written twenty years earlier than those, is the importance of the sheer presence of another person, regardless of whether they appear to be doing anything. If the husband or wife is absent, home may stop being 'home', simply because of the void (p. 212).

Throughout this book Balint's quality of respect, both for the human mind and for the people she is trying to help, is implicit but clearly evident. In this chapter it is explicit. The number of marriages that work, she says, should fill us with respect for the unconscious, and for our patients' hidden loyalties and their desire to put things right.

This chapter was given as a lecture in a series for the general public, and was published in *What Is Psychoanalysis?* (ed. W. G. Joffe, Institute of Psycho-Analysis, 1968). Copyright 1968 by Enid Balint.

Unconscious Communications between Husband and Wife

O ne of the cardinal problems which interested Freud right from the start of his work was how to understand the individual's difficulties in terms of his early history within the family. This means that right from the beginning psychoanalysis recognised that the atmosphere of the family, which is created primarily by the interaction or collaboration between two partners—husband and wife—and later is complicated by the arrival of the children, was of paramount importance for the future development—which more or less means adaptability—of any individual. In spite of this, remarkably little has been written and little research undertaken by psychoanalysts on the dynamics of these marital interactions. There have been some exceptions, mainly in the 1920s (for instance, Groddeck, Deutsch, and Horney had some important contributions to make on this topic), and during the past fifteen years or more, in this country and in America, a few psychoanalysts have turned their attention to the study of marital interactions and have used insights that they had gained as analysts to help them to understand and to attempt to formulate theories about family behaviour.

In the Family Discussion Bureau at the Tavistock Clinic, we have tried, right from the beginning of our work in 1948, to understand marital difficulties by focussing our attention on the interaction between the two partners. That is to say, we have studied the marriage as an entity rather than two people as separate and isolated individuals.

Perhaps marriage somehow goes beyond the natural field of interest of the psychoanalyst whose main concern is with the individual: his urges and drives and his relation to his own private life, including his dreams and fantasies, his hopes, disappointments and wishes, about his family as he first knew—or imagined he knew—them. Whereas, in addition to the individual's internal life of hopes, disappointments, fears, and wishes, his partner's internal life and how these two affect each other, interact or do not interact with each other, must be considered if theories of marital interaction are to be formulated. Furthermore, even these interactions cannot be examined in isolation because the comparative simplicity of the marital relationship is made even more complex when each child is born, not only because of the introduction of a new individual with his own strivings and his own personality into the home but because of the changes in the parents brought about by each pregnancy.

The basic atmosphere, though, in a marriage which is created by the interaction between the husband and the wife will not, probably, be fundamentally changed, and my address will become too complicated if I include the effect of the children on it. So, for the purpose of this paper, I will discuss marriage as if it consisted of two people only, but I will not be forgetting the relevance of the presence of children in a family and the changes brought about by each one.

Our concern, therefore, will be to study how one person's individual life and expectations and hopes and fears dove-tail into and influence another's. We must not forget, however, that this interaction is also studied by sociologists, anthropologists, and social psychologists, partly on the basis of what a third and uninvolved person can observe. They discuss their findings, using concepts like interpersonal relationships, family process, family interaction, etc. They attempt, for instance, to find satisfactory ways of describing the kind of family that produces or contains a schizophrenic or a delinquent child.

Freud, and after him all psychoanalysis, while paying little attention to marital or family interaction, noted and studied in detail the importance of one particular kind of two-person relationship, that which exists between a patient and his analyst. Freud found, for instance, that if a patient's expectations and, one can say, illusions about his analyst are not understood, the analytic treatment does not proceed. He also found that all patients have unrealistic ideas about their analysts. As early as 1895 (Breuer and Freud, 1893–95, p. 302) he called this kind of relationship 'transference'. He said it stemmed from 'the impulses and phantasies which are aroused and made conscious during the progress of analysis; . . . they have this peculiarity . . . that they replace some earlier person by the person of the physician' (Freud, 1905a, p. 116). That is to say, feelings are transferred from that earlier person on to the analyst. After a time he noted also that transference does not only arise in psychoanalysis but that it arises spontaneously in all human relationships. The difference, he says, is that it is revealed in analysis, whereas in other human relationships we are largely unaware of its manifestation. So Freud, although never stating it explicitly, must have been well aware that impulses and phantasies which stem from the past are reawakened in marriage too; and that husbands and wives must have unrealistic ideas and expectations about each other in marriage. The difference is that it is hardly ever recognised between husband and wife as it is between patient and analyst. But clearly it must be of the greatest importance to them and to the family atmosphere which is created by them.

Freud realised that an individual cannot be studied on his own; that is to say, his conflicts and difficulties in relation to another person have to be taken into account as well as his wish to modify his behaviour to suit the other person and his wish to modify his partner to suit him. An individual, in fact, is never in a vacuum. In spite of that, the analyst is concerned with the experiences of one person only. In order to explain these experiences Freud developed a two-pronged theory.

(1) The theory of instincts. In this theory instincts are understood as dynamic forces which are on the borderline between biology and psychology. They create urges or drives which force the individual to pursue certain goals; for instance, his sexual drive forces him to seek a partner. His hunger drive forces him to seek food, and so on.

(2) The second theory is more complicated. It is based on history and accident. Here, once again, there are forces in the individual but these originate from accidents in the special history of that individual and they can be seen to create tendencies or drives in him to repeat what has gone before. For example, he may find himself repeating certain forms of behaviour and find himself unable to accept other forms, however gratifying they might be. He may have a tendency towards reparative acts, towards feelings of resentment, or towards desires for revenge and so on. This theory be called the 'developmental theory'. The two theories, that of instinct and that of development, both have characteristic forces. Both of these theories are needed to explain the internal experiences of one person and both are also needed if we are to understand interpersonal relationships. But things become even more complicated when we intend to study the ways in which two people communicate. Perhaps, in fact, this is a further reason why marital interactions have not been studied by analysts. It is difficult enough to understand the varied and contradictory forces and the fantasies by which they become conscious, that are awakened and transferred in the comparatively simple analytic situation, where only one person's feelings, ideas, and fantasies are verbalised and where only one person transfers, because the analyst has learnt in his training to understand and control his own transference when treating patients. Perhaps the crossed and contradictory transferences in marriage are felt to be too complicated to disentangle and so have been left on one side. But if we are to discuss communication in marriage we must see how much of this kind of interaction can be clarified by psychoanalysts.

So let us start by describing some simple and well-known ways in which husbands and wives communicate.

Words form only a small part of communications in general. We communicate also by the way we move, by our facial expressions, by our silences, by the way in which we give things or do not give things to each other, and so on. When I speak about communication in this paper I shall mean communication in this wide sense. In marriage non-verbal communications are particularly important. Often the person who wants to communicate does not himself know consciously what he wants to say; he may not even know that he wants to say anything at all. Part of our mind is unconscious and this speaks also. In addition, our partner's conscious mind may not notice that anything has been said when we communicate with him although his unconscious mind may set in motion a response. Or to put it another way, a husband may communicate with his wife without being aware that he has. Or the wife may be aware that something has been meant by, for instance, a gesture or a frown, but may not be quite clear what it was and may not know consciously that she has responded to this. Winnicott (1968), in his lecture earlier in this series, spoke of a baby only registering, but not hearing, the mother's silent communication. What I have just said is that this kind of communication is highly important in marriages too, but that, in addition, in marriages it can be seen to be a two-way process. (It probably is also a two-way process between a mother and her baby.)

Husbands and wives fit into each other's needs in the most subtle way, even in the worst marriages, and even, in fact, when there are many areas where they do not fit in at all. For instance, a husband who naturally has a rather small appetite may find himself eating and enjoying huge meals because his wife thinks he likes them. Or a wife who says she is too tired to go out in the evening may unconsciously be doing so because it suits her rather timid and depressed husband. Let us look at some marriages in more detail. For instance, in one case a husband came home from work and his wife told him that she had had a terrible day with the children but everything was all right now and that supper was ready. In saying this, she unconsciously said to her husband that she had had a horrible time and would perhaps like to have a drink, or be kissed and made much of. The husband failed to note the communication and found himself going into the garage to see, instead, if the car was all right. He was unaware that he was responding to his wife's unconscious communication, and she was unaware that his withdrawal to the garage was a result of it. Married couples act constantly on one another in this way; they modify each other's behaviour in the most complex manner and they rely upon each other to do this. This is a part of their daily lives, the atmosphere in the family; the whole feeling of family life would be unthinkable without it.

To an outside, uninvolved person, what appears to be an antagonistic communication can easily be a loving one. That is why it is so difficult for an uninvolved observer to understand what his observations (which can be absolutely accurate) mean to the two partners in a marriage.

When people live together in the same setting over a period of time, they are aware that they are in communication and may value each other's presence when nothing at all seems to be going on between them. For instance, they may not be able to get down to some quite simple job unless they are both in the house together. Each one knows that his activities are enriched by the presence of the other, although neither might become aware of it except in the other's absence. This kind of thing is usually meant when people talk about 'home'. Most people know that they like to be at home, that they may like or dislike getting home after a holiday, and they may not even be aware that they are not really at home when the other one is away. Even if a married couple are on bad terms with one another and feel hostile and irritated about something, they may still want the other to be there—perhaps even more at such times—so that they can carry on with their lives in an ordinary way. In addition to its obvious connection with childhood, there are various theoretical ways of explaining this state of affairs.

For instance, we talk about one person putting part of himself into another person and then feeling lost without that part of himself, but unconsciously recognising it and feeling whole again when relating to it in the other person. This kind of process happens automatically. We are certainly not aware that we do it. We sometimes get rid of parts of ourselves we do not like in this way and blame our partners for having them. Or we may feel empty of our loving feelings, with which we are only in contact when our partner is there. Or we could say that we need our partner to see that we are loving, to confirm our loving feelings, in order to take them back into ourselves and feel good again.

No two homes have an identical atmosphere, no two couples communicate in the same way, but in each there are some characteristics on which that particular marriage is based. These characteristics may not be noticed by either partner as they are there continually and are created by the two of them together, by their two individualities, personalities, and transferences—conscious and unconscious. Here are some examples:

The dynamic structure of one marriage was that the wife had to appear weak and in need of protection. But she had to be just weak up to a point. It was not tolerable for either of them if she was too weak. The wife was happy when she was made to feel rather weak up to that point, and if at these times she enjoyed it when her man was strong, there was harmony between them. If the mutual expectations were apart then there was that much tension between the two. Things could never be absolutely right, for both of them, all the time. Marriages are often, as was this one, a mixture of satisfaction and tension. There is often a subtle balance between the two. Another example: in one marriage the wife appeared to run and control everything. Observers from the outside were rather sorry for the husband, and the husband sometimes complained about his wife's bossy manner. But, up to a point in this marriage, the wife's bossiness suited both partners and when the point was roughly the same for both of them all went well, but if not then there was trouble.

One husband and wife always appeared to be very loving and considerate with each other when they were together. The wife seemed most grateful for her husband's help and care, particularly when she had her frequent, but short, bouts of depression. To an outside observer they suited each other very well; and so they did, but not in the way that showed itself. The wife, in fact, was very frightened of possible outbursts of temper, and her husband prevented these by his kindness. But by so doing, he prevented her using herself and overcoming her fears of what her temper might do. This suited her husband because he also was frightened of violence. Their compulsory lovemaking consisted mostly of petting; penetration was too frightening for both of them. This suggested that the couple could not be violent sexually either, and that was perhaps one of the reasons why they could not achieve a family. The unconscious communication from the wife to the husband was: 'look after me please, save me from my awful violence'. His answer was: 'yes, I will.' So he agreed with her that she needed to be saved from her violence, and this suited him very well too, even though he had to live with a sense of resentment without knowing why.

Another rather similar couple found a different solution. In this marriage the wife appeared to be a timid person who kept to herself in her home and made very few demands upon her apparently jovial, strong, virile husband. The husband was very much admired at parties, and his wide circle of friends pitied him for having such a quiet, retiring, and unamusing wife. They all thought he was marvellous to put up with her so loyally. In reality, though, the situation was very different. The husband was a frightened man and not very potent. He needed to be admired, but kept people at a distance because unconsciously he always feared he would be found out. His wife fitted in with him because she needed to be on her own a good deal and did not like to be interfered with. She wanted to go her own way and encouraged her husband to be sociable. In fact, she was a rather aggressive and tense woman who sometimes exploded and wanted a good row with her husband, partly so that they could get close afterwards and become intimate with one another. But she knew in some way that she had to act with great care and caution because if the row became too heated the husband would feel really threatened and not be able to enjoy the kissing or lovemaking afterwards. Their private hidden satisfactions were not apparent but both husband and wife were careful to keep their public image alive, not only because, in a vague way, they knew that by so doing they were protecting each other, but also because they were only dimly aware of the true state of affairs.

In many marriages there is a basic communication that things should be as they are, but if things become too tense, there is, as a rule, little possibility of a discussion about them because neither partner is consciously aware of his expectations and wishes. Neither of them knows or is conscious of what they are communicating by their actions or by the atmosphere that they create, so that they cannot put things right by words when their actions break down. Degrees of consciousness can vary. Some people are sometimes fully conscious of what to expect from their partner and themselves. Some may not want to admit what they know. Some may be willing to accept it if it is forced upon them, and so on. These kinds of atmosphere characterise a marriage and are kept alive constantly by apparently trivial and everyday kinds of communication. In the marriage I spoke about earlier where the wife complained about the children, the wife's basic expectation was that she should be rather over-pressed and martyred and that she should communicate this to her husband in a roundabout way, and that he should sometimes accept it and do something for her and sometimes reject it and get out of her way. The basic expectation for both of them was that the wife should not say, 'I'm tired, please give me a drink' but that she should formulate her request and her complaint indirectly. Trivial communications sometimes have far-reaching implications. They can convey hostility or love. But they may not be verbalised, nor may they, without grave disruption, go beyond the boundaries which are silently and unconsciously agreed upon between the two of them.

We often find that it is just as difficult for people to express openly that they love and appreciate one another as it is for them to be critical. Many people, in fact, are less inhibited when they are critical than when they are affectionate and appreciative. Sometimes if they do try to express their feelings they may find that what they say is inadequate; it is too little or too much, or it is inappropriate.

If we want to understand these apparent contradictions we must bear in mind that what people feel is only partly conditioned by the present. Everything we say or do is partly influenced by what has happened to us in the past; sometimes events are too closely connected with the past and they cannot be spoken about in a satisfactory way.

There are ways of overcoming these difficulties. For instance, husbands and wives give each other pet names, which when used, express much more than could be expressed otherwise and produce a particular atmosphere. They remind the couple of intimate occasions from the past. The use of the name may re-create a whole scene or fantasy from the past or an event so that there is no need to talk about it in the present. Even here, though, it may be that the importance of the remembered or fantasied event transcends the event itself, and this can be because the event itself was a repetition or a reminder of some even earlier event or fantasy which may have occurred before the husband and wife knew each other. But, in spite of this, it suits both of them.

I have already said enough to make it clear that there are many possibilities of misunderstandings as well as understandings in marriage, and some conscious and many more unconscious ways of dealing with them. How then do these habitual forms of communication originate? On what does a person's ability to communicate depend? We have already seen that it has something to do with transference; with expectations and fantasies which stem from the past and which impose themselves on the present. So let us briefly survey our ideas about how they develop. Before doing so, however, I would like to stress that whatever tendency I describe in an individual is never the only tendency present at any given moment. There are usually many contradictory ones, and at any given time one of them will be the strongest but it may be displaced at the next moment by another. I am referring here to what Freud called the principle of over-determination.

In every human relationship primitive elements are always present. These primitive elements have the structure of an exclusive two-person relationship, which makes them especially important between husbands and wives. We think that they originate from the earliest experiences in the life of every individual when he lived in a primitive world where only he and one other person—his mother—mattered. These early experiences form the basic structures of our personalities. This simple exclusive two-person relationship does not last too long, because we soon become aware of the existence of a third person, our father. This brings all the complications and conflicts of the triangular Oedipal situation. For every individual, however, matters are soon complicated once again by the emergence of other people, first by members of the family, then by neighbours and friends, and then finally by even larger parts of society. The introduction of new people always creates problems and conflicts which must be solved one way or another, sometimes well, sometimes not so well, and sometimes very badly indeed; and very often not one, but many complications arise at any single time.

The individual's position in his family and later the family's position

in society offer or even impose on each of us certain solutions which can
be called family traditions, social conventions, customs, and so on. The
individual's 'vocabulary' of communication depends then on his way of
integrating all these factors and finding a solution to many contradictory
internal wishes and external conditions for himself and for the people he
loves.

   To sum up, a person's ability to communicate and relate depends
firstly on his innate possibilities; these are difficult to isolate but we
assume that they are present. Secondly, it depends on his early experiences, all of which continually act on him and modify him throughout his
life. His adaptability is not settled once and for all at the primitive level
of his relationships, but changes and improves or deteriorates. Although
these processes continue well into adulthood, an individual's adaptability
can never be absolute. He will always have some unalterable prohibitions
and commands forced upon him by his early attempts to find satisfaction
for himself and for the people he loves. His communications are an
expression of the pressure caused by these problems.

   To return to one of our previous examples, I shall isolate one
particular trend in the development of the woman who did not complain
in a direct way and had to engage her husband's sympathy indirectly. She
was the second child in a large family and when she was very young she
was entrusted with the care of her younger brother. It came to light
during her treatment that as a child she could never ask for love directly
from her mother or her father but often got herself into trouble so that
the mother was forced to leave the other children and look after her. The
father was away from home during a good deal of her childhood. All this
made the little girl very guilty and anxious. When, because of her own
guilt feelings, she made it difficult for her mother to look after her in a
satisfactory way, she felt neglected and resentful. All her life she found it
difficult to ask for what she wanted and during her treatment she made it
very difficult for the analyst to help her, although she was miserable
when she got no help. She talked a lot about the problems of other people
in her sessions and found reasons for being late or staying away. In her
marriage her husband responded to this kind of behaviour by appearing to
ignore it, but it came to light in his treatment that he always wanted to be
asked for help and became angry and could do nothing unless he was
explicitly wanted. He felt, in spite of this, some hostility to demanding
women, particularly to those who were nearest to him and whom he
loved the most. He had not been able to feel very close to his much loved
mother, who had been a rather depressed woman and who had needed
help but who had prevented her son from helping her, even in small ways
around the house, because of her depression. So in this marriage neither
the husband nor the wife was able to communicate with each other

directly, but they were able, in spite of this, to find a way to help each other. True, it was a rather indirect and cumbersome way, but it was, nevertheless, available to both of them. This pattern was also a disturbance in their sexual relationship. They enjoyed intercourse, but both prevaricated so much that they seldom had it.

One of the most striking, and perhaps encouraging, things that psychoanalysts have discovered is that people never give up trying to put things right for themselves and for the people they love. Even when they may appear to be doing just the reverse, we often discover that what appears to be the most desperate and useless behaviour can be understood as an attempt to get back to something good in the past or to put right something which was unsatisfactory. Over and over again people come back to their failures in an attempt to remedy them even if they cannot help repeating the same failure over and over again.

We could say, then, that in marriage we unconsciously hope to find a solution to our intimate and primitive problems, particularly to those which we feel we cannot communicate socially in an acceptable way. We are inescapably driven to make relationships in the hope of communicating something which was unacceptable in the past, and we hope to find a person to love in a way which will satisfy ourselves and our partners. Each individual is usually aware of some of his hopes and his needs in relationships, and he may be embarrassed by some of them and unconscious of many. In spite of this, he will still, often unconsciously, hope to find satisfaction for them all in marriage. Unless we are too discouraged we all continue to expect to have someone with whom a gratifying form of communication can be established. Each person hopes to be accepted by and acceptable to his partner, whatever he is like.

Two people, then, partially aware of what they are seeking and not fully capable of expressing it verbally, do, in the end, find each other and decide to marry. They will find reasons for their choice of partner which are sensible and rational to both of them, but in addition, they will be unaware of many of the underlying reasons for their choice. If this is true, and so much is inaccessible to rational decision, it seems remarkable that there can be satisfactory marriages. But we know quite well that there are. This should fill us with respect for the unconscious. In this paper I have tried to discuss some of the forces used by the unconscious to achieve this aim.

In marriage the nature of the relationship is unconsciously agreed upon between the two partners, but it is capable of change for better or for worse as time goes on. No two marital relationships have identical atmospheres or identical characteristics, but in all marriages there are unconscious factors which are important to that particular couple. The individual differences which are present in every marriage are the result of the married pair working out between them a solution which satisfies them both or which is the only solution they are capable of at that particular time. And, finally, these solutions are not consciously decided upon. They just seem to happen. They are the result of a multitude of communications which are expressed partly in words, often in acts, but which may also be silent and barely visible.

Marriage is a uniquely difficult relationship because in it two people voluntarily come together for life and form a relationship in which they hope to satisfy each other in a great many areas of human functioning— not only in the sexual area and the parental one but in many more besides. That this succeeds as well as it does is, as I have already said, perhaps one of the surprising things. However much we may complain about the frequency of marital difficulties and marital breakdowns, I think we ought to credit and be impressed by the fact that there is so much marital harmony and satisfaction. True, the harmony and satisfaction are often more difficult for the outsider to see than the disharmony and dissatisfaction, but if one takes a closer look they can be found to be present even in the most unexpected places.

We have found, in our therapeutic work with marriages under tension, that hidden loyalties and satisfactions are our most valuable allies.

Afterthoughts

chapter 18

Enid Balint Interviewed by Juliet Mitchell

JM: I am going to ask you about your work with general practitioners. [*See the introductory note to Chapter 11.*] It is the area I know least about. I think the papers in the book describe the actual work very clearly and adequately. But why GPs in the first place? I suppose I have always had hunches about why you are so interested in GP work, which I have never really asked you about. I know that it is important to you that analysts should be medically trained, not because you are in favour of psychiatry, but because the body is so important. You have always emphasised the mind–body relationship and argued that there should never be a division between the two; and it is easier not to split the mind and body if one understands the body too.

    I also wanted to ask you whether your whole interest not just in medicine, but in *family* doctors had anything to do with the origins of psychoanalysis. Not only Freud, but more particularly Breuer was a wonderful family doctor. His patients were the Viennese intelligentsia and he was friends with them all. When one thinks of the case of Anna O, it is very much an extension of the sort of work a good family doctor would do, though it was a shock when the transference produced something that wouldn't happen in a purely medical set-up. I wonder if your interest in doctors comes partly out of this sort of doctor–patient relationship?

EB: What you say has validity. I think psychoanalysts are in a way family doctors, although they never see the family. My interest in GP work stems from the same kind of thing as my interest in psychoanalysis, which is that people should not be neglected by being 'understood', in a way which is not understanding but misunderstanding. I see the danger in general practice in recent years, as I did when we started. There was a lot then of what is now called 'psychobabble'; and recently I see that people think they understand when they do not really understand at all. I have heard some horror stories about that. It is more dangerous than when they didn't think they understood and never even tried to, but were just good family doctors 'behind' their patients. The best family doctors may just, quite quietly, watch patients dying without saying so, patients who know they are dying. These doctors understand absolutely nothing, but being protected by their patients are seen as wonderful family doctors. It may seem a poor joke, but there is truth in it; they may understand nothing but still be wonderful, warm, nice people. It is often worse if GPs think they understand the Oedipus complex, or say things like 'if you were nicer to your husband, or if your husband were nicer to you, then it would be all right'. In fact, this is absolutely not what the patients are wanting.

They are wanting something quite different. I suppose I learnt this in the 1940s, during and after the war, when I was looking after, or trying to, people who had been bombed out; and I found that what they were worried about wasn't the being bombed out, but some apparently irrelevant detail about whether their neighbour was pinching their salt or pepper. The smallest things were much more important at that moment, even during the war, than the big things. This is still true. The GPs that I have worked with need to be alerted to the idea that it is not the obvious which has to be understood; it is whatever the patient *wants* understood, and the patient does not know that himself when he comes to the surgery. Of course in medicine a traditional diagnosis does have to be made, and I am not forgetting the importance of skilled physical examination and diagnostic tests.

JM: That seems almost a contradiction of how a lot of analysts would use interpretations. If a patient brings you a complaint about the neighbour stealing salt, one might expect you, as an analyst, to make an interpretation suggesting that what they really mean is something much grander: the primal scene or something like that. One thinks of analysts, and the analytic process, as working from those small things to understand what are the big things behind them. You are saying the opposite: the big thing is obvious, and what matters is what the small thing is about.

EB: The small thing that the patient tells the analyst is probably not in itself what matters, but what matters is not some big thing either. What the small thing leads to may be some other very small thing, perhaps from the past. What often happens in analytic work is that the patient brings something about the neighbour smelling horrible, or something nasty in this particular room this morning; someone who has been there, perhaps. You listen. You don't say anything then; you don't make an interpretation which turns it into something important, about the smell of a mother, or whatever. If you do that, you may be neglecting and misunderstanding the patient by understanding too quickly. You have to wait and see what it is about, and perhaps you find that it is about a smell when the child was small, or perhaps something quite different. You don't know to begin with, but if you come in too soon with an interpretation, you might miss a dream, for example, by interrupting the flow of association. In my view it's much easier if you have an association, then maybe a dream, then more associations; and then you get back to the bad smell at the beginning. But if you come in too soon, you are doing just what I am most anxious about at the moment, both in general practice but more so, much more so, in analysis, which is that people may hang on to set-piece interpretation. I think we have given up the idea of its being all the Oedipus complex, or all parental neglect, or all anything. We get tiny little important details which really make the thing alive for the patient, and then, once you do that, the patient tells you something different and unexpected. That is the transference in the true sense, not just in the 'here and now'.

JM: You mention your coming to psychoanalysis through your work at the end of the war, and suddenly realising it was not the obvious thing that mattered but something else, maybe something extremely small. Now if I look at your early papers they are very much about an interaction between two people, with yourself as the person who listens. I know you write about the mirror, and being there as a mirror for the patient to see her- or himself in, but nevertheless the papers are about two people relating, and I suppose I want to ask you, do you still think therapy is about relating? Your later work is more about somebody not having a relationship to a person, and then having to grow into a relationship to a person.

EB: This raises all the interesting questions, because what you have said just now is right. I am still interested in, and listening for, what is happening between two people, although I bear in mind that there may be three people, or no distinct person at all. It may sound too dramatic, but that is roughly what I mean. I am really interested in what is happening in a room with a patient and what it reflects, both in the present and the past, and what it is the opposite of, because there are contradictions and paradoxes throughout, so you never get anything simple. But I think I am more interested now in what is not said than what is. I am as interested in the pre-verbal as the verbal, so I always have my chair in a position where I can see my patient's face if possible, although some patients see to it that you can't. I sit to one side, a bit but not totally behind the couch, and I certainly watch hands, feet, and body, and that is part of what I hear when the patient talks. Both make sense together, or sometimes don't. I have to stop and think and try to find my way, and of course I never do get it quite right to start with, or if I do it's by chance. But if you get somewhere near it and stick to it for long enough (not non-stop, of course), the patient may at the end of the session, or sometimes during it, give you something that tells you where he is going, or where people intruded on him, or where he was totally alone with nobody else there. Then he may have had to start inventing someone else, perhaps by looking in mirrors or hallucinating, when in fact he had no relationship with another person, or even part of a person. With some patients I make a conscious decision that I don't want to get to that level of the mind; I might have too many patients of that kind on my hands at the moment. With a particular patient I may just not want to do it and then I don't, which sounds wicked, but I think I have always done that.

JM: What do you do instead in those cases? Where do you stop?

EB: I suppose I don't look at what I don't want to see. Perhaps a patient can be sufficiently helped if we cope with a difficult two years: say, from the age of three to five when the mother was depressed, or the war was on, or the child was sent away to boarding school because there was no one to look after him. There may have been an external reality disaster. I will not listen to what happened before that period. I don't deliberately cut off, but I find myself not knowing.

JM: You obviously still think that everything is really determined by, and goes back to, the very early infancy.

EB: Another very difficult question; I don't know. I seem to have done quite good, indeed very successful, work with some patients where I have deliberately not gone back, because I probably decided, diagnostically, at the beginning where to go. I have had one patient for five years now and thought that when she was a baby her relation with her mother was quite good, that the mother liked having a baby and the baby liked having a mother. It worked all right, but then there was a sudden change. Another child was born and the mother was depressed. The mother's mother had been severely ill when the mother was three, and things had gone wrong for her at that age.

After the mother's depression, things did go wrong and the first child, my patient, was grossly neglected and not 'tuned in' to. Over the years we have been dealing with her extreme fragility, her tendency to be absolutely thrown off balance if the expected understanding from, nowadays, her husband or me is not there. She doesn't just become frightened, she gets in a panicky, almost incoherent state where rage predominates, and so our work has to be to do with that. But in two or three years' time, assuming I am still working, if I find, as I have done with other patients, that that is not good enough and I have to go further back, and let her tell me about much earlier stages, then I shall have been wrong, and I ought to have done that earlier on. I have sometimes made that mistake. But it isn't always wrong; I think the mother or the environment can be 'good enough' for a time, but then if it stops it may be worse than if it was never all right. I am beginning to wonder whether for the very young baby sudden changes and inconsistencies are not worse than a general low level of caring and understanding. Low-level care can lead to neurosis. Shock will lead to rage, impoverishment and, very likely, to withdrawal.

JM: How would you fit this area of very early relations and their absence, or a break in them, together with something else which you emphasise all the time: the importance of the unconscious?

EB: This is obviously very difficult. I immediately find myself trying to think of a session to discover what I mean; that is my addiction and I don't seem to be able to get out of it. I think of unconscious phantasy life, which is there all the time, as part of the structure; that there is a stream of images going on in our lives. I see the structure as a world of phantasy regulated by defences where fear, anxiety, and catastrophic events are registered, but not necessarily experienced; where everything happens, but only a certain amount is realised. I am talking descriptively now, not structurally. I am really asking myself why the human mind has developed in the way it has, why we have built up this system of defences, and I can only imagine it is because of the volume of fear associated with unconscious phantasy life and with the reality of the fears which threaten to overcome civilisation.

JM: There is work in the unconscious. I am thinking, for example, of a topical issue, child abuse; when it really happens. I think Ferenczi, in some ways, was right to redirect our attention. Real abuse shatters the possibility of an unconscious phantasy about it; because the unconscious is a way of working out anxiety and horror, and if there is too violent an impingement, too much actual physical or mental abuse, I think you may erode the possibility of unconscious phantasy about it. Perhaps a really abused person cannot phantasise, even unconsciously.

EB: This might be true. It seems to be the case when you are working with abused patients, but I am not sure that it really is so. My mind goes to the work I did years ago with a boy whose mother had been murdered by the father, and he had seen it. All I did with this boy for about a year was to be there when he came, but at the last session he stole a small bit of china; so he took something away with him which makes me think his unconscious phantasy life had not got lost. He could symbolise.

     I don't really know what happened in that case, but I am not sure about the work of the unconscious. I find that a puzzling concept. I see other parts of the mind having to do the work.

JM: The unconscious just being there?

EB: Yes, relentlessly; more and more shut out by the defences, in some people who cannot perceive at all. In order to perceive, imagination is needed; and of course I may be including projection. If you look at a small baby, it seems that it is born with an ability to experience in a particular way. I do not mean verbal thinking, but there is some kind of registering going on. If the mother is in pain, the baby will cry too. So you start off with a communication of mutuality. This can only happen if the baby has a mind or receptive 'organ' responding to another person. You have to hypothesise that the baby has some instrument of knowing, and I suppose I would see that as part of the unconscious mind, but not the repressed unconscious.

JM: We say our work with the unconscious is the distinguishing mark of psychoanalysis. Why?

EB: I think that when I listen to a patient I hear something which I don't hear at a dinner party. People think you do this all the time. You don't. You couldn't. You sit down in your analytic chair and your patient comes in and your mind switches on, to hearing and looking and feeling in terms of unconscious concepts and images. We do it automatically. The patient says it's a fine day and he had a horrible journey and there was a lot of traffic. I immediately begin thinking, 'Oh, what's he talking about? What's this all about? Is he distracting me from yesterday's dream, or is this actually more to do with what he dreamt?' If one is constantly distracted, then is that because one is being made to feel that there is no unconscious communication?

JM: In this last example, what is going on? Why does a patient do this?

EB: I don't know, but one would say that there is a defence against any unconscious communication. The fear of whatever sort of damage can be so great that you are just not allowed to penetrate the defences. There are patients like that, and if we see them in consultation we may think they are not analysable because they are so defended. I saw one like this the other day who wanted a diagnostic interview, and I did not even get as far as giving her that. I knew it was impossible. She would break down and was not ready for it.

We have to be terribly careful. It may take years before a bit of repressed material can be borne. Patients who are very defended can only take tiny bits; their world is structured in such a way that a tiny change is shattering. If you are healthy enough, you can stand being shattered a bit, but these people we are talking about can't stand it.

I think of the unconscious as a very active process in the mind, both in sleeping and waking states, which structures people's lives. People come to analysis in order to have a bit of it modified, a little tiny speck of its defences, whatever we can get at in about six or seven years, so that something new can be perceived by the patient, or something dreadful that happened can be repeated in the transference, perhaps several times, then modified, then repeated again if need be. I don't think Michael's idea in *The Basic Fault* of 'scarring over', helps me clinically a great deal with this. I think what needs to happen is for something to be created; something was wrong, it has to be accepted, and then something else can be put in its place.

JM: That seems to me to go to the heart of your therapeutic aim. I suppose one could call it a new beginning, but I don't think you would want to.

EB: For me that phrase implies a gratification, and there is none. Perhaps it does not mean that, but when Michael and I talked about this I always got a feeling that gratification was implied, whereas there is no gratification in it whatsoever. It is painful, it is hard for the analyst, it is terrible for the patient, and it is not done once, but several times, and there is no gratification when it is over, if it ever is, and the patient is living that bit of his life in a different way. No gratification; no gratitude either. It's very odd. Of course some people never do change. Their failures continue; they can only be repeated, even perhaps enjoyed, but it seems nothing else can be put in their place. They are hung on to. The patient would feel he had lost something, that he wasn't himself without the failure.

JM: Driving down here on the motorway, I was thinking about a patient that I supervise, and therefore about the supervisee as well, and about their relationship and theirs with me, and I found myself saying to all three of us in my mind, 'Well, analysis is about going to hell and back'. What do you think about that?

EB: Yes, I think that is good. You must take somebody by the hand and show them the way, and think, 'I have been there before, perhaps. They do not have to come with me, but I do know the way'.

JM: I was just thinking about why this is. Why not take drugs, instead? I suppose it was in that context my thought came to mind, and I was thinking about the training analysis as well. What if one has not been there, and one has a patient who actually needs to go to some further part of hell; what can one do?

EB: That's an absolutely fundamental question. Even if you have had a training in psychoanalysis, as you and I have, it does not mean we have been to that bit of hell ourselves. We have been to some bits of hell and some bits of bliss, which is when some particular bit of hell disappears.

 I am thinking of a patient whom I analysed some time ago who had had what seemed to be good mothering, from her mother and an aunt as well. It seemed they had both adored her, but it was puzzling to find in the analysis that she had never really had any warmth, and was living very efficiently in her skin without being able to let herself go or trust herself to be held close to anybody; I mean physically close to one person. I felt she had sat on her mother's and aunt's laps, but at a distance from their bodies. It took me quite a time to be able to realise how fragile this patient was, because she gave the impression of being extremely competent and not easily broken. Her father had disappeared from the scene when she was quite young, so she had never really had a father. She seemed, in fact, to have less difficulty in getting near to men than women, because her father had not been close enough to be longed for. At one stage in her analysis, we came to a terrifying moment when I interpreted that she felt she must remain a boy and never become a woman with a woman's body. She got extremely frightened and her face showed terror. From then on, though, we were able to find out that she needed to feel she was a woman but did not dare. She wanted to feel close, in the way a newborn baby should immediately feel close to its mother's body. But then we spoke about her fear of becoming a woman and her need to be a boy instead, not a girl but a boy who would remain a boy for ever, and, as I say, she was very frightened. On that occasion I did in fact put my hand, very firmly and rather harshly, on her shoulder. The episode lasted a few seconds, and I acted from a spontaneous feeling that she needed a sample of closeness which was not comforting, but was alive; a closeness that was necessary for her if she was to develop or even to survive. That episode was never repeated, but changes took place rather quickly in the patient. For many years she went back, from time to time, to her feeling of isolation and lack of contact, angrily denying its importance; but she became a woman.

JM: That makes me want to go back to the number of persons in the consulting room. I felt a shift, which I had not seen at first, from your early papers to the later ones in Part I: let's say from 'On Being Empty of Oneself', which is a marvellous paper, through to 'Unconscious Communication'. I might want to formulate it as a move, metapsychologically speaking, from an object relations theory to some kind of three-person structural theory. I think the first papers are in dialogue with a lot that was happening in the 1960s which seemed quite controversial. People were saying that we just needed a humane relationship to the patient, that establishing a 'good enough' situation meant comforting and not saying no. Your early papers do not agree with those ideas, but they still seem to be arguing within that framework while the later ones are not. They no longer have the same two-person frame of reference. Do you think there is a shift of that sort between your earlier and later work?

EB: I think you are quite right about this. When I started writing papers, I was very aware of the thing you are talking about, and I was angry at this idea that all you had to do was to be nice to your patient like Laing was thought to be (totally unfairly quoted, I am sure); and I felt very much that that was not what was needed. That was what I was writing about, or at least what I hoped I was writing about. Winnicott always warned me that I had a reassuring personality and I had better watch out. So it could be, in spite of thinking that I was not being nice to my patients, that I was. In fact I have found, thirty years later, that various patients tell me quite different things—some that I was so very nice, and some that I was absolutely horrible—so it must be transference anyway. Or am I nice to some, which might mean that I neglect them? Still, the important question you are putting is whether in, say, the last ten years, I haven't been paying attention to the two-person relationship, but just to a patient by himself. I sometimes criticise myself when I realise I am doing that, but what I have been finding in my work is that these are the patients with whom I am working at some depth. There are only three relevant patients now, all people who appear, one of them certainly, never to have had an object relation of what I call imaginative perception with anybody. This has changed over the years, and one particular patient is now in a relationship with me, which she talks about but which is not structured in the way that I wrote about in the 1960s. It is structured in quite a different way, and I have not yet formulated how. Perhaps there are two of us, but the patient either ignores me or sees me as another aspect of herself.

With another patient my relationship could be felt to be more like a relationship to a twin or an image in a mirror, but there are two of us. This patient quotes what I said a year ago, so I do exist. It does not feel to me as if I were a mother with a baby. It feels much more as if I were a person talking to a bit of himself which is not himself at that moment. It is not an object relation in the sense in which I wrote about object relations before, although this patient has plenty of 'relationships' with other people. They do not concern him privately and what I am does concern the private part of himself. His private life is rich when he is alone and he tells me about it; publicly he is another person.

JM: Let's vulgarise that and oversimplify it to see whether we can make any pattern. Suppose that in the early 1960s you had looked at your patient in 'On Being Empty of Oneself' in the same way as you do now, and worked technically in the same way as now, which you probably didn't then; maybe it took quite a few years to notice that you had changed. Would that 1960s patient look different?

EB: Yes.

JM: Can you try and imagine that patient in today's world for a moment? What I am hypothesising, far too crudely but it will let us get rid of the idea if it is wrong, is that nowadays you might be saying that there was not an established object relationship. In 'On Being Empty of Oneself' it was a question of a mother who misperceived completely: perhaps a 'dead' mother in André Green's sense, or a misperceiving mother or a cruel one. There are many ways of misunderstanding, or understanding falsely as you have talked about. Now some people might, through some capacity which has come from somewhere else, nevertheless be able to create something in that space, which then won't be exactly themselves, nor exactly a self watching, nor exactly another; but it will be some sort of other part of themselves that enables them to live. It is usually just part of themselves, but you are saying that it becomes you. What's happened in the process of the therapy is that what was just them, in some blurred way, has now separated out into what was in fact originally two people, one of whom, however, was not really there outside. But that person is there inside somewhere, because there has to be someone else. A baby on its own cannot survive; it is actually impossible.

EB: That is true enough, but I find myself thinking of some of the things Bion talked about. I am glad you brought up the 'On Being Empty of Oneself' patient, because there is a lot of similarity between her and the other patient I have been talking about, and I do think that if I had had the experience or the courage, or had felt safe enough, I could have worked with her in the way I am working with this patient now. She must have had some relationship before at an early stage. They had different experiences in their earliest years. I think there might have been something which got completely shattered with the one patient, because there was a lot about shattering and rocks coming down on her head, and she remembered all sorts of associations to that. With her I think there was something that got shattered, but with the other patient there never was anything. As I now know for a fact, his mother was withdrawn and depressed from the start, because of how identified she was with a close relation who died. But I think that now I am sometimes a separate person. He even perceived that I had a cold last week, and when various things happen we can talk about it. When I don't know where I am, or am not sure whether I exist at all in this particular session, I can use the word 'babble'. I think we must be careful about this word, because I do use it. At the beginning of the analysis he used to babble incoherently for nine-tenths of most sessions. Now that is rare; but if I am muddled, or make a remark or put in an interpretation which has nothing to do with him, he will start to babble. I may wait for the end of the session and then he or I will say 'It's been one of those sessions'. The nice thing about this particular analysis is that, unlike the other ones I have been writing and talking about lately, he does not mind when I am no good or let him down, when I am really muddled or confused beyond bearing; and he does try to confuse me, too. He shows that it is perfectly all right, whereas with most patients of the kind I am writing about it is an injury, a real neglect if one does not understand. With this patient it's not at all; it's totally different now after ten years or so.

JM: I think you are saying now that the mind is not formed only by other people or the absence of them; it is also when the baby gets the sunlight through the leaves in the trees, or is wet in a cold nappy. The mind is not only a question of object relationships or their absence, but other things do come in to form it, particularly the unconscious mind.

EB: I agree. I am really glad you have put it that way. My only reservation is that although I think this is true of everybody, there are also differences. For people who have a relatively healthy development the two go together. There is the light through the trees and a feeling of coldness and wetness, and there is also somebody with whom one is in a relationship that one can tolerate and who can tolerate being in a relationship with a confused baby. But with some patients there doesn't seem to be any relationship with the other person, or anybody who did tolerate them, so there is only them. They do survive, which is odd; one would think they wouldn't survive on just the sight of the light through the trees. I am not sure about this. Perhaps there was in fact a nanny or someone to make some kind of relationship with the mind, and the feelings, the sense of touch, and so on. Sound is important too: what is going on around. There is a lot of noise, after all, in a room, which we don't hear but babies do.

JM: But doesn't one have to have had another person?

EB: I would say, Yes, one does. If somebody is alive and twenty years old, it means they have had someone. But there are people who come to analysis who are breathing, but they don't seem to be alive. There is no creative life in them; it's just a body breathing. However well educated, perhaps very clever, they may be, they are still not properly alive yet; as people, they appear dead. Their minds are alive, but their psyches or souls are dead. They are compliant, clever, orderly minds.

Over the years I can think of different examples of this with quite a number of patients, but as I was not thinking generally in these terms I was always dealing with it as a matter of individual cases. I must take responsibility for having, until the last ten years at least, structured the work on the assumption that there were two of us, even if the patient did not know it; and in doing that I have influenced what happened and what I could observe. It is only relatively recently that I stopped assuming there was more than one person in the room, and that there was a relationship even if the patient did not think so.

JM: If you can do important work for somebody for whom you are not there, that seems to challenge object relations theories of analysis. If you are not there, what can you be doing?

EB: What is actually there if the patient does not perceive anything? I think one has to hang on, not go away, and find out. I found this very hard: to acknowledge that I do exist, can hear and try to understand even though the patient does not perceive me. You, with your patients, also have to acknowledge that you do exist even if you are not perceived.

JM: Yes, it's extremely difficult. What difference does it make? You continue to live, just! But what does it do for the patient?

EB: Well, I suppose I work on the hypothesis, without a great deal of conviction, that in due course the patient also allows you to exist. I think this happened with Sarah, the patient I wrote about in 'On Being Empty of Oneself'. I did exist for her. I believe I existed for her in some form or another from the beginning, and then she lost me and then I existed again. So I don't think she is somebody for whom there was no object from the beginning. But for the patients where there hasn't been any object from the beginning, I feel that if I insist that as far as I am concerned I do exist, I don't necessarily feed that to the patients. I don't tell them all the time that I am here too, although I might from time to time, if I get too fed up. But I work on the hypothesis that even though I do not exist now, in due course I will exist and they will perceive me.

JM: If there really wasn't an object from the beginning, where is that perception going to come from? Is it from your knowledge that you exist, and is it going to have to be your imagination that enables the patient to see you?

EB: I have thought about that. It is either what you have just said, or it's to do with the mirror image. With the patient who doesn't mind if I am muddled, confused, or even if I let him down, mirrors are very important. I see him as relating to himself in the mirror, and finding someone else; and then not being able to, and then being able to again. I think, but I am not sure about this, that gradually I am being seen in the mirror when he looks at himself. There is the looker, and there is what is in the mirror.

JM: It is you being seen there. Otherwise one could say that Narcissus might have gone on living if only he had not reached out for himself in the mirror. If he had just looked, he would have been all right.

EB: He would have been all right, but entirely by himself. We have got a theory that one is not all right by oneself.

JM: That could take us on to another one of your interests—creative life and creative work. Maybe some people are all right by themselves, even if they go mad or something.

EB: Could we try and define madness? Is it a state when you are on your own, but in order to maintain the boundaries in your life you have to be creative? To be on your own without being creative is not being alive. Being on your own and being creative might be being mad, but it is being alive.

JM: In that case an old wives' tale that psychoanalysis is actually bad for creative people could have a nucleus of truth in it, if offering a creative person somebody other than themselves means that that person will eventually emerge in the mirror. One might in some sense be interfering with that creative process whereby they are alive through a madness within themselves.

EB: I have had a certain amount of experience of working with artists who have not been able to work or have some difficulty. I have seen one quite recently. My experience of it is that one can undo a block in their creativity which enables them to go on creating, but when you do that they don't throw you out. My very first patient was a creator and he had a block; and I was included in his first creation which got him going again. He created me and then got on with it, and was able to go on creating. I think when you see a creative artist who has a block you don't say: 'I am going to undo this'. You let them create you; then they can carry on. Your being there in the room with them means nothing; but if they can create you (and I had this recently in a very few sessions) then they see you as real. They perceive you creatively. Then they are not alone.

JM: So maybe with people like the patient you were describing, with whom you are nobody, it is not that in time he will get a mother, or another object in the object relations sense, who looks after him or whom he relates to; but that in a way you can become a painting for him, or a ray of sunlight in the mirror.

EB: Which is a distortion of me, but an imaginative creation.

JM: He has got blocked because the room was empty. He couldn't see himself; he couldn't see anything in the mirror. What can emerge in time is a new thing, which is in fact you. He needs you to offer yourself, to be what comes into the mirror.

EB: That may be right. It certainly hasn't been my experience that artists should keep away from analysts. Mind you, if analysts make interpretations about the artist's work, which I find horrifying in the extreme, that is a real killer. But if you let the artist do it, create you imaginatively, that is OK. But how you do that is another matter.

JM: That could explain why it does not hurt your patient if you are muddled.

EB: When I started I made ordinary interpretations about breasts, which I think were perfectly correct, since he was looking around for a breast in a very obvious kind of way, with his hands on the pillows and so on. But those interpretations were totally useless. They weren't what he needed to live. His search was pre-verbal, to find the images, to invent the words. Later, what he found were symbols.

JM: So really what you come to be is an experience of the external world which the creative artist must see for himself. At the time of the block there are no symbols available for the external world.

EB: I think so. Some artists do say they don't need the external world at all, because it all comes from their imagination. But I wouldn't agree with that.

JM: I don't think that is possible; it must come from something. What you would get, as you did with that patient, is a fantasy without imagination. He was going on and on using old stories, which then become in a way emptied. You can see that in creative work of all sorts. If someone comes to an analyst like yourself at that point he may, in time, be able to use you to shift, to refill, and imaginatively start all over again with an external world. What you are is a new, or renewed, external world.

EB: I am not a person, I agree. I would say an object, a bit of the external world, but not a person: maybe an experience, a realisation of outside.

JM: Yes. It might be a bit of a person. You may turn out to be a painting, but what matters is that you are enough of a reference point to be something to feed the imagination.

EB: That sounds right to me, but I think we both need to think about it.

JM: The imagination can't feed on itself for ever, only for a certain amount of time. Then it has to be re-fed.

EB: I think of the word 'perception'. The imagination has to be able to perceive a bit of the world that it can accept. The artists I have worked with, not only painters but musicians and writers too, have to be able to hear or perceive through ears or eyes or sense of touch, something which they haven't perceived before; and if their ability to perceive gets cut off then they are finished. They can only repeat themselves. Their perceiving is terribly painful; don't let us forget that. For analysts as well, to perceive something you have not perceived before is terribly difficult; we fight against it like mad. I do this with the GPs too, of course.

JM: I am still harping on about objects. The artists are certain people who have not had enough: not nothing, but not enough. Is it that they use their imagination to make more of the not enough?

EB: Could one say that the not enough which they have had is something that has never been turned into a whole person? So there has never been a mutuality, a relationship, or concern for the other.

JM: There is something there which has to be re-used, re-found.

EB: Or re-created, but I don't know what we mean by that. I suppose we have all had this experience. One may go to a Shakespeare play, or open a book and find two lines of prose, and it comes alive; or something comes alive in you. We all need that all the time.

JM: When those two lines come alive, it is because there is something inside that has got lost. In that sense it is not a new beginning but a re-creation. Something has been there before.

EB: Something must be there, otherwise the two lines would not echo. Maybe the something never was two lines. It was disorganized: a readiness, a preparation.

Bibliography

Alexander, F. (1932) *The Medical Value of Psychoanalysis.* London: Allen & Unwin.

Alexander, F. (1933) A note on Falstaff. In *The Scope of Psychoanalysis, 1921-1961.* New York: Basic Books, 1961, pp. 501-510.

Alexander, F. and French, T. M. (1946) *Psychoanalytic Therapy: Principles and Applications.* New York: Ronald.

Balint, A. (1939) Love for the mother and mother love. In M. Balint (1952), pp. 109-127.

Balint, E. (1969) The possibilities of patient-centred medicine. *Journal of the Royal College of General Practitioners* 17:269-276.

Balint, E. and Norell, J. S., eds. (1973) *Six Minutes for the Patient: Interactions in General Practice Consultation.* London: Tavistock.

Balint, M. (1937) Early developmental states of the ego. Primary object-love. In M. Balint (1952), pp. 90-108.

Balint, M. (1938) Strength of the ego and its education. In M. Balint (1952), pp. 200-212.

Balint, M. (1952) *Primary Love and Psychoanalytic Technique.* London: Maresfield, 1985.

Balint, M. (1957) *The Doctor, His Patient and the Illness.* London: Pitman.

Balint, M. (1958) The three areas of the mind: Theoretical considerations. *International Journal of Psycho-Analysis* 39:328-340.

Balint, M. (1959) *Thrills and Regressions.* London: Maresfield, 1987.

Balint, M. (1960) The regressed patient and his analyst. *Psychiatry* 23:231-243.

Balint, M. (1961) *Psychotherapeutic Techniques in Medicine.* London: Tavistock.

Balint, M. (1965) The doctor's therapeutic function. *Lancet* i:1178-1180.

Balint, M. (1968) *The Basic Fault: Therapeutic Aspects of Regression.* London: Tavistock.

Balint, M. and Balint, E. (1961) *Psychotherapeutic Techniques in Medicine.* London: Tavistock.

Balint, M., Balint, E., Gosling, R. and Hildebrand, P. (1966) *A Study of Doctors: Mutual Selection and the Evaluation of Results in a Training Programme for Family Doctors.* London: Tavistock.

Balint, M., Ornstein, P. and Balint, E. (1972) *Focal Psychotherapy: An Example of Applied Psychoanalysis.* London: Tavistock.

Bion, W. R. (1962) *Learning from Experience.* In Bion (1977).

Bion, W. R. (1963) *Elements of Psychoanalysis.* In Bion (1977).

Bion, W. R. (1970) *Attention and Interpretation: A Scientific Approach to Insight in Psycho-Analysis and Groups.* In Bion (1977).

Bion, W. R. (1977) *Seven Servants.* New York: Aronson.

Bollas, C. (1987) *The Shadow of the Object: Psychoanalysis of the Unthought Known.* London: Free Association.

Breuer, J. and Freud, S. (1893–1895) Studies in hysteria. *Standard Edition* 2.

Deutsch, H. (1946) *The Psychology of Women, Vol. 1: Girlhood.* London: Research Books.

Drury, J. (1988) Master artists, like God himself, realize their representations. *The Independent,* June 11th, London.

Eigen, M. (1985) Towards Bion's starting point: Between catastrophe and death. *International Journal of Psycho-Analysis* 66:321–330.

Eissler, K. R. (1953) The effect of the structure of the ego on psychoanalytic technique. *Journal of the American Psychoanalytic Association* 1:104–143.

Elder, A. (1987) Moments of change. In Elder and Samuel (1987), pp. 54–67.

Elder, A. and Samuel, S., eds. (1987) *While I'm Here, Doctor: A Study of the Doctor-Patient Relationship.* London: Tavistock.

Erikson, E. (1950) *Childhood and Society.* New York: Norton.

Federn, P. (1926) Some variations in ego-feeling. *International Journal of Psycho-Analysis* 7:434–444.

Federn, P. (1932) Ego feeling in dreams. *Psychoanalytic Quarterly* 1:511–542.

Ferenczi, S. (1919) On the technique of psychoanalysis. In Ferenczi (1926), pp. 177–189.

Ferenczi, S. (1923) The dream of the 'clever baby'. In Ferenczi (1926), pp. 349–350.

Ferenczi, S. (1926) *Further Contributions to the Theory and Technique of Psycho-Analysis,* 2nd ed. London: Hogarth, 1950.

Ferenczi, S. (1931) Relaxation and education. In Ferenczi (1955), pp. 236–238.

Ferenczi, S. (1933) Confusion of tongues between adults and the child. In Ferenczi (1955), pp. 156–167.

Ferenczi, S. (1955) *Final Contributions to the Problems and Methods of Psycho-Analysis.* London: Hogarth.

Freud, A. (1936) *The Ego and the Mechanisms of Defence.* London: Hogarth, 1976.

Freud, A. (1954) The widening scope of indications for psychoanalysis: Discussion. *Journal of the American Psychoanalytic Association* 2:607–620.

Freud, S. (1900) The interpretation of dreams. *Standard Edition* 4–5:xxiii–621.

Freud, S. (1905a) Fragment of an analysis of a case of hysteria. *Standard Edition* 7:7–122.

Freud, S. (1905b) Three essays on the theory of sexuality. *Standard Edition* 7:130–243.

Freud, S. (1909) Notes upon a case of obsessional neurosis. *Standard Edition* 10:155–318.

Freud, S. (1910) 'Wild' psycho-analysis. *Standard Edition* 11:221–227.

Freud, S. (1912) Recommendations to physicians practising psycho-analysis. *Standard Edition* 12:111–120.

Freud, S. (1914) On the history of the psycho-analytic movement. *Standard Edition* 14:7–66.

Freud, S. (1915a) Repression. *Standard Edition* 14:146–158.

Freud, S. (1915b) The unconscious. *Standard Edition* 14:166–204.

Freud, S. (1917) Mourning and melancholia. *Standard Edition* 14:243–258.

Freud, S. (1919) Lines of advance in psycho-analytic therapy. *Standard Edition* 17:159–168.

Freud, S. (1921) Group psychology and the analysis of the ego. *Standard Edition* 18:69–143.

Freud, S. (1923a) The ego and the id. *Standard Edition* 19:12–59.

Freud, S. (1923b) The infantile genital organisation (an interpolation into the theory of sexuality). *Standard Edition* 19:141–145.

Freud, S. (1925a) Negation. *Standard Edition* 19:235–239.

Freud, S. (1925b) Some psychical consequences of the anatomical distinction between the sexes. *Standard Edition* 19:248–258.

Freud, S. (1926) The question of lay analysis. *Standard Edition* 20:183–258.

Freud, S. (1927) Fetishism. *Standard Edition* 21:152–157.

Freud, S. (1931) Female sexuality. *Standard Edition* 21:225–243.

Freud, S. (1933) New introductory lectures on psycho-analysis. *Standard Edition* 22:5–182.

Freud, S. (1939) Moses and monotheism: Three essays. *Standard Edition* 23:7–137.

Freud, S. (1940a) An outline of psycho-analysis. *Standard Edition* 23:144–207.

Freud, S. (1940b) Splitting of the ego in the process of defence. *Standard Edition* 23:275–278.

Gitelson, M. (1958) On ego distortion. *International Journal of Psycho-Analysis* 39:245–257.

Gogh, V. van (1958) *The Complete Letters of Vincent van Gogh* (introduction by V. W. van Gogh). London: Thames & Hudson.

Green, A. (1986) *On Private Madness*. London: Hogarth.

Greenacre, P. (1950) General problems of acting out. *Psychoanalytic Quarterly* 19:455–467.

Greenacre, P. (1953) *Trauma, Growth and Personality*. London: Hogarth.

Hampshire, A. S. (1972) *Freedom of Mind, and Other Essays*. Oxford: Oxford University Press.

Hartmann, H. (1950) Comments on the psychoanalytic theory of the ego. *Psychoanalytic Study of the Child* 5:74–96.

Hartmann, H. (1955) Notes on the theory of sublimation. *Psychoanalytic Study of the Child* 10:9–29.

Hoffer, W. (1950) Development of the body ego. *Psychoanalytic Study of the Child* 5:18–23.

Hoffer, W. (1952) The mutual influences in the development of ego and id: Earliest stages. *Psychoanalytic Study of the Child* 7:31–41.

Holmes, J. and Lindley, R. (1989) *The Values of Psychotherapy.* Oxford: Oxford University Press.

James, M. (1960) Premature ego development: Some observations upon disturbances in the first three months of life. *International Journal of Psycho-Analysis* 41:288–294.

Jones, E. (1929) The psychopathology of anxiety. In Jones (1948), pp. 294–303.

Jones, E. (1948) *Papers in Psychoanalysis,* 5th ed. London: Baillière.

Josipovici, G. (1971) *The World and the Book: A Study of Modern Fiction,* 2nd ed. London: Macmillan, 1979.

Khan, M. (1962) The rôle of polymorph-perverse body-experiences and object-relationships in ego-integration. In *Alienation in Perversions.* London: Hogarth, 1979, pp. 31–55.

Klein, M. (1932) *The Psychoanalysis of Children,* 3rd ed. London: Hogarth, 1949.

Klein, M. (1935) A contribution to the psychogenesis of manic–depressive states. In Klein (1975), vol. 1, pp. 262–289.

Klein, M. (1946) Notes on some schizoid mechanisms. In Klein (1975), vol. 3, pp. 1–24.

Klein, M. (1975) *The Writings of Melanie Klein,* 4 vols. London: Hogarth.

Laing, R. D. (1960) *The Divided Self.* London: Tavistock.

Lampl-de Groot, A. (1928) The evolution of the Oedipus complex in women. *International Journal of Psycho-Analysis* 9:332–345.

Laplanche, J. and Pontalis, J.-B. (1973) *The Language of Psychoanalysis.* London: Hogarth.

Little, M. (1958) On delusional transference (transference psychosis). In Little (1981), pp. 81–91.

Little, M. (1960) On basic unity (primary total undifferentiatedness). In Little (1981), pp. 109–125.

Little, M. (1981) *Transference Neurosis and Transference Psychosis: Toward Basic Unity.* New York: Aronson.

Loch, W. and Dantigraber, J. (1976) *Changes in the Doctor and His Patient Brought about by Balint Groups.* Helsinki: Psychiatrica Fennica.

Luborsky, L., Singer, B. and Luborsky, L. (1975) Comparative studies of psychotherapies: Is it true that everyone has won and all must have prizes? *Archives of General Psychiatry* 32:995–1008.

Malan, D. (1963) *A Study of Brief Psychotherapy.* London: Tavistock.

Malan, D. (1976) *Toward the Validation of Dynamic Psychotherapy: A Replication.* London: Plenum.

Milner, M. (1950) *On Not Being Able to Paint,* 2nd ed. London: Heinemann, 1957.

Milner, M. (1952) The role of illusion in symbol formation. In Milner (1987), pp. 83–113.

Milner, M. (1987) *The Suppressed Madness of Sane Men: Forty-Four Years of Exploring Psychoanalysis.* London: Tavistock.

Pines D. (1986) Working with women survivors of the holocaust: Affective experiences in transference and countertransference. *International Journal of Psycho-Analysis* 67:295–307.

Rosenfeld, H. (1964) An investigation into the need of neurotic and psychotic patients to act out during analysis. In *Psychotic States: A Psychoanalytical Approach*. New York: International Universities Press, 1966, pp. 200–216.

Roustang, G. (1982) *Dire Mastery*. Baltimore: Johns Hopkins University Press.

Russell, B. (1946) *A History of Western Philosophy*, 2nd ed. London: Allen & Unwin, 1961.

Schilder, P. (1923) *Das Körperschema: Ein Beitrag zur Lehre vom Bewusstsein des einigen Körpers*. Berlin: Springer.

Schilder, P. (1936) *The Image and Appearance of the Human Body*. London: Kegan Paul.

Scott, W. C. M. (1958) Some embryological, neurological, psychiatric and psychoanalytical implications of the body-schema. *International Journal of Psycho-Analysis* 29:141–155.

Searles, H. (1958) Positive feelings in the relationship between the schizophrenic and his mother. *International Journal of Psycho-Analysis* 39:569–586.

Searles, H. (1961) Anxiety concerning change, as seen in the psychotherapy of schizophrenic patients, with particular reference to the sense of personal identity. *International Journal of Psycho-Analysis* 42:74–85.

Stern, D. (1985) *The Interpersonal World of the Infant: A View from Psychoanalysis and Developmental Psychology*. New York: Basic Books.

Strachey, J. (1961) Editor's note on 'Some psychical consequences of the anatomical distinction between the sexes'. In S. Freud, *Standard Edition* 19:243–247.

Tarkovsky, A. (1989) Lecture quoted in 'Directed by Andrei Tarkovsky'. Posthumous television documentary, Channel 4, January 7, 1989. London: Artificial Eye.

Trilling, L. (1950) *The Liberal Imagination*. New York: Viking. (Oxford: Oxford University Press uniform ed., 1981.)

Tustin, F. (1972) *Autism and Childhood Psychosis*. London: Hogarth.

Tustin, F. (1981) *Autistic States in Children*. London: Routledge & Kegan Paul.

Vel'vovskii, I. (1973) The health service—if your nerves play you up. R. Edmonds, unpublished trans. *Pravda*, Moscow.

Winnicott, D. W. (1945) Primitive emotional development. In Winnicott (1975), pp. 145–156.

Winnicott, D. W. (1948) Paediatrics and psychiatry. In Winnicott (1975), pp. 157–173.

Winnicott, D. W. (1954) Metapsychological and clinical aspects of regression within the psychoanalytical set-up. In Winnicott (1975), pp. 278–294.

Winnicott, D. W. (1956) The antisocial tendency. In Winnicott (1975), pp. 306–315.

Winnicott, D. W. (1960) The theory of the parent–infant relationship. In Winnicott (1965), pp. 37–55.

Winnicott, D. W. (1962) Ego integration in child development. In Winnicott (1965), pp. 56–63.

Winnicott, D. W. (1963) Communicating and not communicating leading to a study of certain opposites. In Winnicott (1965), pp. 179–192.

Winnicott, D. W. (1965) *The Maturational Processes and the Facilitating Environment: Studies in the Theory of Emotional Development*. London: Hogarth.

Winnicott, D. W. (1968) Communication between infant and mother, and
    mother and infant, compared and contrasted. In *What Is Psychoanalysis?*
    W. G. Joffe, ed., London: Institute of Psycho-Analysis, pp. 15–25.
Winnicott, D. W. (1971a) Transitional objects and transitional phenomena. In
    Winnicott (1971b), pp. 1–25.
Winnicott, D. W. (1971b) *Playing and Reality*. London: Tavistock.
Winnicott, D. W. (1975) *Through Paediatrics to Psychoanalysis*. London: Hogarth.
Winnicott, D. W. (1988) *Human Nature*. London: Free Association.

Index